GUESTS AND ALIENS

Also by Saskia Sassen

Globalization and Its Discontents:
Essays on the New Mobility of People and Money

The Mobility of Labor and Capital

The Global City

Cities in a World Economy

Losing Control? Sovereignty in an Age of Globalization

SASKIA SASSEN

GUESTS
AND
ALIENS

THE NEW PRESS

NEW YORK

Originally published in Germany © 1996 Fischer Taschenbuch Verlag,
The New European Encyclopedia. GmbH, Frankfurt am Main

Published in the United States by The New Press, New York
Distributed by W. W. Norton & Company, Inc., New York

LIBRARY OF CONGRESS CATALOGING-IN-PUBLICATION DATA

Sassen, Saskia.
   Guests and aliens / Saskia Sassen.
     p.   cm.
   Includes bibliographical references and index.
   ISBN 1-56584-481-5 (hc.)
   ISBN 1-56584-608-7 (pbk.)
   1. Emigration and immigration – History. 2. Refugees – History.
  3. Emigration and immigration – Government policy – History.
  4. Refugees – Government policy – History. I. Title.
JV6021.S27 1999
304.8'094 – dc21   98-33126

The New Press was established in 1990 as a not-for-profit alternative
to the large, commercial publishing houses currently dominating the
book publishing industry. The New Press operates in the public interest rather than for private gain, and is committed to publishing, in
innovative ways, works of educational, cultural, and community
value that are often deemed insufficiently profitable.

The New Press,
450 West 41st Street, 6th floor,
New York, NY 10036

www.thenewpress.com

Printed in the United States of America

9 8 7 6 5 4 3 2 1

For Richard Sennett

CONTENTS

When Eric Hobsbawm asked me whether I would consider writing a book on 200 years of migration history in Europe, all I could say was "Pardon?" Even more surprising to me was perhaps that during the research for this book I found that to understand the place of migration in Western Europe I had to go back further than 200 years, that it would not do to begin the story where it is usually started – with the mass outmigration to the new continent. While doing my post-doctorate research on migration in Western Europe at Harvard's Center for International Affairs, I had come across Abel Chatelain's two volume history of seasonal migrations in France in the 1700s and 1800s. Ever since it had stayed with me as Europe's other history, one unrolling in the penumbra of the historical record as passed on through mainstream culture. As I returned to Chatelain's work I became convinced of the necessity of breaking the iconography of Europe as a continent of mass emigration.

I knew that the only way I could sustain several years of research and writing on this book was to put myself in the shoes of an ivestigative journalist and bring to light that other history of migration in Europe, now largely buried in often obscure scholarly texts and the preserve largely of those knowledgeable about history. A good part of this book is an effort to provide a more balanced view of Europe's migration history. It shows the extent to which international and inter-regional labor migrations have been both a widespread and a strategic component of Europe's urbanization and industrialization history over the last three centuries, whether it was the seasonal long-distance migrations of the Hollandgänger from Westphalia to Amsterdam in the late 1700s or the migrations of Italians to build railroads and cities in Germany in the 1800s. Migrant workers from far and near came to the Paris region to built Haussman's extensions and renovations, lay water pipes and build boulevards. At one point Paris had quite a community of German immigrant workers living there. Europe has not escaped what seems to be the destiny of all areas experiencing rapid growth: the need to bring in labor supplies from the outside.

One of my concerns is to explore to what extent this past history can help in re-framing the immigration question today, develop a more intelligent and effective approach to immigration policy, and rethink the cherished notion that Europe is not a continent of immigrants. It certainly is not in the colonizing way that the New World was, where it is embedded in a history of conquest. But it is in a different fashion. As I proceeded with my research, searching in obscure documents and legislative debates for clues to the role of immigration in the economy, in politics and in society, I began to think of the current discourse on the past as constituting in many ways a narrative of eviction when it comes to labor migrations in Europe's development. This book is then clearly a response to an absence in this discourse.

Similarly, in researching the history of refugees and exiles, it seemed important to me to recover the extent to which the refugee and mass refugee flows are a profoundly European process, deeply caught in the history of the formation of the inter-state system and the modern European state. Today, when most refugee flows are in Africa and in Asia and are largely internal refugees, we often forget this profound articulation of the modern state and the formation of the refugee and mass refugee movements.

The possibility of writing a book with a strong position made all the difference to me. The editors at Fischer Verlag clearly asked for such a book. It is impossible in such a short book to write a comprehensive history of migration over two or three hundred years. Inevitably many subjects were not covered. This is not a survey. It is, rather, an attempt to trace a line through the shadows of history. This is not a line in the sense of a continuous process, since there were massive discontinuities—indeed, one of the important issues for me is the extent to which migrations are born, have a duration and come to an end. I have sought to pull out from the shadows of history a few strategic instantiations of what is a multi-faceted dynamic of migration and refugee flows as it intersects with economies, societies and polities.

This book could not have been written without the existence of an enormous body of scholarship on migration and refugee flows and on many of the related subjects, notably urbanization, demography, industrialization, war, politics. Today there is a vast number of researchers doing important work on a broad range of immigration and refugee issues in Europe. Many of these are included in the bibliography; but many are not given space constraints. I often chose to list a more obscure source rather than the better known one. I apologize to all those whose research could not be acknowledged in this brief book and short bibliography.

There are three texts that were unusually important in my effort because they represent enormous archival research and compilation. I am deeply grateful to the authors of these books for the astounding work they represent: they are Abel Chatelain's *Les migrants temporaires en France de 1800 a 1914,* originally published in the 1930s; Jan Lucassen's book based on his doctoral research on the archives of the Napoleonic Inquiries, *Naar de Kusten Van de Noordzee. Trekarbeid in Europees Perspektief, 1600–1900,* and Michael R. Marrus, *The Unwanted: European Refugees in the Twentieth Century.*

There are many friends and colleagues whom I owe a debt of gratitude for conversations and exchanges of papers over the last twenty years. I am particularly thankful to Sophie Body-Gendrot, Catherine Wihtol de Wenden, Yan Moulier-Boutang, AbdelMalek Sayad, Mirjiana Morokvasic, Czarina Wilpert, Aristide Zolberg, Rainer Munz, Jochen Blaschke, Enzo Mingione, Rainer Baubock. Although the research and writing of this book took place over the last three years, it is a subject I have woven in and out of over two decades, slowly gathering information, insights, ideas. There are many people and research centers who have played an important role in the gestation of this book over those decades, among them most importantly, Daniel J. Koob, the first one to alert me to the importance of international migrations in Western Europe over 20 years ago while I was just beginning my doctoral studies, and Joseph Nye, Jr. of Harvard's Center for International Affairs for supporting my postdoctoral research on migrations as an instance of trasnational relations. More recently, I benefited greatly from fellowships, scholarships, and visiting professorships at, among others, the Wischenshaftszentrum Berlin, the Institute for Advanced Studies in Vienna, the Russell Sage Foundation in New York City, the Salzburg Seminars, the American Academy in Rome, the Institut d'Urbanisme of the University of Paris, the Summer Institute of Lancaster University. Finally, several people helped me with the research and manuscript preparation; I am especially grateful to Todd Kenworth for his generous and intelligent assistance.

I also thank my wonderful Dutch parents who, without much ado raised me in five languages and then, when I turned thirteen, informed me in all innocence that it was time to learn a foreign language. Never have I been as glad to know these languages as during this particular research project.

My husband, Richard Sennett was a careful and generous reader of most of the book; his advice was invaluable. And my son, Hilary Koob-Sassen, was a vigorous interlocutor on the immigration and refugee question today, one of growing interest to the people in his young generation.

All mistakes are mine.

It has long been argued that Europe and the United States have radically diverse immigration histories. They do. Left unspoken in such general assertions, however, is the extent to which Europe in the nineteenth and twentieth centuries saw the enactment of a series of dynamics usually associated with immigration in the United States and only with Europe over the last decade: anti-immigrant feelings, racialization, a crisis mentality about controlling immigration, rapid fluctuations from periods of acute demand for foreign workers to mass unemployment blamed on these same workers.

It is certainly true that Europe has a distinctive history with respect to the production of refugees. With its endless series of wars and "revolutions," Europe throughout the nineteenth century and in the aftermath of two world wars created what is now seen as a "Third World" phenomenon. In fact the drama of people in motion in Europe shows with great clarity the intimate connection between the formation of independent nation-states and the creation of the refugee, the displaced person, the asylum seeker. Nation-states in Europe contributed to the production of the refugee through their aspiration to administrative sovereignty, particularly in their assertion of the right to determine entitlement to citizenship. In this century alone millions of persons in Europe were displaced after each of the major world wars. After World War II an estimated sixty million civilians were displaced in one way or another. The world had never experienced what happened after each of these world wars. Whole states were eliminated from existence by the wars' victors. Yet in each case the victors mostly refused to accept the people who had been citizens of those states.

Not a single European nation came out clean – not a single victor gave full priority to humanitarian concerns or "the rights of man." Instead the victor nations after World War I pursued above all their narrow interests. Collectively the pursuit of these narrow interests created such an unmanageable condition after World War I that the League of Nations established a High Commission for Refugees in large part to handle the floating mass of millions of displaced persons. When I read the archival materials about this history, I found it difficult to agree with today's general commentary that the wars of ex-Yugoslavia are somehow a specific Balkan "distortion." On a basic level they are simply the result of a larger unspoken European history.

The United States has produced its own off-shore history of refugee flows through its actions as a global military power. Indochina in the 1960s and 1970s and Central America in the 1980s are two examples. Although the resultant displacements are minor in comparison to those of Europe, and much of it happened outside the United States, it has had to confront the consequences by admitting a portion of these refugees and recognizing their claims.

It is, then, largely in the area of immigration rather than refugee history that Europe offers insights which may prove valuable to the United States. Understanding this history might help illuminate both the basic features of labor migrations and the dynamics of racialization, as well as help Americans reconsider our options in immigration policy. This book attempts to make a contribution to the U.S immigration debate by addressing these three areas.

What precisely might an examination of 200 years of labor migrations in a range of European countries teach us? Can we detect empirical regularities – is there a set of basic features that observed labor migrations seem to share? The regularities and basic features matter because they ought to determine policy. Recognizing them might help the United States and Europe move away from their current mentality of immigration crisis and mass invasion.

The evidence about cross-border migrations in Western Europe in the nineteenth and twentieth centuries shows that these migrations are patterned, bounded in scale and duration, and conditioned on several particular processes. Migrations were not simply an indiscriminate flow from poverty, as suggested in the imagery of "mass invasions." If poverty were enough to produce emigration, then the developed countries would indeed be threatened with massive invasions. But only a very tiny fraction of poor people emigrate, and they do so from very specific areas and toward equally specific destinations. This book discusses a number of very detailed ethnographic studies about these flows which give us information about why one village in a given poor region developed emigration flows while others next to it did not, and why certain people in that village became emigrants and others did not. Western Europe in the nineteenth century also shows us, then, that notwithstanding significant uneven development in the region, most people did not migrate from its poorer sectors to its richer precincts.

And this was so even at a time when states did not have the technical and administrative capacities to control their borders. Further, many territories fell under multiple systems of rule making; the notion of state control over borders was not really established. The fact is that even though they could have moved to richer zones, most people did not want to leave their home communities. Interestingly, we see two variants of this phenomenon today in the European Union (EU). One is the movement between East and West Germany. In the first years after the Berlin Wall came down and east-to-west migration within Germany was still counted, there was a sharp increase in moves from the east to the west. But soon this trend subsided, and only a small minority of easterners migrated to West Germany. The second case is the option to free movement within the EU among EU nationals. Because the latter are free to move to any other country of the EU and there remain significant differences among countries in socioeconomic conditions, we might expect migrants to move to EU countries with better occupational opportunities, salaries, etc. Yet only five million EU nationals out of a total population of well over 350 million today reside in a EU country which is not their country of origin.

The Western European experience also shows that most migrations end. Most cross-border migrations in Europe took place within the duration of twenty years. One of the reasons for this is that migrations tend to be embedded in the cycles and phases of the receiving areas. Dramatic examples of this are the large-scale migrations of Italians and Spaniards to Northern Europe. These flows of hundreds of thousands of workers were in full swing in the 1960s and basically ended in the 1970s. Today, when Italians and Spaniards are free to move within Europe, there is almost no new migration. That particular phase of labor migration, embedded as it was in the postwar reconstruction of Europe and then in the expansion of the 1960s, came to an end when these conditions no longer held. This reveals perhaps the most important feature of migrations. They are conditioned on various other particular processes. It is this conditionality of migrations that contributes to make them limited in time and scale.

A second set of insights concerns the question of racialization. Whether the complaint is of "cultural distance" in Europe or the "quality of immigrants" in the United States, racialization of immigration populations is a common condition. Europe's history, especially of the nineteenth and early twentieth centuries, shows the extent to which the status of the outsider—the one that does not belong to the extant community—marks the immigrant. Phenotype, religion, or "culture" have never been, in fact, the most important markers. In the nineteenth century large numbers of migrant laborers moved from one area of Europe to another, typically at fairly short distances, usually also within the same broader ethnic/cultural setting. More often than not the migrants looked like the locals, typically had the same diets, the same religion, similar music, similar life rituals such as christenings, weddings, burials. No matter: they did not belong to the local community or town.

It is possible to detect in this history a racialization that instructs us about immigration in the contemporary United States or Europe. A few situations today are similarly illuminating. Perhaps the most familiar example is how Germans from the former East Germany are treated as a different ethnic group in the West.

We easily lose sight of this dynamic of racialization when it is embedded in actual differences in cultures, religions, life rituals, language, and often phenotype. The debate about Islam or "Africanization" in France, for example, easily gets derailed onto notions of an essential difference between "Africans" or "Muslims" and "French." The actual differences in culture or religion or phenotype come to be taken as an "objective" difference and hence "problem." But a look at Europe's past makes it clear that the simple fact that the immigrant is an outsider might be the chief factor behind the experience of a difference.

A third area where Europe's experience offers us several lessons is policy and the role of the state in regulating migration flows. The policy experience of the EU when it comes to immigration has been shaped by the constraints it has had to face while building a union and the innovations it has had to produce in response. Member countries have *had* to negotiate the tensions between economic policies that lift border controls for the flow of capital and migration policies aimed at strong border controls for people. In the United States there is a refusal to recognize the incompatibility between the new economic regime aimed at neutralizing borders and immigration policies aimed at total control of borders. The EU *has* to come up with ways to accommodate the free movement of its residents, including those who are not EU nationals. And it has to do so multilaterally. This set of pressures is forcing a more enlightened manner of handling cross-border flows of people than currently practiced in the United States. Although it would be a stretch to say that the EU has attained an entirely enlightened policy, one can say it is putting some of the pieces of an enlightened policy in place. The renationalizing of political rhetoric evident in most of the EU countries today threatens to derail this process, but the institutional infrastructure being set up to handle immigration probably cannot be derailed in the long run.

In contrast, immigration policy in the United States today features an emphasis on policing as a way of regulating immigration, and the insistence on unilateral power over the matter. The latest U.S. immigration law, passed in 1996 strengthened these features. Policing and unilateralism were a response to what was perceived as a crisis in the state's authority to control its borders. In 1999 immigration is still seen as a threat – to the employment opportunities of natives, to the "American culture," to the government's authority when it comes to borders, drugs, and crime.

Of course this is not the first time this century that immigration has been portrayed as threatening. Nor is it the first time that many in the United States have clamored for strong unilateral state action. But today's context is radically different from past periods. The shift has three main features. National states currently face a set of new economic conditions that push toward the neutralization of borders and diminish, or at least alter, state sovereignty and unilateral state action. Further, when it comes to immigration, states confront a set of international factors that can limit their autonomy. The emerging human rights regime makes the individual regardless of nationality, a possessor of rights. It also means that the state is no longer the exclusive subject of international law. The individual also emerges as such a subject, even though as yet a very minor one. Finally, states under the rule of law today confront the accumulation of a whole range of judicial and even constitutional changes that have the effect of strengthening the rights of citizens and, in many cases, the role of civil society. This strengthening of citizens' rights may well constrain the state's expansion of policing as an approach to regulating immigration.

The weight of these three new conditions on immigration policy has been far greater in the EU than in the United States. One sees the same resistance to relinquishing unilateral sovereign control over immigration among the member states as exists in the United States. But the reality of the EU has forced recognition of the tensions between the new economic regime and the traditional approach to sovereignty.

Pulled on the one hand by economic globalization and on the other by the growth of civil rights and the international human rights regime, the U.S. government has responded to immigration by invoking the same old tenets: control, including militarized, over its borders and its absolute unilateral sovereign power on immigration questions. The contradiction between diminished sovereignty in some matters and invocations of absolute sovereignty in immigration, on the other, has not been recognized as an issue by the media in the United States. It is also rarely discussed by the policy makers. But the sovereignty contradiction has clearly become a difficult and visible policy problem in Europe.

Why this difference? The elaborate institutional framework established for the economic union has made it impossible to ignore the question of cross-border movement of EU residents. In contrast, NAFTA and the GATS, with their far less-developed institutional frameworks, can push the issue aside–at least partly. Not even NAFTA or the GATS could completely ignore the issue in the formal text or the agreements, let alone in the actual operations of cross-border flows of trade and investment in services, capital, and information. Both agreements include special clauses about the cross-border circulation of service workers, who are principally professional (Sassen 1998, chapter 2).

It is apparent, then, that once the formation of a common trade and investment zone reaches a certain level of institutional development, the cross-border movement of people can no longer be ignored. A high level of institutional development also puts in motion dynamics that have the effect of reducing the unilateral sovereign control of the state over immigration.

The global context has also changed regarding the emerging human rights regime. This is clearly seen in the recent experience of Europe. Human rights instruments are more available to judges–and they are far more likely to be used–than ten years ago. Europe has a much longer experience using international human rights instruments in *national* courts than does the United States (Jacobson 1996). Institutions such as the European Court of Human Rights today have considerable power, the court regularly overrides decisions by member states even though it is made up of jurists from those states.

As yet, there is no analog for this in the United States. But in both Europe and the United States, far more human and civil rights instruments are available today to judges, and a trend toward the constitutionalizing of civil rights is developing. A global concept of civil society – a somewhat autonomous sphere that contains its own forms of empowerment and options for citizen action – is also emerging. Strategic sectors of the citizenry have asserted their right to criticize and even take to court various government agencies, particularly police agencies. One example is the group of unauthorized immigrants from several African countries who holed themselves up in a church in Paris when the police sought to deport them. After several weeks a judge granted some of the protestors the right to stay, and most were granted one type or another of permit to remain in the country. There are similar instances in all the EU countries.

Finally, regulating immigration through the old lenses of national crisis is simply both unsustainable and undesirable because of the rule of law. Political and civic order in the world's highly developed countries is strongly conditioned by the aspiration to the rule of law; precarious and partial as the concept of the rule of law may be, and imperfect as its implementation is, it is nonetheless an impressive tool in the struggle for a better and more democratic society. The rule of law refers, in good part, to the right of citizens to be free from abuses by the state. It is not enhanced by the expanded use of policing as an instrument to maintain control over immigration, as evident in several recent measures in the United States, notably the elimination of some levels of judiciary review of immigration police conduct in the 1996 act. The simultaneous intensification of police approaches to immigrant regulation and of recognition of civil and human rights creates a tension, and this tension has consequences. When the objects of stronger police action include an ever-expanding spectrum of people – immigrant women, men and children – sooner or later the state will get caught in the expanding web of civil and human rights. It will then violate those rights, interfering with the functioning of civil society.

Such conditions make the EU a testing ground for the changing balance of power between the national state and supranational or transnational actors. Institutional changes linked to the EU have necessitated a shift of competences in immigration matters, away from nation-states and onto the EU level. State regulation and administration of various cross-border processes require specific institutional arrangements when shared with EU institutions. This occurs in areas ranging from trade and investment to crime and culture. It also appears in the need to form specific cross-border regimes to handle immigration and refugee issues. Much as EU states have resisted and found it incompatible with protecting their sovereign power, they have had to relinquish some forms of border control and have had to accept court rulings which support the human rights of immigrants and the civil rights of their citizens to sue their own government, often in connection with infractions of immigrant and refugee rights. And the world did not come to an end. Nor did this destroy the capacity of the nation-state to regulate immigration.

This may be a good time for innovation in immigration policy. Observers agree that a profound gap between immigration policy intent and immigration policy reality has developed in the world's major immigrant-receiving countries. In their impressive study, Cornelius, Hollifield and Martin (1994) found that the gap between the goals of national immigration policy (laws, regulations, executive actions) and the actual result of policies is wide and growing wider in all major industrialized countries. The researchers noted the declining efficacy of immigration-control measures and found that immigration officials in the nine countries studied were less confident about the effectiveness of policy than officials were fifteen years ago.

The clash of two very different regimes – one for the circulation of capital and one for the circulation of immigrants – poses problems that cannot be solved through the old rules of the game. The European Community (EC) and the national governments of member states have found the juxtaposition of the divergent regimes for immigration flows and for other types of flows rather difficult to handle, but have faced up to the need for doing so. The United States has basically not even recognized there is an issue. But there is one. A recent proposal to check trucks at the border between Mexico and the United States as part of drug-trade policing, with an immigration-control component, ran into enormous complaints from Mexico–U.S. trade-related parties. They argued that the policy would have disastrous consequences for free trade in the region, a micro-level illustration of the tension between the different regimes.

The evidence for Europe does suggest that several key features of international migrations signal the possibility of more and better policy options than the United States has thought feasible. If we understand international migrations are conditioned, patterned and bounded processes, we might move away from a mentality of national crisis to one of management–of a difficult yet manageable process. Whether dealing with the World Trade Organization or International Monetary Fund bailouts or environmental emergencies and military interventions, both Europe and the United States have had to develop new ways of handling complex processes as well as a more multilateral understanding of processes and conditions. Regulating immigration remains a complex and difficult matter, and it requires considerable innovation. But it can be done.

1

INTRODUCTION

T oday immigrants appear as threatening outsiders, knocking at the gates, or crashing the gates, or sneaking through the gates into societies richer than those from which the immigrants came. The immigration-receiving countries behave as though they were not parties to the process of immigration. But in fact they are partners. International migrations stand at the intersection of a number of economic and geopolitical processes that link the countries involved; they are not simply the outcome of individuals in search of better opportunities. Part of the problem of understanding immigration is recognizing how, why, and when governments, economic actors, media, and populations at large in highly developed countries participate in the immigration process.

Refugee flows are also at the intersection of various processes. And for much of the twentieth century it has been recognized that refugees were unwilling departees, pushed by circumstances completely out of their control rather than by the desire for better opportunities in a rich country. Policies and conventions among states recognized refugee flows as an outcome of the actions of other actors – particularly the actions of states. This understanding is increasingly under scrutiny if not attack. Slowly the same imagery prevalent regarding international migration is gaining ascendance: refugees are now often seen as individuals in search of better opportunities in a rich country.

International law, statecraft, and everyday discourse about immigrants and refugees are out of touch with the political and economic realities which govern their existence. If it were true, for instance, that the flow of immigrants and refugees was simply a matter of individuals in search of better opportunities in a richer country, then the growing population and poverty in much of the world would have created truly massive numbers of poor invading highly developed countries, a great indiscriminate flow of human beings from misery to wealth. This has not been the case. Migrations are highly selective processes; only certain people leave, and they travel on highly structured routes to their destinations, rather than gravitate blindly toward any rich country they can enter. The reason migrations take this highly structured form has to do with the interactions and interrelations between sending and receiving countries.

When policy makers and the general public misunderstand migration as caused simply by the poverty of or persecutions in poor countries, they are left with very few policy options. The seemingly logical response to a mass invasion would be to close all the borders. Xenophobia and racism are but the most extreme expression of this option in a country's political culture; milder versions of "closing the gates" to immigrants and refugees are appearing in all highly developed countries.

My purpose in this book is to widen the options we envision for dealing with immigrants and refugees by making a broader interpretation of why these people in motion exist in the first place. To do so means looking at Europe itself, at its own history of migration and exile, for within that evolving European context there developed the active participation today of the rich nations in the system of migration flows.

In particular, I have sought to explore how the history of migration and refugees in Europe over the last two centuries might lead to an interpretation which sets us free from the imagery of "mass invasion." I show how various migrations in the past and today have been, first, patterned and bounded in durations and in geography. Second, I show how such migrations transcend the brute facts of persecution, poverty, and overpopulation. Of course I could not and would not deny the spur of such forces, but argue that these brutal motivations are raw ingredients which combine and metamorphose within larger political and economic structures so that people are set in motion. When persecution, poverty, and overpopulation are seen as no longer sufficient explanations in themselves of migration flows, then images and metaphors based on invasion will no longer satisfy us, and policy-making concerned with immigration could be more innovative, because it would address a confined event, a shaped experience, a manageable process.

Understanding the place of migrants in the development of Europe leads back into the beginnings of modern industrialization, in particular the shift to factory-based manufacturing and the development of the railroad. The shifts in the economy from the late eighteenth to the late nineteenth century were complemented by new ways in which states dealt with religious and political refugees. Shifts in modernization of course occurred at different times in different countries and regions, and at different rates. But generally these shifts occurred during an era of little border control and the lack of bureaucratic and technical state capacities for such control. The migrations occurred in patterns sufficiently complex to set limits to the size and duration of flows, and determine the geography of flows. I explore if this shaping of flows tempered the will of individuals to migrate, and set limits to the numbers who wound up migrating. And I probe, more analytically, whether and how such systemic conditioning of migrations might have had an effect akin to a quasi-equilibrating mechanism.

We know that high-growth situations have required mobilizing "foreign" labor supplies throughout the period of colonial expansion. Such recourse to foreign labor has assumed many different forms: vast forced-labor movements for work in mines and plantations, the most extreme form of which was slavery; but also millions of indentured workers from the Indian subcontinent shipped to the Caribbean, white European indentured servants to North America, and forced-labor systems imposed on indigenous populations in South America, such as the mita and the encomienda. Because it was not known to have any other resources, Venezuela was raided for labor to supply the plantations in the Caribbean islands. These are familiar features; they are generally recognized to be an integral part of the economic history of the Americas, of Africa, of Asia. In this context it is also worth noting that Japan, untill recently perhaps the single highly developed country that had negotiated massive growth in the 1950s and 1960s without resorting to labor imports, has had to resort to immigrant workers for agriculture, fishing, and manufacturing and is expected to need large numbers of people for low-wage service jobs that are being vacated by elderly Japanese ready to retire.

But what about Europe? The master images about migration and

Europe are the millions who left the continent. How important and how integral a part were labor migrations within Europe over the last two centuries? The West European nations have steadfastly maintained that they are not immigration countries, that immigration in Europe basically began in the 1960s – an exceptional measure due to the massive destruction of the war and the need for reconstruction. I try to show how historical reality diverged from this belief.

Though my data are mainly numeric and geographic, this alternative history cannot be told without considering the cultural and political representations of the migrant in different periods and under different conditions. Today it is frequently asserted that one of the problems with contemporary immigration is racial, cultural, and often religious distance – all factors which can be seen as creating barriers toward the assimilation of immigrants. I therefore ask, were racism and antiimmigrant sentiment less likely when the immigrant was of the same race and, broadly speaking, the same West European culture?

These issues culminate in exploring the meaning of borders. Today we see a combination of drives to create border-free economic spaces and drives for renewed border control to keep immigrants and refugees out. The context in which today's efforts to stop immigration assume their distinct meaning for me is the current transnationalization of flows of capital, goods, information, and culture. Governments and economic actors in highly developed countries are increasingly seeking to reduce the role of national borders in such flows, to create transnational spaces. Current immigration policy in developed countries is increasingly at odds with other major policy frameworks in the international system and with the growth of global economic integration.

The European Community and the national governments of member states have found the juxtaposition of these divergent regimes rather difficult to handle. Indeed, all highly developed countries have received rapidly growing numbers of legal and undocumented immigrants over the last decade; none has found its immigration policy effective. These countries are opening up their economies to foreign investment and trade, and deregulating their financial markets. The emergence of a new economic regime sharply reduces the role of national governments and national borders in controling international transactions. Yet the framework of immigration policy in these countries remains centered on older conceptions of the nation-state and of national borders. Immigration policy has to account for the facts of rapid economic internationalization, the corresponding transformation of national governments, and the new meaning of borders when it comes to economic transactions.

A parallel dilemma is shaping up on the refugee front. Beginning with World War I, West European states had developed the full technical and bureaucratic capacities to control their borders and regulate a growing share of activities and events taking place in their territories. A crucial component of this process is the strengthening of the interstate system. The definition of refugee coming out of the Geneva convention shortly after World War I, is a very narrow definition of refugee and a function of the interstate system. It basically describes those fleeing from communism. The state participates in the identification of refugees and in their regulation. This definition held for the next fifty years, the period of the coming of age of the interstate system.

But in the two decades preceding World War I and the subsequent decade, Europe was awash with millions of refugees, marking the beginning of the modern mass refugee era, a profoundly European history. And then again in the 1930s and after World War II Europe saw millions of refugees. I have explored the mechanisms which allowed European states to negotiate the divergent conditions represented by a very narrow definition of "the refugee," the reality of a mass of refugees classifiable or not, the absolute sovereignty of the state in refugee matters, and resulting rigidities of the interstate system.

The interstate system has played a crucial role in the definition of the modern refugee beginning with the end of WWI. But in the last ten years a redefinition is emerging. This is partly because of the changing role of the interstate system in an increasingly global world. Partly because the end of the Cold War calls for a change in the formal definition of the "refugee." Partly because the drama of large-scale refugee shifts is being played out today in Asia and Africa. Within the framework of the West European states, the question "Who is a refugee?" is finally complicated by the growing belief that these are economic migrants masquerading as political victims. Who is a refugee? Are those driven by economic despair which may come from war and generalized oppression as was the case with the 2.5 million Jews who

left Russia and East Europe between 1880 and World War I, "legiti-
mate" refugees? Does such a broadening of the definition undermine
the status of refugee? Is control by the state over the definition of
refugees tenable in the new political and economic reality of Western
Europe, one characterized by growing transnationalization?

These questions about immigrants and refugees, and about the policy
dilemmas they evoke, organize this book. Displaced, uprooted, migratory people seem to have dwelled in the penumbra of European history, people living in the shadows of places where they do not belong.
But I call immigrants and refugees "today's settlers" to indicate that
old concepts of belonging do not fit present realities. Migrations are
acts of settlement and of habitation in a world where the divide between origin and destination is no longer a divide of Otherness, a
world in which borders no longer separate human realities.

2

1800

A s the Napoleonic wars unfolded, forming swords and cannons into the master images of the epoch, hundreds of thousands of men, women, and children were otherwise engaged than in war. Mountain people in France descended to the Mediterranean plains for a few weeks to work in the grain and grape harvests in annual seasonal migrations that continued throughout the nineteenth century. Peasants from Westphalia, the so-called Hollandgänger, annually migrated to the North Sea region for three months to cut peat, dredge bogs, cut hay. Peasant households throughout Europe sent their sons and daughters away to be farmhands or domestic servants on annual contracts that took them from one master to another. But until quite recently these were peoples "without history," in Eric Wolff's evocative phrase.

War and religious persecution, however, shaped the understanding of migration among Napoleon's generation, and indeed migrations resulting from war and intolerance are more vivid in our own understanding of European history than are labor migrations. The expulsion and departure of half a million Huguenots from France after 1685 and the expulsion of Lutherans from Salzburg in 1732, were the types of population movements commonly evoked when it came to the seventeenth and eighteenth centuries. The ancien régime well remembered that war between the Ottoman, Austrian, and Russian empires led to large population shifts in southeastern Europe and Asia Minor. Modern scholarship has elaborated such memories. We have learned that the emergence of nationalist/ethnic movements in the

Ottoman Empire, often supported by Western and Central European powers keen on weakening that empire, also produced massive population shifts. Subjugated ethnic minorities were often encouraged to emigrate: Prussia sought to expel the Poles on the land it had taken from former Poland, and the Austrian Empire encouraged Croats to emigrate.

Yet, although war and religious persecution have been the dominant causes associated with population movements, Napoleon's own military planners knew that they had also to think about labor migrations. During the course of the latter eighteenth century temporary migrations for work expanded throughout Europe, creating a mobile–and therefore mobilizable–mass of bodies. The French army, concerned about recruiting men for its expansionary wars, launched the first government inquiry into temporary labor migrations. This Napoleonic Inquiry, which took place between 1808 and 1813, sought to establish the manpower resources of the empire, an empire at the time covering today's France, Belgium, Luxembourg, the Netherlands, westernmost Germany, and parts of Italy and Switzerland. Today that inquiry forms the main source of detailed information on seasonal migrations for that period, and constitutes as well an ironic document in economic history; many migration routes stagnated precisely because of the imperial wars and their attendant economic upheaval.

When the Napoleonic wars began there were several major labor migration routes that brought workers to the North Sea region, the Mediterranean plains, Paris, Madrid, and London. These had evolved in turn from the temporary rural migrations that began to take place at the end of the Middle Ages. All urban areas in preindustrial Europe had migrants: small and large cities gathered in both poor and well-to-do migrants. Exact historical knowledge today draws most reliably on records about burghers, that is, urban citizens. Such German records for the eighteenth century show, for instance, that about half of the burghers in trading towns were migrants. The absence of registers for many less prosperous urban residents makes it difficult to know the share of these migrants in preindustrial European cities; the Napoleonic Inquiry found it could learn more about ordinary people in the countryside the empire had overrun than it could about those in cities.

Today we have established that there was great movement both in and out of ancien régime cities. Migrants were a key factor in stabilizing or raising population size in these cities at a time when there were more deaths than births in most cities (de Vries 1984). Two centuries before railroads were built, temporary migrants were also circulating throughout Europe. Poussou (1988) has shown that life during this period was not as sedentary as is often believed. Clark (1979) has found, for instance, that mobility was the norm in Southern England from 1660 to 1730. Indeed, in the view of Chatelain (1976) migrants circulated more effectively than merchandise.

If these migratory people mattered to Napoleon's surveyors as potential cannon fodder, they matter to modern historians in understanding the political economy which came into being after Waterloo. Writing in the 1920s and 1930s Chatelain – a pioneer in the reconstruction of the history of labor in the nineteenth century – argued that temporary labor migrations, though neglected by historians, were not at the margins of economic dynamics: they importantly shaped the economic and social life of the nineteenth century, as did rural industry. Today we may be in danger of a new form of historical amnesia, because these temporary migrations have become insignificant in the course of the twentieth century. The written history of labor migration within Europe in the 1800s now emphasizes other types of migrations taking place in that century, such as the more permanent moves to cities and mass overseas emigration during the second half of the nineteenth century.

This chapter attempts to give a balanced picture of both the temporary movements of workers and more permanent migrations made up to the middle of the nineteenth century. It focuses on the world Napoleon's surveyors sought to map, and the geographic, economic, and social forces which were altering that map. It ends with a detailed picture of one of the migratory systems plotted by the Napoleonic investigators, as reconstructed by the modern scholar Jan Lucassen (1987): the annual seasonal migration of peasants from Westphalia to the North Sea region dominated by Amsterdam's thriving economy. If much of this history has received little attention, if many of its features have disappeared, its structure yet contains much that is helpful in understanding migration in Europe after our own equivalent of Napoleonic conquest and defeat, Europe after the Second World War.

THE STATE IN EARLY LABOR AND REFUGEE FLOWS

Before the nineteenth century Europe had experienced many different types of migrations related to work. The migration of craft workers beginning in the Middle Ages is perhaps the best known. After an apprenticeship which could last up to ten years, a master sent his pupil to a larger center where he could advance his training or simply to another center to practice his skill. These guild-regulated migrations eventually led to more generalized migrations of craft workers and particularly members of the emerging engineering profession who moved from one work site to another. The "Tour de France" and the "Gesellenwanderung" are emblematic of these types of migrations. There was recruitment of skilled workers throughout Europe: Italian stonecutters and tile layers were in demand in much of Europe; German cabinetmakers were recruited for France; Swiss dairy cattle workers were recruited to Germany.

Long-distance seasonal-migration systems were another form of migration, common to all prosperous regions in Europe during the seventeenth century (Hart 1974; Lucassen 1987). These circular-migration systems eventually developed the elements of chain migration as some migrants stayed at their destinations and started families, thereby building linkages for more migrations from their communities of origin.

What makes such migrations alien events to us today is that they were welcomed, on the whole, by the receiving community. The wandering journeyman brought scarce high-skill labor to remote places; the seasonal migrant who stayed in a new place swelled its population in a Europe where disease frequently decimated even the most prosperous regions.

Amsterdam well illustrates the positive economic consequences of migration. A commercial and financial capital of the seventeenth century, the city was greatly enriched by wealthy and poor immigrants: from 1600 to 1650 Amsterdam grew from about 60,000 to 175,000 inhabitants. To be sure, some of these were refugees fleeing the intolerance and persecution in France or wealthy traders fleeing intolerance in Spain and Spanish-controlled Antwerpen. But the economy and social life of Amsterdam became increasingly and more largerly dependent on foreign workers. Nearly sixty percent of its sailors and seamen were foreigners, mostly from Germany and Norway (Hart 1974). By 1700 about 15,000 German workers went to Amsterdam every year. By 1730 between 15,000 to 20,000 Germans migrated annually to Holland; by the end of the century, before the wars of the French Revolution, this migration may have reached 30,000 (Lucassen 1987). These foreign workers, called Hollandgänger in Germany, were part of a vast system of seasonal migration directed to brick-making, peddling, hawking, canal construction, dock work, and agriculture.

Economic migrants and religious refugees intersected in ancien régime Europe at the point where the state entered the migration process. The sixteenth and seventeenth centuries saw large numbers of refugees as a consequence of religious persecution and religious wars that occurred in Europe during and after the Protestant and Catholic reformations[1] There were over one million refugees in Europe in these two centuries, a level that declined significantly in the eighteenth century. Where and when the state-building process centered on creating a more homogeneous nation politically and culturally, religion served as a key marker of allegiance. Groups with a strong alternative religious identity were seen as undesirable, suspect in their loyalties, threatening to political authority: Jews in Spain, Protestants in France and the Spanish Netherlands, Protestants or Catholics in states and principalities in Central Europe during the Reformation era. The swath of religious refugees was broad: Serbs fleeing Ottoman rule from the seventeenth century on, who crossed into Hungary; English, Irish, and Scottish Catholics who followed their monarch into exile after 1688; various Protestant sects leaving Scandinavia and Central Europe in the eighteenth century.

Religious wars had devastating economic consequences, engendering further economically induced flight. A tolerant city such as Amsterdam receiving these religious refugees reaped a corresponding economic gain. The paths of economic migrants and religious refugees crossed just here. In the ancien régime, receiving polities did not seek to restrain migratory and refugee inflows as they eventually would in the twentieth century. Mercantilist policy, for one thing, considered in-migration of people a positive matter, an addition of resources. In-migration compensated, again, for the high mortality rates, short life expectancy, famines, and multiple wars which decimated the European population, a population which did not begin to grow significantly until the mid-nineteenth century. In many regions the process of building up a city's population from the surrounding hinterland and from "foreign areas" formed explicit state policy: in-migrants were given citizenship rights if they had wealth comparable to that of resident citizens.

Many governments in the seventeenth and eighteenth centuries indeed actively sought people with talents and resources who for one reason or another were forced or felt obliged to leave their countries.[2] Frederick William of Prussia invited Protestants to settle in 1685 when they were expelled from France through the revocation of the Edict of Nantes; later Prussian edicts continued this policy. Peter the Great and Catherine the Great sought to attract immigrants, a process that eventually drew ten million settlers to Southern Russia and later also to Siberia. Beginning in 1763 such settlement was encouraged in the "New Russia" through a policy of low prices for land and various privileges for immigrants. Under Catherine II there were significant numbers of German settlers and later, when the Germans proved difficult to integrate, Slavic settlers.

The obverse of this process was that many governments in the late seventeenth and eighteenth centuries imposed restrictions on emigration. Colbert made it illegal for residents to leave France and went so far as to institute the death penalty for those leaving illegally. Emigration was illegal in Scandinavia and for certain types of skilled workers in Britain. British ironworkers and loom builders were forbidden to leave because they might take their trade secrets with them, as did Samuel Slater; he memorized the construction of the Arkwright frame and created a new cotton industry center in Rhode Island that competed with the looms of his abandoned homeland. More generally, in an age which combined people-intensive wars with low population growth and short life expectancy, governments were keen to hang on to their population. Labor shortages marked a wide swath of Europe, from the North Sea system to the Mediterranean plains. State policy on emigration was hemmed in by this general labor shortage on the one hand, and on the other by the desire to build national cohesion by expelling those who deviated or dissented.

A particular state's position on emigration partly reflected its fortunes in the world economy (Zolberg 1978; Hansen 1961; Plender 1972; Thomas 1973). By the early 1800s the most developed country, Britain, felt strong enough to relax its anti-emigration stance and introduce a more liberal policy. Although Britain did not suddenly abandon barriers to emigration, at least three factors contributed to their decline: a fifteen percent population growth, as shown in the 1811 census; continued internal migration supplying labor to the new urban industrial centers; and the growing influence of the political economists who viewed emigration and settlement as a way of creating foreign markets for British goods. Other European states such as France, some of the German states, and Russia maintained their strong antiemigration policies into the nineteenth century because their economies were less dynamic. France, for example, had sound reasons to be opposed to emigration. Industrialization and the generalization of the labor market were not as fully developed there as elsewhere in Western Europe during the Napoleonic Era. Full-time farming remained widespread; the farms were small in size, managed by single families; the emigration of one son induced a crisis in the farm's viability. Moreover, demographic growth was slow in France, a sluggishly breeding population in a country in desperate need of soldiers for its colonial empire, which unlike the British did not significantly enrich the mother country through trade. France's internal economic structure, and its place in the global economy, thus created interests different from those of Britain.

To be sure, even within the well-integrated North Atlantic region controlled by Britain, restrictions on the movements of goods and people were more commonplace and effective than a purely laissez-faire view might suggest (MacDonagh 1961). Attempts to control emigration continued through regulations, preferential fares, and restrictions. But the comparison between these two nations, like the history of Amsterdam, shows a general if simple truth which ruled the political economy of the ancien régime: emigration was more of a threat than immigration to needy nations, while immigration was a blessing for all.

THE ECONOMIC CONTEXT
AT THE TURN OF THE CENTURY

Save for the massive disruptions of the wars in Europe from 1792 to 1815, the modern economic order dawned on a Europe at peace. Although this new order grew in the shadows of recurrent famines and widespread poverty, these privations differed structurally from the devastating traumas such as war or plague which wracked early modern Europe and threatened the entire European population in sudden blows. From the second half of the 1700s Europe knew steady if unevenly distributed economic and demographic growth. Europe's population grew from eighty-one million in 1700 to 123 million in 1800;

most of this growth took place after 1740.[3] It is in the context of both
these types of growth that labor migrations emerged as a significant
and widespread process involving ever larger numbers of people,
making them an integral part of the social and economic history of
Europe. Wars and plagues do not promote labor migrations (although
famines to some extent may promote migration, as they did most
sharply in the mid-1800s in Ireland and in the 1880s in Germany). In
place of the blows of fortune, now Europeans had to make sense of
the seemingly inseparable, structural union of misery and wealth;
migration made manifest both sides of that union.

In one way we are no better equipped today to map this "great
transformation" than were Napoleon's surveyors, who counted
people sporadically and by whim. In this period there were no universal censuses, population registers varied greatly in quality; above
all, the past has left us poor migration statistics. The scholarhsip on
early industry, and on the development of economic linkages between
the countryside and the city, often provides only indirect information
on labor migration (Tilly 1983). Social conditions at the time aggra-
vated these statistical deprivations. For instance, rural servants
owned no property and were typically hired on one-year contracts
with an estimated two-thirds changing employment annually; the
peregrinations of such servants are thus difficult to trace (Kussmaul
1981; Todd 1975). Instead, we need to rely on detailed historical accounts of particular places and regions where and when they exist.

From such sources we do know that population growth and the
entry of capital into the economy of the countryside contributed to the
proletarianization of small landholders.[4] Population growth entailed
the subdivision of parcels often already too small to sustain their oc-
cupants. The introduction of taxes and various required payments in
cash to the state or feudal lords created sharp pressures on small
landholders to work for wages. Migration was the only way to gain
access to cash for many. And yet the rapid growth of waged jobs did
not stop the downward economic slide of growing numbers of individuals and households. Many of the jobs were extremely low paid,
creating a whole new class of impoverished Europeans. We see in
this century the rapid spread of severe marginalization: former landholders too poor to remain in their villages and winding up in poor-
houses, too poor to keep their children with a corresponding growth

in the numbers of foundlings. At the limit, migrants come to be seen as vagabonds.

This impoverishment of Europeans took different forms in different political systems. In England landlords were free to expel peasants from the land, to enclose the land and engage in whatever type of production they decided on. Productivity was raised at the expense of peasants who became dependent on wage labor for survival. In France small landholders continued to own the land, and the nobility was restrained by an absolutist state and kept from displacing small-landholders; but that same absolutist state extracted a maximum of taxes and tribute from the small-landholders. As if this were not enough, the nobility continued to extract feudal dues from small-landholders it could not displace, thereby further pushing them into poverty.

In the eighteenth century the major European countries had fairly similar levels of productivity and technical development if looked at as a whole. Thus Bairoch (1982) estimates that Britain, Belgium, and France had similar levels of production and were only slightly ahead of Germany and Italy; Switzerland was somewhat behind these other countries. It was not until the next century that England took an overwhelming lead over the rest of Europe and became the industrial powerhouse of the world.

But a more detailed geographic analysis shows that growth and technical development in the eighteenth century brought with them a sharpening in spatial polarization, with a growing number of prosperous regions alongside increasingly poor regions. The available evidence shows that there were a limited number of regions with major concentrations of rural industry (Guttman 1988). Take for example the manufacture of wool cloth and linen. In Britain the largest employers in rural industry included wool manufacturers concentrated in West Riding, Yorkshire, and linen producers in Ulster. Linen, the major industry on continental Europe, saw significant concentrations of producers in Netherland's Overijssel Province, in several areas of Westphalia and in the lower Rhineland, in Saxony, Bohemia, Silesia, and lower Austria. The plain of Flanders was the center of linen manufacturing.

The growth of linen production created thriving regions with rapidly growing numbers of jobs, and significant in-migration. In some of the major production centers, a majority of the population might be employed in linen production. Women and children were spinners, and men worked as handloom weavers. Because it took at least four and often up to ten spinners per handloom, women were a significant presence in the industry. Lace making also was very labor intensive and employed large numbers of women, while nail making, typically a male occupation, employed fewer. These and other activities suggest that rural industry probably employed more women than men.

Rural industry produced thread, cloth, nails, tools for merchants serving often distant markets. A growing mass of rural industrial workers became dependent on world markets, international trade agreements and international politics. For instance, the implementation of the 1786 treaty allowing British textile imports into France meant that thousands of workers in northern France lost their jobs and experienced great poverty (Gullickson 1986).

Labor migrations were a key part of survival for those in poor regions; and they were a key component of the labor force for expanding prosperous regions. A marked division emerged between those who had to leave home to make a living and those who could do so staying in their home villages. The growth of rural industry created new economic spaces insofar as cities became key elements in the new configuration: they were finishing and marketing centers and created many jobs. In the eighteenth century we see the emergence and expansion of many medium-sized cities, a new pattern after the tendency for growth to be concentrated in large capitals and port cities in the seventeenth century. After 1700 towns of 5,000 to 9,900 people were the most likely to grow. In the 18th century there were about 3,000 to 4,000 urban centers for marketing, administration, and production (de Vries, 1984). Villagers in such regions could find jobs outside agriculture in towns and cities and hence did not have to engage in long-distance circular migration.

The most exhaustive account of migration to cities is Poussou's study of eighteenth century Bordeaux, which became a major international port city in that period. It grew from 45,000 in 1700 to 111,000 in 1790, a growth fed by multiple regional and national migrations. A quarter of the city's brides were migrants from a dozen cantons outside the city. Women dominated local migration; they were two thirds of migrants from the region. Circular migration from the more distant uplands was exclusively male; it was not until the nineteenth century that women became part of these migrations and in so doing contributed to the formation of chain migrations as they settled permanently in Bordeaux.

In areas where rural industry was particularly dynamic, families did not depend on such migrations: Ulster in Ireland, the lowlands of northern France, the Netherlands, the Rhineland, and what is Belgium today. Vigorous rural industry may have made subsistence migration less essential for family survival (Head 1979). According to Lucassen (1987), in the case of the Hollandganger of Westphalia, in the eighteenth century only the very poor were forced into these types of migrations.

So as the nineteenth century opens, the older, crude ancien régime imbalance between emigration and immigration took on a new character, particularly when we explore it in terms of economic regions rather than nation-states. If labor migration was more restricted in prosperous places, more a matter of a complicated web of movements woven locally, still the fact of labor migration contributed importantly to the development of these dynamic regions (Souden 1984). And it did so not only in the sense of providing a flexible labor supply, but also in the sense that migrants came to regions where there was freedom to settle and to occupy buildings in new ways. Levine (1977) notes that rural industry grew in England in those villages that had freeholds where lords did not restrict settlement; rural industry languished where there were restrictions on settlement of newcomers and subdivision. Kisch (1981) notes that in regions where free settlement was restricted by feudal lords, rural industry only thrived in areas where migratory labor formed part of some workers' obligations to their feudal lord, as was the case in Silesia. The interaction between freedom of movement and the development of rural industry also is made evident in the case of the Austrian Waldviertel: here, in a region given over to linen production, law restricted settlement, the division of landholdings, and new cottage construction. This meant that men could work in linen production only when they were not working the fields, and much work relied on women and children; according to Lutz this limited the development of rural industry in Austria because it was a system that excluded precisely those most available for maximum employment: those without land and other resources and hence most in need of waged employment.

The webs of locality affected the very rewards of work. Nail makers and spinners were among the lowest paid workers in rural industry.

If these rural industries operated in generally poor regions, such as the central highlands in France, then the earnings were meager (Poitrineau 1985); if these same activities occurred in generally prosperous regions such as the lowlands in France, then earnings were better. The web of locality could, moreover, become almost microscopically tight. For instance, French and Spanish records show how local subsystems operated within a region's migration patterns: an inventory of French migrants in Cadiz, on the Atlantic, shows that they came from about eighteen villages less than twenty miles from each other; and that migrants in Valencia on the Mediterranean came from about seventeen villages not more than eighteen miles apart (Poitrineau 1985).

There were formal migrations run through family companies, capable of mobilizing capital and involving both high rank and laboring migrants. Poitrineau (1985) describes the case of the Société Chinchon, with headquarters in the town of the same name located just south of Madrid. Its members all came from southern Auvergne, and specifically from about twenty parishes just north of Aurillac. It traded in wools, linens, pins, buttons, needles, ribbons, etc. The French members sold these wares as peddlers and in the twenty-five stores the société owned throughout Spain at its height.

These are among the developments in the countryside that set the stage for the massive growth in labor migration in the nineteenth century. The productive relation between rural industry and migration is an extremely important issue, and one not fully incorporated in our common understanding of the development of the modern economic order.

Certain aspects of migration during the nineteenth century are grippingly familiar to us, dramatized by social reformers and political revolutionaries alike. The increase in urban, proletarianized labor, and the corresponding decrease in the wealth-share of peasants and of rural industry are part of this painful history, signs of a radical transformation in the nature of labor migration (Tilly 1983, 1990). After 1780 subsistence migration increased as poverty rose, and vagrancy spread as a result of poverty and severe unemployment. Yet the new economic order also began to organize migration in more coherent, if less familiar forms.

There was a distinct range of jobs where migrants were likely to be employed. Workers coming to the Paris basin worked in the harvest and as vineyard laborers; in the city they were employed as water carriers, laborers, construction workers, and petty laborers. Most of these workers came from the central highlands in France. Further, some groups came to be associated with particular types of jobs (Chatelain 1976). The Hollandganger from the eastern territories in Germany had long worked as agricultural laborers, dike workers, sailors, servants (Lucassen 1987). Those migrating to London and its surrounding area worked either in the fields harvesting grain and cutting hay or in the city as construction workers, peddlers, and laborers (Redford 1976). Workers going to Corsica, Rome, and central Italy worked in the grain harvest and in the vineyards, in heavy construction work, trade, and services. Workers going to the Po Valley worked in the rice fields, and in construction, trade and services in Turin and Milan (Lucassen 1987). The conditions were similar in the other major migration systems – those going to Spain or the coastal plain of the Mediterranean. The new economy drew on these clear lines of movement, established over time.

There was one necessary obscurity in both organized and disorganized movement: we know much less about women in these movements than about men.

GENDER AND LABOR MIGRATIONS

Most families found themselves engaged in a multiplicity of economic subsystems in the eighteenth century and the first years of the nineteenth century. It was rare that one particular industry or economic subsystem totally dominated a region the way it eventually happened with industrialization and industrial towns. The family formed the nexus for allocating different members to different types of economic activities, according to age and gender.

In many regions there were several economic subsystems which engaged a family: agricultural production, production for local markets, and rural industry producing for export to other regions. Labor migration for part of the year was also common. In addition to household production and fieldwork, women frequently earned some cash working in lace making and ribbon weaving, while men earned extra cash making nails.

Leaving home to work as a farm laborer or domestic servant was already common in the seventeenth century (de Vries 1984; Moch and Tilly 1985). Most young migrants worked as rural servants; they were called valets de ferme in France, Gesinde in Germany, servants in husbandry in England. The available evidence from parish lists shows that there were as many women as men among rural servants. Migrant men travelled in large groups, often work teams, for protection and support and because they would leave their villages at the same time (Chatelain 1976). Migrant women were placed in domestic service and worked as seamstresses or in silk mills with housing for women attached (Garden, 1970). They did also travel in teams to the vineyards.

Yet the place of women in nineteenth century society obscures what we can know about their migrations. Women were not needed by the army and hence their movements of less interest to the state than the whereabouts of men. Because women were more likely to be part of small, private domestic arrangements, their migration for labor did not show on historical records or government inquiries (Berkner and Mendels 1978).

We know at least that as rural industry developed many women took wage jobs which typically involved short-distance movements; long-distance temporary migration seems not to have been very common among women. The immense hazards and hardships of these treks may have also prevented many women from going. Receiving communities could be risky places as women migrants had no rights and no protections. Away from their families and kin, migrant women were in a weak position to defend themselves from men.

We also know something about the relation of pregnancy and migration. From the eighteenth century onwards there is some evidence that most single mothers in towns and cities were migrant women. There is also evidence that many of these women had lost a parent; for instance, over half the single mothers in Lille had lost their father and seventy percent had lost one parent (Lottin 1970). And it seems that only a minority of these were rural women who came to have their pregnancy completed in the city in the hope for anonymity and then planned to return to their villages. Instead, single women with children migrated to cities and stayed there to work (Tilly, Scott and Cohen 1976).

MAJOR LABOR MIGRATION SYSTEMS
IN THE NAPOLEONIC ERA

We have seen what prompted people to migrate and the differing values put on immigration and emigration in the ancien régime. As economic life began to take a new turn, the regional webs of migration became more complex, as did the social experience of migration. The Napoleonic surveyors, imbued with received ideas about war and religious persecution, had only a few evident categories into which to slot other forms of human displacement. One of these derived from the European experience of colonization; another derived from the seasonal movements of workers which could be observed every year throughout the continent.

In fact neither of these categories was misleading. There had been several prominent colonizing migrations within Europe. To take only German examples, there were Germans who were recruited to settle the plains of southeastern Europe after the defeat of the Turks in the seventeenth century; 60,000 colonists arrived by official invitation in Hungary from 1748 to 1786, followed by 180,000 private settlers. About 37,000 Germans arrived in Russia's Volga districts and near the Black Sea from 1763 to 1800. About 300,000 Germans moved east to colonize Prussian territories, encouraged by Frederick the Great (Fenske 1980). Germans recruited other colonizers to their own lands, notably Dutch workers experienced in draining bogs.

Outside Europe, North America became a significant destination for colonizing Germans. By the end of the eighteenth century 125,000 Germans had settled in North America, mostly in Philadelphia, and 17,000 German mercenaries who had fought in the independence war in North America also stayed and settled. America represented to all Europeans, indeed, the very model of a colonize-able society, a "natural" home for refugees and entrepreneurial economic migrants, its "natives savages" without viable claims on their own soil.

British and French colonizing migrations to America which had increased in the later seventeenth century were followed by a period of little migration during the early eighteenth century. The conclusion of the Seven Years War in 1763, which consolidated Britain's control over North America, launched a new massive transatlantic migration of settlers. About 1.5 million emigrated from Britain alone in the eighteenth century, as did smaller numbers of Irish, Swiss, and Germans.

Between 1760 and 1775, there also arrived 84,500 enslaved Africans (Bailyn 1986). After the Napoleonic wars, economic devastation and crop failures in Europe would produce an annual flow of about 30,000 to 40,000 migrants to North America; in 1840, with the expansion of famine in Europe, an even greater mass emigration would commence.

Seasonal migration was the other major type of movement at this time. Mountain people had developed particularly strong seasonal-migration practices, in good part fed by the climate, the characteristics of livestock grazing, and the need for trading. Modern scholars have fleshed out the Napoleonic-era descriptions of such events (Poitrineau 1966; Chatelain 1976; Lis and Soly 1979). They describe the descent of mountain people from the Pyrenees to work in Spain, the growing city of Bordeaux, and the lowlands of western Languedoc; and they describe people from the central highlands in France descending in large numbers to Spain, to the cities and plains of southern France, and to Paris. Other seasonal migrations consisted of workers from southern Sweden who went to the Danish island of Sjælland, from the North Sea coast to Schleswig-Holstein, from southern Lorraine to Alsace. Probably the largest labor migration in the eighteenth century of this sort was the annual migration of Westphalian men to the fields of Holland.

Yet we also would want to describe the migrations of people who lived in Napoleon's time using other categorizations than they used to understand themselves. We know more about the political economy of their time, and its relation to economic regions rather than nation-states, than they did. We might want in particular to draw on the work of Lucassen (1987), who estimates that there were seven major intra-European migration systems operating at the end of the eighteenth century. These formed a key part of the economies of the various sending and receiving regions, which together stretched across Europe. These systems involved a total of about 300,000 workers moving annually to three major destinations in the north and four major destinations in the south. Lucassen estimates that the distance between the center of the receiving areas and the center of the sending areas ranged from 300 to 700 kilometers. The distance travelled by migrants rarely would exceed 350 kilometers and most travelled far shorter distances.

Lucassen drew his picture of the seven systems on the basis of the data gathered by the Napoleonic Inquiry, so it is not simply an imposition of the present on the past. That inquiry showed him, and us, the following:

The first significant system of movement lay in eastern England: every year about 20,000 migrants came to work in the harvest in Lincolnshire and East Anglia, to do garden work in the counties around London, and to jobs in London, including jobs in public-works projects. Most of them came from the far west in Ireland, particularly Connaght. This flow also included Scotch, Welsh, and English workers.

The second region of migration formed around the Paris Basin: every year about 60,000 workers came to this region, mostly to the city itself where they filled jobs in public-works projects, services, and trade; in the surrounding region migrants were employed largely in the grain harvest. Most came from the Massif Central, and to a lesser extent from the Alps and the west of France.

The third took shape in Madrid and its region, Castille: at least 30,000 migrant workers came every year, mostly from Galicia, and to a lesser extent from Asturias. Up to the Napoleonic wars there were also annual migrants from France. They came for the grain harvest, for jobs on public-works projects and in services. Napoleon's invasion of Spain led to hatred of the French migrants and their forceful expulsion.

The fourth stretched along the Mediterranean coast from Catalonia to Provence: This was a flow that resumed after the Napoleonic wars and reached its highest levels toward the end of the nineteenth century. In the earlier period about 20,000 migrants came mostly to work in the grain harvest, and to a much lesser extent in the grape harvest, at that time a relatively small crop. When the vineyards expanded later in the century the numbers of migrant workers were ten times as large. Migrants came mostly from the mountain areas: the Alps, the Massif Central, and the Pyrenees. (The next chapter contains a detailed description of this flow.)

The fifth lay in the Po Valley: Each year about 50,000 workers came to work in agriculture, particularly rice cultivation, and in cities such as Milan and Turin for jobs in public works and services. They came largely from the surrounding mountains: the Bergamasque Alps in the north and the Ligurian Apennines in the south.

The sixth lay further south in central Italy, including the south of

Tuscany, Lazio and the islands of Corsica and Elba: about 100,000 workers came each year to work in the grain harvest and other agricultural work, and in construction, trade, and services in the cities, particularly Rome.

Lastly, there was systematic movement around the North Sea: 30,000 migrants came every year from eastern and southern areas mostly in Germany.

To convey what systems of migration conceived in these ways reveal economically and socially, I describe in some detail the last of the seven, the patterns of movement organized around the North Sea.

THE NORTH SEA SYSTEM: THE HOLLANDGANDER

The North Sea economic region as described in the Napoleonic Inquiry and elaborated by Lucassen covered an elongated coastal area of about 250 kilometers from Calais to Bremen, about 50 kilometers wide. It was characterized by intense economic development and high levels of transportation infrastructure, including harbors and roads. It drew migrants from as far as 300 kilometers. In this broad region there were multiple push areas; but there also were multiple areas which were not touched by labor migrations of any significant size, areas where there was no in- or out-migration.

The main source of evidence for specifying the characteristics of these systems is the so- called Questionnaire of 1811, part of the Napoleonic Inquiry on Temporary Labor Migration. It asked specific questions about travel from and to every department in the French Empire, with specific information about areas of origin and destination of workers. It also asked about kinds of labor, dates of departure and arrival. But it needs to be supplemented with other types of information; the questionnaire does not help in understanding the types of households migrant workers came from, the work structure in them, what share of household income was represented by migrant earnings, or whether migrant households were different from nonmigrant households, or why some households in the same areas sent migrants and others did not. It was a minority of people from identifiable areas that migrated for labor. For the North Sea system it was three percent of the population in push areas; a narrower delineation of areas of origin allows us to see that this share could rise to twelve percent and at even smaller scales, to twenty-six. But it was always a minority. Nor does the questionnaire allow us to understand the timing question: the precise timing of the high season in receiving areas and the migrants' timing of their departure.

1. Who Left and Who Stayed

One of the questions Lucassen seeks to answer is why some regions emerged as sending areas and others did not. He finds that areas with extensive domestic industry, particularly weaving and metal work, were unlikely to emerge as sending areas. Thus what he calls the Flemish corridor and the Bielefeld corridor further east are major flax spinning and linen producing areas where there were about fifty looms per thousand population, a very high number because it meant that about one in every four households had a loom. It also seems that at this time these fairly dynamic economic areas were not drawing migrant workers either, though there may have been some very localized use of migrant workers. Further, areas where agriculture required full-time work and could sustain a household, development of labor migrations also seems to have been unlikely. Domestic industry based on weaving was thriving in several areas in the broader sending region: in some places 40 to 60 looms per 1,000 inhabitants were counted. Because weaving required at least four spinners per handloom, it meant that weaving was absorbing considerable labor. In brief, these particular combinations of resources contributed to migration-neutral regions: labor demand was satisfied locally and there was enough work to sustain the livelihood of most households.

There is evidence that in some push regions where linen production was significant, migrants would come from specific areas in the region where linen weaving was a secondary occupation, done often in the wintertime when there was little agricultrual work. In these areas there was a far greater concentration of small farmers who rented their land. They were the so-called Heuerlinge, who typically made up about twenty percent of the families in these push areas. As tenants they farmed an average of 1.14 hectares in the early nineteenth century and many even less. In the areas within sending regions where farms were larger, Heuerlinge were less common and home weaving was a strongly established activity, these three conditions seem to have made labor out-migration far less common. Lucassen finds that spinning was probably far more common in the migrant household: there was a large demand for spinners, and spinning took place largely in the winter which suggests that spinning was easier to combine with labor migration. Any member of the household would work in spinning and it required little capital. Spinning was a poor household's type of domestic industry. In my reading of Lucassen's analysis we see here the formation of a certain kind of labor market segmentation: migrant households were more likely to be poor, rent their land, and spin, a more lowly paid activity than weaving. For Westphalia as a whole Lucassen finds that domestic industry based on linen production, and particularly weaving, was incompatible with labor migration.

Areas with very intensive domestic industry were not labor sending areas in the early part of the century. Textiles and metal work were key components of the rural economy in the region east of the Rhine: the Prussian Regierungsbezirke Arnsberg and Düsseldorf, and the Landkreis Mülheim had particularly developed domestic industries at the beginning of the nineteenth century. Further to the west and south, around Aachen and Verviers, there was a highly developed wool-textile industry, and around Liege, mining. Finally, in the departement du Nord, around Lille, there was also a high level of industrial development.

Similarly, there were agricultural areas which did not send nor draw migrants. Lucassen examines the nature of the agricultural economy in these areas and finds that considerable inequality in the distribution of land may have been a key factor explaining the absence of labor migration. Small landholders were small and poor enough to have to sell their labor to the large farmers who could then secure the needed workforce through local labor. Further, given the small size of their plots, small landholders would have been likely to have a surplus of workers in their household once children reached maturity, and hence be able to allocate labor to the large farms. For this system to work in a largely agricultural economy, however, the nature of the crops grown by small and large landholders would most likely have to be different in terms of timing of labor inputs. Indeed, Lucassen finds in various detailed accounts about areas in Belgium that did not have labor migration, that large farms grew different crops. Grains were viable on large farms, but not on small ones; on the other hand, small farmers in Brabant seem to have engaged largely in producing vegetables for the market and potatoes for their own consumption. Similar accounts exist for other areas in Belgium. There is insufficient evidence to show this for all "neutral" areas in terms of labor migration.[5]

The migrant household typically had very small landholdings, about 1.5 hectares, and engaged in types of production that made it possible for one or more men in the household to go away for three months of work in the North Sea system. Grain production would not have allowed this, nor would it have been profitable on such small scales. Thus it seems that migrant households were likely to grow potatoes for their own consumption and vegetables for the market, crops that other members of the family could also handle. Lucassen also finds that it is particularly in certain stages of the household cycle that migration for labor is likely to have emerged as a strategy: when there are children and hence extra needs, when the number of "producers" in the household has become larger than the household requires as some children have reached their teens.

Wages in the North Sea region were relatively high, so it typically paid off to go for three months of work. But illness, crop failures, economic failure in any of the industries hiring migrant workers, could mean very low earnings. The cost of living was also much higher than in areas of origin. Thus migrants tried to take as many provisions as they could with them, and would travel loaded down with food and other essentials, as well as often a bolt of linen to sell at advantageous prices. (It is not clear whether the migrant's household had woven the linen or just done the spinning and had the weaving done by another household.)

Some migrants had short distances to travel, but many had distances that took multiple days. Because water needed to be crossed, there were particular points where migrants would gather to take the boats. Thousands would come together at these points and shuffle to get on as quickly as possible. Time was of the essence for these workers. A day spent waiting for the crossing was a day lost in earnings and a day when resources, even if just of food, were used up.

It was an east-to-west movement and to some extent also a south to north one. Along the road there were markers where workers would meet and gather every year: a particular tree that got named Friessische Eiche; certain inns where migrants would stop every year; an enormous boulder located between Ankum and Üeffeln, called Breiten Stein.

2. *Hollandgänger*

Lucassen reconstructs one particular route travelled by these migrants, one originating in Münsterland in the south of Oldenburg (Ems Superieur in 1811) and going to a central area of the North Sea region, the peat bogs south of Amsterdam. In each of the particular sending localities workers would gather and begin the trek together sometime in March. Music and song seem to have been part of the experience: the wanderbursche were well known for their singing. As the trek proceeded other groups coming from other localities would eventually travel the same roads. By the time they reached the Breiten Stein they numbered in the hundreds or more. This was a well-known gathering place for migrants. There was a geography and an iconography to these treks. It seems that the migrants liked to stop at the same spots, whether a particular tree, rock, or inn, year after year.

At Lingen they had to use a ferry to cross the Ems, up to the time when a bridge was built. By then they would number in the thousands and would proceed via Neuenhaus and Uelsen in Bentheim to the Netherlands at the border point of Venebrugge and then on to Hardenberg in Overijssel. At this point quick action was critical: the purpose was to be able to deliver one's backbreaking baggage to be carried by boat in order to proceed, thus freed, as fast as possible on foot straight to the Zuiderzee on the "Hessenweg" that ran north of the towns of Dalfsen and Ommen in Vecht, and just south of the peat bog. Again here there was probably fierce competition to get one of the places on the ferries to cross the Zuiderzee at Hasselt or Zwolle or several other towns.[6] On the way to Hasselt there was a small Catholic shrine, which it seems was an important place for Catholics bound for Holland. It dated from the early fourteenth century and had been endowed with a papal indulgence of 100 days because of a miracle that had taken place on the spot. Many of the migrants stopped there. They crossed the Zuiderzee with their baggage, which by then would have arrived, 100 workers at a time in ferries otherwise used to transport cattle.

The one-day crossing would leave them in Amsterdam, close to the Oude Brug. Upon arrival migrants would have to pay a municipal tax on any meat brought in, a practice that continued up to 1865. In that same area, also called the Moffenbeurs, or German Exchange, they would find places to sleep, eat, buy tools. The next day they would proceed to their destinations: the peat dredgers would take a barge down to the bogs, while the grass mowers would go up north later in the season

On dairy farms migrants only mowed grass and prepared hay; they were not allowed to do other types of jobs. In 1811 at least 12,000 migrant workers came to these farms. There seem to have been two recruitment forms. One was the employment year after year of the same workers, if this was what the dairy farmer wanted, who would then also hire other workers recommended by his crew. The employer would then let his mowers know when he thought his grass would be ready and when he expected them to come. The second way was for the migrant simply to go and offer his services from farm to farm or go to day-labor markets. Because grass mowing was late in the season, many of these workers combined it with work in the peat bogs or dikes earlier in the year or with other agricultural tasks.

Those who worked in the grain harvests came in groups of ten to the southern areas and hired themselves out as a group to farmers. Later in the season there was work digging madder whose half-meter-long root needed to be extracted whole. By then migrants would have worked on the dikes or bogs, and then some midsummer work such as grain harvest.

There was a broad array of industries in which migrants were employed in the high season, ranging from agriculture to peat cutting, excavation work, and manufacturing. Migrants worked in the flax and potato harvest, and in the stripping of oak. Migrants also worked excavating, dredging, and cutting peat in land-reclamation projects, maintenance of dikes and harbors, and dredging of bogs. They held industrial jobs, transport jobs, and jobs in trade and services. Work in teams was frequent. Migrants had little contact with local workers and little contact with their employers.

CONCLUSION

Historians have long ceased drawing a thick line separating the ancien régime from the onset of the modern political economy. Yet the history of migration is not one of smooth changes between the distant and the nearer past. Economic migration in the ancien régime often overlapped with the movements of refugees in relation to the state; the economic migrant and the refugee represented two sides of the state's dilemma in curbing or causing people to move. Other states, regions, or cities tended to benefit from this dilemma, when migrants and refugees arrived at their gates.

Migration related to work had a particular character in the ancien régime; in the seventeenth and eighteenth centuries, whether local or regional, labor migration tended to be cyclical, a pattern of going and returning. At this time we do also see the emergence of some chain migrations – Germans settling in Amsterdam, French in Spain. But career migration was a phenomenon restricted to people of high rank in government and church; that is, geographic mobility among workers was not tied to social mobility in the way it would become linked in the nineteenth century. The labor migrant in Europe was neither a man on the make nor a destitute vagabond. Only in the process of colonization does the migrant of the ancien régime appear as an economic actor in search of a new economic status.

What changes after 1750 is the sharp population increase and sharp growth of rural industry. Though it took very specific combinations of local conditions, we see a tendency of increased migration out of areas with little rural industry where population growth had created additional pressures on agricultural land, and a decrease in migration out of areas with rapidly growing rural industry. The expansion of rural industry pivots on the movement of capital into the countryside which in turn puts pressure on agriculturally based forms of subsistence. During the second half of the 1700s and the early 1800s two patterns emerge: one is the rise of communities with large numbers of people and insufficient land holdings where it became increasingly necessary for men and women to migrate to supplement earnings; the other is the rise of thriving communities based on rural industry with rapid population growth and dynamic economies where labor migration was not common. Eventually these conditions created a large population of poor migrants after 1750.

The rapid expansion of cottage-based manufacturing in the countryside also brought new growth to many of the cities. City and countryside were part of one economic system in the eighteenth century, something that would change radically in the nineteenth century with the development of factory-based industrialization in cities. Cities were servicing and trading centers, and they were centers for certain skills; they were geared toward the products of rural industry which was mostly for export markets. These manufacturing arrangements began to insert workers even in remote villages into chains of production connected to world markets and make them vulnerable to fluctuations in these markets, a process that would accelerate rapidly with the growth of commercial and industrial capital.

If the surveyors of the Napoleonic Inquiry could not understand these changes, even as they recorded some of their manifestations, as in the North Sea migratory system, neither could they foresee their consequences in the future–consequences to which we now turn.

NOTES

1 The first expulsions of Jews from the Iberian Peninsula were in 1492. There were religious wars in France (1562–1593); the revolt of the Netherlands against Spain (1562–1593); and the Thirty Years War, which devastated many parts of Germany (1615–1648). England had religious conflicts and eventually a civil war from 1642–1660.

2 Instances do occur earlier. After the Spanish-enforced expulsion of Jews from the Kingdom of Naples in 1511–under Bourbon rule at the time–some cities asked the king to allow the return of Jews claiming that without their services they could not pay their taxes to the king. Sennett (1994) describes how the Jews in the Venetian ghetto had secured a certain position/protection because their money services were, precisely, essential for the running of a good part of the economy in Venice. Because Jews were part of European-wide networks, we know for instance that the Jews in Venice were in contact with the Jews in Frankfurt, they were able to mobilize capital on a scale that few indigenous operators could.

3 The German population grew by fifty-one percent from 1680 to 1820; the French by thirty-nine percent, the Spanish by sixty-four percent, the Italian by fifty-three percent, and the English by 133 percent (Guttman 1988; Wrigley 1983; Anderson 1988). Life expectancy at birth rose sharply in this period. In England it is estimated to have risen from about thirty-six to forty-one years; in Sweden from thirty-eight to forty-six; in Denmark from thirty-five to forty-four; in France from twenty-nine to forty-one. The survival rates reflected the new conditions that lengthened life expectation. Thus in England, somewhat below a quarter of all boys born in the early 1740s were dead before they reached one year of age and half were dead by about twenty-eight. By the early 1830s, sixteen percent of boys died in infancy and half reached the age of forty-four. France reached a similar level with the 1830s cohort; but it represented a far sharper improvement since of boys born in the 1750s half were dead by the time they were nine years of age (Anderson 1988, 81).

4 See, for example, Blaschke (1967) who shows that from 1550 to 1750 nearly half of the population of Saxony had become proletarian, both in cities and countryside. In Leicestershire village of Wigston Magna, forty percent of the land was held by peasants as late as 1765; by 1831 the peasantry had disappeared, forced to sell or rent out their land. In France, Soboul (1970) estimated that forty percent of the rural population was semi-proletarian or proletarian by 1790. Similar processes took place in cities (Lis and Soly 1979); for instance, in Strasbourg the share of wage laborers rose from twenty-nine percent in 1699 to forty-five percent in 1784 (Moch 1983).

5   Lucassen does find that in one of the migration-neutral regions, that of the great rivers in the center of the Netherlands, the uneven quality of the soil led to great variety in crops and activities. This ensured year-round demand for labor. A year-round supply of labor appears to have been assured through extensive participation of women and children in various job markets. Lucassen cites a report evaluating the early years of compulsory education in the Netherlands, a system dating from the early nineteenth century, which found that the highest rates of absenteeism among schoolchildren were to be found precisely in this region.

6   There was sharp competition between Hasselt and Zwolle and other towns to transport the migrants. Hasselt had made various agreements with the shipping guild in Amsterdam to get the exclusive right to transport the migrants. Zwolle responded by using various tactics to confuse and ensnarl migrants into coming to Zwolle, at one point including setting up signs along the road telling migrants where to go and attaching penalties to other routings. When this did not work Zwolle brought in soldiers to force migrants to go to Zwolle; when that failed, Zwolle made a secret arrangement with the baggage shippers not to deliver the migrants' baggage at Hasselt but at a "friendly" town. Lucassen gathers that probably most migrants did wind up going to Hasselt because it was the most convenient point for the crossing.

3

AFTER 1848

Though specific dates are suspicious markers of sweeping historical changes, 1848 can be justly called a turning point in European affairs. The revolutions of 1848 intensified radical calls in the early nineteenth century for the building of unified nation-states and the destruction of dynastic family regimes. The radicals calling for these changes in 1848 often became political exiles from their own countries. 1848 marked the point, however, when the political refugee, usually a highly educated or an affluent patriot, was lost in a new crowd of displaced persons who were economic refugees without means. These hapless displaced persons were one class of victims of the new economic order, which rapidly expanded after the Revolutions of 1848 failed.

Karl Marx argued that the radical collapse in 1848 legitimated the draconian rule of capital over labor in the development of industrial capitalism; Europe woke, he said, from the dreams of St. Simon Fourrier that there could be cooperation between these two great forces. Whatever the truth of this argument in general, it was certainly true that after 1848 the movements of laborers changed as the larger economy changed. The building of cities, the laying down of railroads, the growth of factory-based manufacturing, all created a vast demand for workers. This growth entailed loss and decline, notably in the final stage of proletarianization of the peasantry. The elimination of serfdom in Russia and Austria, following in the steps of earlier reforms in Prussia, created a vast mobile, landless mass of workers and growing misery.

In the wake of these continental changes, colonization took on a new meaning, becoming a massive flight from distress rather than an act of conquest. Much transatlantic migration was a migration for survival: the famine of mid-century in Ireland which killed one million people and sent another million across the Atlantic is probably the best-known case. The invention of the steamship reduced the cost of overseas travel fivefold, and so gave millions of poor people access to transatlantic travel.

In the new economic order, generating profit from manufacturing depended largely on efficient transportation of goods and raw materials. Eighteen forty-eight (or more precisely, 1849) marks the point at which the design of railway undercarriage supports and the laying of continuous track took important technological steps foward, making possible heavy-duty, long-distance rail travel. These advances, too, affected the mobility of labor, in particular seasonal migration, Europe's most ancient form of labor migration. As the completion of the railroads reduced the cost of travel in Europe, the seasonal migrations for work covered longer distances, travel made by a mass of increasingly proletarianized migrants who went rapidly from city to city, factory to factory, from one construction site to another.

Some recent scholarship has reinterpreted the history of industrialization, emphasizing the central role played by movements of capital and labor and criticizing an exclusive emphasis on technology as the driving force in the process of industrialization (Tilly 1983; Guttman 1988). But the migrant of the age of High Capitalism knew that the advent of new machinery was inseparable from his or her own experience of uprooting – machinery which had destroyed the old ways of making a living on farms or in workshops, as well as machinery which now carried him or her in search of a remedy.

The routes of seasonal migration up to the mid-1800s were mostly stable, typically involving the same destinations for workers coming from the same places year after year. The geographies of migration in the late nineteenth century became far less stable: the building of new cities, new factories, new railroads and tunnels, meant the destinations were always changing. And because of the growing proletarianization of the rural economy, the worker's points of origin were also changing, because migrants had no farm or cottage to return to. Capital took on a new meaning in these workers' lives. As the factory system grew and the rural economy became decimated after 1848, the vast majority of small landholders and cottage owners became dependent on cash earned elsewhere rather than on the products of their land or cottage. Like the new colonists, these seasonal migrants moved prompted by the struggle for survival in a cash-bound world.

In the ancien régime, the religious exile and the mobile laborer represented two sides of a state's dilemma; a ruler often wanted to cause the one to move, while keep the other from doing so. From the vantage point of the state the movements of the exile and the laborer differed in kind. After 1848 they tend to be increasingly confounded, in a political economy in which mobility is more and more an act of desperation.

Yet history draws no thick, unbreachable lines between what is and what was. An example of this truth, which is explored at the end of this chapter, lay in seasonal migration to the vineyards of Europe, a migration flow that began in the seventeenth century and, notwithstanding multiple crises, continued into the twentieth century. Even so durable an economic institution, however, reflected many of the transformations of the nineteenth century: economic expansion, the impact of new technologies and new ownership structures, weakening attachments of people to the rural economy.

EXILES AND REFUGEES

After 1848 the pedigrees of displacement changed rapidly in Europe. The term "exile" is as old as Western civilization itself. But up until the nineteenth century the word "refugee" referred mostly to Protestants forced to leave France at the end of the seventeenth century; French and English dictionaries referred to "refugees" specifically as the victims of the revocation of the Edict of Nantes. The first change appeared in the Third Edition of the Encyclopedia Britannica issued in 1796: "refugee" was extended beyond that particular case of Protestants to anyone leaving his or her country in times of distress, a general term also covering specific cases like the word "emigré," applied to aristocrats who left France during the French Revolution. Marrus (1985) notes, though, that there is little evidence that this shift in meaning of "refugee" was at first widely adopted.

In German there was no term for refugees until the mid-nineteenth century. "Heimatlos" or "staatenlos" began to be used to denote certain categories of stateless refugees after 1870. It was only after World

War I that the current term "Flüchtlinge" came into use. Yet 1848 stands as a turning point in these pedigrees of the displaced in terms of the human beings to whom these words applied.

In the early nineteenth century, well-educated, cultured exiles embodied the sort of refugees who were politically motivated to leave their own countries, not the masses of poor, homeless people who figure in twentieth century history. London, Geneva, and Paris were important cities of refuge for such exiles, places where these small groups of often talented individuals were mostly well received. The refugees included Polish nationalists who escaped after 1831, and refugees from Spain, Portugal, Italy, Germany, all involved in various political causes. In 1848, as one uprising after another fell to counterrevolutionary repression, a new wave of such people washed over Europe, now Germans, Austrians, Czechs, Hungarians, Italians. Switzerland was probably the main recipient of these political refugees, taking in about 15,000, mostly from Germany and Italy. In the 1850s, however, London had become the major European center for exiles in Europe, a palimpsest of generations of displaced people plotting return and revenge.

The friendly reception accorded these refugees should in one way surprise us, because the governments in power receiving them were not noted for native revolutionary ardor. Mazzini, for instance, set up the Young Italy movement in Marseilles in 1831, affirming to the world the aims of an Italian Republic and the cause of republicanism everywhere in Europe—at the time when a king ruled France. Yet he encountered no real difficulties from the state, though his establishment of the Young Europe movement in 1834 did cause the authorities to worry.

Though some form of refugee legislation was passed early in the nineteenth century in various European countries, it addressed largely the condition of those exiles who were members of elites. Thus in 1832, when France received a wave of largely aristocratic Polish exiles, King Louis Philippe codified the standing of these and other exiles from Spain, Italy, Portugal, and Germany in law. The French state was allowed, on paper, to expel them and to exercise various types of control over them; but these powers were seldom exercised, instead state policy came to provide stipends and support for the refugees according to rank.

Apart from solidarity among elites, perhaps another source of such toleration lay in the fact that the refugees from the years 1830 to 1848 were not taken seriously, and those from 1848 were failed men. Few in number, idealistic, they seemed to pose no serious threat to interstate relations. In the 1850s and 1860s the political-exile communities shrank, as their countries of origin granted amnesties and many of them returned home.

The refugees of 1848 were the last to have this honeymoon abroad. In the last third of the nineteenth century conditions changed. The wars of German unification of 1864–1871 created a new type of refugee and in far larger numbers. During the Franco-Prussian War, the North German Confederation had twelve million men fighting against France (which is twice the size of the army Napoleon sent into Russia in 1812). The destruction of villages and towns during this war produced refugee flows of a sort that begin to foreshadow the experience of the twentieth century.

The spread of nationalist fever to masses of people in the later nineteenth century also produced larger refugee flows, in that people were less willing to be ruled by "foreigners" than had been the case earlier. Thus a very large number of central European emigrants between 1867 and 1871 originated in provinces that had been annexed by Prussia. Rule over foreigners came to seem more problematic: France expelled about 80,000 Germans when Alsace-Lorraine was annexed by the newly formed German Empire, while 130,000 French left the region for France. Poles from the eastern provinces in Germany became refugees, seen as a threat by the authorities supposedly because of ongoing aspirations to form an independent Poland. Indeed, the line between involuntary expulsion and voluntary emigration became ambiguous, as when Germans who had lived in Russia since the days of Peter the Great became refugees and fled to Germany: between 1900 and 1914 about 50,000 Volhynian Germans left, and eventually others left from the Baltic region.

The refugees produced by these developments were often poor, typically blending with the native working class. Many of them were politically active as union organizers and socialist agitators. Tsarist Russia produced a whole new slew of radical revolutionary refugees who were active organizing the parties of the eventual revolution while in exile. The often deadly campaign of the anarchists beginning

in the 1890s also distinguished these political refugees from the ideal-
ism and romanticism of the earlier generation of exiles of the 1830s
and of 1848.

The mercantilist policies that held sway in ancien régime cities
such as Amsterdam considered the in-migration of people a positive
matter, an addition of resources. Obviously terrorists and anarchists
could not be viewed in this light, and the later nineteenth century saw
expulsions, as well as state collaboration with countries of origin in
returning radicals. France reversed its traditionally liberal policy, for
instance, and expelled more than 1,600 foreigners as anarchists between 1894 and 1906. It should be said that this was not the case everywhere in Europe. Great Britain, Belgium, and Switzerland refused to
collaborate and maintained their liberal policies, including the protection of the rights of refugees.

The more general issue, however, was the place of political refugees whose circumstances and whose numbers meant that they could
not be treated blithely according to mercantilist assumptions, as human resources added to the receiving society. In this, the condition of
the political refugee began to meld with the condition of the migrant
laborer in the age of High Capitalism, an age in which it was no
longer the case that the shortage of human beings meant all additional hands were welcomed.

THE MULTIPLE MEANINGS OF ECONOMIC GROWTH

Beginning in the third decade of the nineteenth century, the European
population exploded. Population growth in the nineteenth century as
a whole far surpassed even the thirty-four percent growth of the second half of the eighteenth century in some countries. From 187 million in 1800 Europe's numbers rose to 266 million in 1850, then nearly
doubled to 468 million by 1913. During this century population in Denmark, Finland and Great Britain more than tripled; in Belgium, Holland, Germany, Austria-Hungary, and Italy it doubled or more than
doubled. France's population growth at fifty percent was slow in comparison.

Food production rose as more land came into cultivation and new
crops were introduced, notably root crops such as turnips and potatoes. In England, for instance, food production tripled between 1700
and 1870, the greatest growth appearing from 1840 to 1870. Fewer

wars, fewer famines, fewer plagues, and more food ensured that mortality declined. For example, Armengaud reports that whereas in the early 1800s sixty-two percent of women survived to age twenty, by the early 1900s, three-quarters survived into their full childbearing period.

Paradoxically, the extremely rapid growth of population and food made it more and more difficult to ensure a livelihood in the rural economy, because of a sometimes rapid, sometimes gradual disintegration of a rural economy based on a peasantry and on cottage industry. The entry of capital into agriculture and manufacturing, including rural-based industries, and the explosion of factory-based manufacturing in cities, undermined the viability of production centered on small-scale ownership, typical of peasant agriculture and cottage industries. Tilly (1983) notes that by the mid-1800s the European countryside, a mostly peasant population in the sixteenth century, was now only one-fifth peasant; most people owned no land, except for their homes and a garden, if that.

We might imagine that the presence of more food would have sustained the existence of people in the countryside. But increased food production resulted from the entry of capital into agriculture and the development of cash crops. And these developments worked in the opposite direction: they concentrated ownership and control over food, far more so than had been the case when small peasant holdings ruled agricultural production. Governments reinforced the concentration of food in a few hands through policies supporting land consolidation, enclosures, and privatization of common lands that had once been used for grazing. The rural landscape became far more productive than it had been in the ancien régime, but far less capable of supporting its residents.

Rural manufacturing did not fare much better. The tools and machines used in cottage industry became obsolete causing the ruin of many households. Handicrafts production had supported hundreds of thousands of villagers. With the development of factory production not only did markets for cottage industry shrink if not disappear, but factory production increasingly expanded in large cities, leaving whole regions without much manufacturing of any sort. Without markets for their goods and with rapidly falling wages, the cottage industry could no longer support the local workforce (Levine 1987).

Many of these villages shrank in size and became almost exclusively agricultural (Pinchemel 1975).

The disintegration of rural economies affected home life and the relations between men and women. Thanks to the work of a modern scholar – Gullickson (1986) – we can chart these effects in depth on a particular French village, the village of Auffay. Here the decline of the rural textile industry affected courtship, marriage, and childbearing. When the weaving jobs of men declined, men left the villages leaving behind women. The women, however, were less mobile. Courtship became a troubled event in the village, because the young men knew they wanted to leave, while families tried to keep their daughters at home, away from the city, particularly the provincial capital of Rouen. There thus occurred a fall in marriage rates and an increase in births out of wedlock. The effect of the rural economic crisis on Auffay was repeated in many other villages (Grafteaux 1985; Chatelain 1976).

The timing of the transformation of the countryside varied considerably across regions; some rural industry continued to grow in Germany even toward the end of the nineteenth century, while most such efforts had begun to disintegrate in England by the end of the eighteenth century. But across Europe, these changes took a consistent form in the duration of labor: long-term jobs tended to be replaced by short-term jobs. As rural industry declined, agricultural labor remained the only option for many, but it was increasingly in the form of short-term work gangs working for hourly wages, and at often extremely low wages; people worked as vine trimmers, hoers, flower cutters, hay mowers, potato diggers, all jobs of short duration. The introduction of new crops, such as sugar beet, and of new machines, such as the thresher, again concentrated the annual demand for labor into bursts of activity during the summer.[1] This left long, jobless seasons where the mass of laborers lay idle.

The disintegration of the rural economy thrust more and more people into migration, looking for work. The end of annual contracts, in particular, led to year-round migration streams of workers in search of any job available, no matter how short, risky, and lowly paid.

LABOR MIGRATION AND THE BUILDING OF EUROPE

In the second half of the nineteenth century there thus arose new migration systems covering far longer distances than earlier systems and involving multiple destinations. The new cities of the Ruhr became the destination for people from eastern regions in Germany who had not migrated heretofore or had been part of the migration system to Holland. Irish went in large numbers to English cities. The crisis of the 1840s brought the workers, both men and women, from Flanders to work in the French countryside and cities. The end of serfdom in early 1848 in Austria and 1861 in Russia also set workers in motion. Austrian and Russian Poles migrated to Germany and France after 1861.

Such displaced rural people could go to other places which needed temporary agricultural labor. By 1841 seasonal Irish agricultural workers in England numbered 50,000; they came between the time they planted their own potatoes in February and dug them out in November (Harris 1989). By the mid-1800s there were over 350,000 seasonal agricultural workers in France, well over a fourth of whom were women. In addition there were almost a million seasonal jobs in the vine harvest (Chatelain 1976). (It should be noted that some of these jobs were held by the same person at different periods of the harvest; these are counts by employers.)

Massive new migrations were also supported by the vast amount of construction which occurred in the late nineteenth century, in cities and in the completion of railroads. Railroad construction required enormous amounts of digging, carving tunnels, building bridges. It took place throughout much of Northern and Western Europe and was largely work done by migrant workers: Britain had already employed them in the 1830s and 1840s, followed by the low countries, France and Germany, which laid thousands and thousands of miles of railroads from the 1850s until World War I. It was hard, dirty, and dangerous work, and evidence suggests that foreign workers were far more willing to accept the hardships of the jobs and the extreme discomfort of camp living than were natives (Chatelain 1976; Bade 1980; Rosoli 1978).

Several scholars (Chatelain 1976) describe the work of migrants on the railroads. For instance, to install the railroad through the mountainous fifty-one kilometers north of the coalmines of Ales in the south of France, workers from the central highlands and from the Piedmont built forty-seven tunnels through sixteen kilometers of mountains. The tunnel of Frejus in the Alps on the French-Italian border was another enormously difficult and arduous task. It took from 1857 to 1871 and employed about 2,000 men on a regular workday at the height of the construction of this thirteen-kilometers-long tunnel. The tunnel at the Gothard pass took nine years to build. Rosoli (1978) describes the migrations of Italians who worked on railroads and roads in the Alps: in 1900, 44,000 Italian men were employed in railroad construction in Switzerland alone. Italians constituted the main seasonal labor supply for railroad construction throughout Europe.

The installation of the railroad engendered new seasonal migrations insofar as deliveries of seasonal products – from flowers to fresh vegetables – could aim at a far larger geographic market area. Seasonal migrations into the Mediterranean plains were involved not only in the traditional grain harvest but also in the harvesting of fruits, vegetables, and flowers shipped by rail. There were multiple seasonal circular migrations aimed at specific areas and crops: women picked strawberries in the Rhône Valley in May and June, followed by men later in the summer who came to pick tomatoes; large numbers of Montagnards came for the grape harvest in the Mediterranean plains; east of the Rhône, 15,000 Italians came every year to Provence where the women planted and picked flowers, vegetables, and olives, and the men worked in the vines and gardens; Breton seasonal migrants picked strawberries and green beans for Paris and new potatoes for the London market (Boyer 1934; Rosoli 1978).

Changes in the actual produce of the land also set people in motion from place to place. When sugar beet became an important crop, for instance, it engendered very large seasonal migrations because of its extreme labor intensity and rapidly expanded demand. In Germany some of the earliest seasonal migration to beet fields began in the 1840s with *Sachsengangerei,* or "going into Saxony." By 1914 the beet fields drew about 450,000 foreign migrants from Italy, Scandinavia, White Russia, Ruthenia as well as Russian and Austrian Poles.

The largest migrations were of course overseas. The expansion of colonial empires and the development of the steamship made it possible for masses of people to flow into the transoceanic migration systems toward Latin America, Australia and New Zealand as well as North America. Over fifty million Europeans left for overseas destinations in this century before World War I. By the late 1840s 200,000 to 300,000 were leaving Europe each year. Betweeen 1840 and 1900, an estimated twenty-six million Europeans left, followed by another twenty-four million up to World War I. Of these, thirty-seven million (or seventy-two percent) went to North America, eleven million (or twenty-one percent) to South America, and 3.5 million to Australia and New Zealand.

Extreme distance was not, however, only to be experienced in journeys by sea. Migrations also occurred in the southern plains of European Russia and later in Siberian territories. The estimates for the number of such settlers vary widely; one of the more reliable is that ten million migrants arrived from 1815 to 1921 (Dollot 1965). The figures are smaller than those of settlers to North America, but they are significant because cheap land was available in southern and Asiatic Russia, and not only in the United States or Canada (Hoerder 1985).

These then were the circumstances of migration. What did they mean to those on the move?

We might begin to answer this question by considering again the villagers of Auffay. Though the villagers of Auffay, as elsewhere, may have sought to keep young women at home, economic need often did not permit that desire to be satisfied. As in the past, young women continued to make more or less temporary moves to cities to work as domestic servants, as mill workers, and needle workers. But some women made an entirely different sort of move, changing where they lived to become upwardly mobile. They were "career migrants," in the case of women a growing cadre of school teachers who found training and jobs far from their homes.

The strengthening of the modern nation-state, of overseas empires, and the formation of new states (the German Empire in 1871 and Italy's reunification in 1870) also opened up other opportunities for career migration for men, as post office officials, court-system clerks, and colonial police (Moch 1988). Career migration, as Max Weber pointed out, formed an inseparable part of the growth of modern, rational bureaucracies. These bureaucracies were meant to be open to anyone who was qualified, rather than closed, inherited offices; advancement through their ranks was to be similarly open. Weber believed that as nation-states consolidated, their bureaucracies would invite career moves and change of position throughout the nation-state as vacancies occurred.

The great novelists of the nineteenth century depict the drama of migration in this expanding economy almost always in terms of career migration, though seldom in these bureaucratic terms. We think of Balzac's depiction of Lucien Rembrempre in *Lost Illusions*, of Julien Sorel in Stendhal's *The Red and the Black*, of Becky Sharp in William Thackeray's *Vanity Fair*. The lure of city lights, the mobilization of ambition, the sheer hatred of stability: these mobile individuals dominate the literature of the nineteenth century, while few literary sources make heroes of workers moving to cities out of economic desperation, looking for work in construction or factories.

The fact that a novelist lacks sociological expertise, however, does not mean the writer lacks social vision. The sense of opportunities to be found through migration conveyed in these novels reflected a real world in which expansion of both economy and state bureaucracy created the possibility for career mobility. And the imagery of the beckoning city reflected a real world in which opportunities, such as they were, were more likely to open up in town rather than in the country. What is missing in the novel of "career migration" is both the interconnections of town and country, and perhaps even more importantly, the fact that a particular city, or foreign country, was not always a fixed destination for those on the move.

In the real world people frequently would or could not stay even in the great capitals such as London, Paris, or Berlin. There was considerable movement back and forth, both among local, intra-European, and transatlantic migrants (Langewiesche 1977; Hochstadt 1988). Return rates were particularly significant in transatlantic migration, because they challenge the commonplace assumption that migrants who went abroad in search of opportunities stayed there. Recent data show, for instance, that about one-third of overseas migrants to the United States returned to their countries of origin from 1899 to 1924 (Thernstrom and Orlov 1980). German and British migrants also had higher return rates than is usually assumed. The story of nineteenth century migration contains life histories with uncertain destinations; some of the German settlers that had moved to Russia, for instance, eventually moved to the United States when their privileges were reduced, some of the Finns who had moved to the United States eventually moved to Russian Karelia in search of less oppressive work conditions (Kero 1975). There is a parallel here with rural-to-urban migration: recent scholarship has also shown that this was not always a one-way movement.

When Balzac wrote about people on the move, he imagined his characters motivated by the desire to start a new life, to abandon the life they had known. In the more prosaic experience of people off the page, much migration – both abroad and to cities within Europe – aimed instead to raise family income to maintain an existing rural household, or buy more land, or make one's agricultural production and cottage industry viable.

The relations between art and life are perhaps most difficult to assay in the matter of how many career migrants succeeded, and how many, like Julien Sorel or Becky Sharp, failed. In the nineteenth century novelist's imagination, the ambitious migrant is undone by the very immoderation of his or her desire to rise. In the world off the page, ambitions were more focused and restrained; Sennett (1970) has shown that for most workers, ambitions were centered on ownership or secure possession of a new dwelling. Recent scholarship also finds that there was far less upward social mobility for migrants in the United States than is typically assumed, though it was higher than in Europe (Kaelble 1981). It is probably fair to conclude that career migration was a limited event, most achievable for those like teachers or colonial bureaucrats whose jobs were tied to the state. For others the immense geographic mobility brought about by industrialization did not translate into correspondingly significant upward mobility.

In this the condition of the new migrants approached, again, that of the political refugees. The struggle for survival consumed their energies rather than a coherent narrative of ambition. For the new masses of migrants and refugees, the geography of movement became a vector of change without a secure destination. They revolved on fortune's wheel, rather than pursued a fate.

CONTINUITY AND CHANGE: SEASONAL MIGRATIONS TO THE VINEYARDS

At the opening of this chapter, I remarked that history does not draw a fixed line between what is and what has been. It seems fitting to conclude this sketch of what happened to people in motion after 1848 with a more probing, local look at how the past also shaded into the present. We shall do so in exploring human movements in and out of the vineyards of France, drawing on the work of the modern scholar Chatelain.

Vineyards were already an important part of France at the beginning of the nineteenth century. Most regions sought to grow vineyards for their own consumption, only a few were truly massive concentrations of production for export. Their sharpest growth occurred after mid-century and the early twentieth century. In 1873, before the devastating phylloxera epidemic, 2.5 million hectares were under cultivation; by 1879 production had reached seventy million hectoliters, but declined to fifty million by 1900 and up to World War I. This massive expansion throughout the century required access to vast supplies of temporary seasonal labor.

The evolution of the vineyards over time and place, through crisis and prosperity, marks one of the many histories of temporary migrations. Migration to the vineyards was of two sorts. One originally occurred in the early spring, but this work eventually became year round, as the tasks associated with setting up a good vineyard multiplied. The other, at harvest time, remained the province of temporary seasonal workers.

Chatelain calculates that toward the end of the Second Empire about half a million seasonal migrants travelled the roads of France to go work in its vineyards. After the Second Empire, and the recovery from the phylloxera crisis, the numbers never again were as high. The 1929 agricultural survey found slightly under 108,000 seasonal migrants working in France's vineyards in the four Mediterranean departments. Over this century there occurred a significant change in the sources of temporary seasonal migrations: while the Montagnards from the Massif Central kept on migrating to the vineyards, migrations from the Alps and the Pyrenees dried up. As the mountains accounted for fewer and fewer of the seasonal migrants, laborers in the vineyards came from the cities, organized by recruitment offices and agencies. This change affected large vineyards. Small growers continued to make do with the help of family and neighbors.

In the first half of the century it was the South Atlantic region that drew more temporary migrations than the Mediterranean plains. This region was well connected through its Atlantic ports to northern

France and beyond. To the South Atlantic region came two types of migrants. The montagnols or *défricheurs* who came in the winter, mostly from the Pyrenees, were men and were hired for the heavy work of planting, défrichage, and fumage. The second migrants who came for the harvest, in September and October, consisted of men and women. From the Lot-et-Garonne, for instance, came 400 men, women, and children to work in the vineyards of the Gironde. They walked by foot for three days; they carried the tools of their trade, their bedding, and their food. From the Charente-Inferieure came 850 mostly youth fifteen to twenty years of age; they returned to their home communities with a total of 8,500 francs, which was about 100 francs each. Beyond the two peak seasons, the Gironde also had to import laborers during off-season periods.

After the Gironde, the Mediterranean vine producing region — Roussillon, Bas-Languedoc, and Basse Provence — was the second largest vine-growing region. The report for an 1808 inquiry provides a useful account. It tells us that teams of vineyard harvesters came every year to the eastern Pyrenees region from the Aude and the Ariege. A total of about 1,000 men and women came for about fifteen days working at modest salaries: the men worked at 1.80 franc per day and the women at 1.20 franc; food was not provided. Thus again, as in the Gironde the earnings were meager — even for the times — given the hard labor involved. A Dr. Morelot records they were excessively exploited and surveilled, badly fed and with miserable lodgings, and given extremely low pay for the amount of hard work.

The vineyard owners viewed migrant workers as untrustworthy, needing continuous surveillance to ensure productivity and that they would not eat too many grapes as they worked. Dr. Morelot mentions that wives of owners were sometimes sent to follow the workers, picking the grapes that the workers had failed to pick and making sure they would not eat too many grapes. They would be served two meals, one frequently early in the morning before leaving for the vineyards, the second one or two hours after mid-day: the first meal was typically a plate with potatoes or haricots seasoned with a bit of milk, and a piece of poor quality bread; the second was a form of garlic bread.

A lowly paid, feared, often despised population, yet indispensable to the vineyard owners, the migrants knew how their employers viewed them, as expressed in the lyrics chanted by migrants on their route to Bourgogne:

> Allons en vendange pour gagner cinq sous
> Coucher sur la paille, ramasser des poux
> Manger du fromage qui pue comme la rage
> Boire du vin doux qui fait aller partou

Yet there was growing competition among neighboring departments for seasonal workers throughout the latter half of the nineteenth century. Some vineyards went to recruit workers in departments where they had hitherto never recruited before. The concern among growers was such that some called for a halt on emigration of French workers to the Americas, that the government should not allow them to leave given the labor needs in France – a continuation of the calls for the state to bar labor emigration which had arisen in the ancien régime. A report from late nineteenth century complains about massive departures of up to 6,000 workers, "deceived by the promise of great riches" by labor contractors taking them to the Americas. The situation was similar in other regions of France. As wine cultivation expanded labor shortages appeared everywhere, in the Saône and Loire, in Côte d'Or, in Bourgogne, in Loire-Inferieure.

The new industrial world being constructed in the cities via the railroad provided to some growers the explanation for the modern experience of an ancient shortage; they blamed the expansion of public-works construction because it employed growing numbers of migrant workers. The miserable conditions of work the employers had imposed on migrants did not figure in this explanation, though in certain regions some growers recognized that they had to give workers better treatment and pay, which they did.

Again, the new economic order intruded as the partial mechanization of certain tasks in the cultivation and preparation of fields sharply reduced the demand for labor in the spring season after the 1860s. But the need for a vast supply of workers in the fall harvest remained, indeed, as production expanded, grew ever more acute.

The end of the Second Empire marked the highest expansion of the vineyards. A crucial factor behind this expansion was the rapid growth of the market for wine thanks to the development of railroads. This particular period of about twenty years of great expansion and sharp shortages of labor came to an end with the devastating phylloxera plague.[2] More workers abandoned the vineyards in their travels due to the death of the vines caused by the phylloxera mite – which ate away at the root of the plants. The phylloxera crisis also set in motion new labor migration dynamics: it prompted some local workers and small growers to become migrant laborers themselves. For instance, some of the local workers in the Languedoc went to Algeria, where grape production was expanding. But this meant in turn that when the Languedoc vineyards recovered and began to expand again, the problem of an adequate labor supply returned with a vengeance. Recruitment of French migrants especially Montagnards began once more, but it was not enough.

After the plague passed it became necessary to recruit workers from foreign countries, notably Spain and Italy. Spaniards had already come to the Mediterranean plains as part of construction crews on the railroads. Italian workers were recruited by growers in Provence. Because foreign migrant workers accepted lower wages, vignerons in many regions began to prefer Spanish and Italian workers over French migrants. Not surprisingly the French workers did not take kindly to foreigners, who were seen as pulling down the wage scale. Seasonal Spanish workers in the vineyards numbered 18,000 in the years preceding World War I, a migration that was to resume after the war and reached its highest number in 1922 with 24,755, of whom almost 11,000 were women. They arrived in large numbers on chartered trains; waiting carts took them to the vineyards where they would be working, filling all the roads with enormous traffic.

By the beginning of the twentieth century, the migrant laborer ceased to be part of a migration system whereby he went every year to the same places and then returned home with all his or her savings. Often the new migrant workers had no permanent home and were forever searching for jobs. This impermanence increasingly marked the lives of the Spanish and Italian newcomers as much as the native French migrant laborers. The familiar rhythms of work movements were disappearing. Yet as this short history also makes clear, that effacement was not the sudden work of the railroads, the construction projects, or the conversion of rural labor into short-term wage contracts. Rather, these changes widened tears in the fabric of rural life made in earlier generations.

NOTES

1 The thresher did the work that had taken eighty percent of a farmworker's time in the winter season; in addition, threshing had to be done toward the end of the summer, thus eliminating a key source of off-season jobs.

2 The phylloxera plague began in Gard as early as 1863 but the massive devastation of vineyards did not begin until 1872.

4

NATIONS AND MIGRATIONS:
GERMANY, FRANCE, ITALY

Low did the nation-state figure in these emerging patterns of migration? Germany, France, and Italy in the nineteenth century revealed three ways the nation-state was and was not engaged by migration. Germany represented the ideal of temporary immigration within the nation-state. France acted on the principle of permanent immigration – the more immigrants the better and make them all French. Italy, still a more amorphous land by the end of the nineteenth century than Germany or France, emerged as a major emigration country shortly after national unification. There seems to have been a minimal role of the nation-state in emigration, though significant enough eventually to exempt Italy in the 1951 Geneva Refugee Convention from the obligation to take in refugees given its history as an emigration country.

To be sure, the nineteenth century nation-state played a less defined role than it would with World War I in identifying and categorizing "foreign" populations and in regulating their movement, entry, exit, and conditions for residence. But the nineteenth-century shows us how contemporary issues in immigration policy became deeply embedded in questions of nationhood and political culture, as well as in economics and geography. It also shows us that even as a country can keep reproducing itself as a labor exporter, there is considerable patterning to this process, both in its duration and scope. This holds even at smaller geographic scales, such as regions within a country.

In terms of economics and geography, the three countries formed a sharp contrast to each other. Germany's nineteenth century migration history was dominated both by disintegration and growth; as noted in the last chapter, the agricultural economy and rural industry disintegrated as a factory-based industrial economy, with an increasingly proletarianized population, grew. The disintegration of earlier forms of livelihood based on the rural economy produced conditions for emigration while industrialization produced conditions for the demand and employment of low-wage migrant workers. In the late 1880s Germany sent a million people overseas, mostly to the United States. By the beginning of World War I, there were over three million Germans overseas, and Germany, in turn, had received one million foreign workers.

France has had a longer continuous migration history than other major countries in Europe. Immigration played a far more important role in nineteenth-century France than emigration. Unlike the Germans, the French never were part of nineteenth-century mass emigration from Europe to North America. The maintenance of a significant agricultural sector until well into the twentieth century ensured the possibility of a livelihood in the countryside, and created a demand for immigrants. The rapidly growing cities in France created a further demand for workers, though the French did not become urbanized on the scale of the English until after World War I.

Italy, along with Ireland, has been until recently the quintessential European emigration country, an image formed by overseas migration. Less familiar is the draw of other European countries upon Italian emigration during the nineteenth century. Early in the nineteenth century, indeed, in the eighteenth century Italians flowed into France and Switzerland, then to Germany and Sweden. The Italian migration to Europe appeared to outsiders to be a temporary seasonal event that lacked the definitiveness of an overseas journey. But for the Italians these European migrations were both highly structured and often disturbing events.

This chapter provides more detailed information, for in these facts and figures there appears the shape of the conundrums of migration which nation-states face today.

GERMANY: THE IDEAL OF TEMPORARY IMMIGRATION

Until the late nineteenth century Germany had significant emigration flows: besides mass emigration overseas, there were the earlier migrations from Westphalia to the North Sea as described in chapter 2, and Germans migrating for work to France and to Switzerland in the early nineteenth century. In the late second half of the nineteenth century the development of mines and factories, railroad construction, and the building of cities drew significant levels of foreign workers from Southern and Eastern Europe to Germany. The elimination of serfdom and the associated proletarianization of peasants also generated massive internal migrations and overseas emigrations in search of employment (Bade 1987; Benz 1985).

The northeast of Germany emerges as a major area for these different flows in the late 1800s. It was here that recruitment for Germans to go overseas was most intense; it was also where most of the East European migration to Germany came; and it was a principal source of internal migration to areas in western Germany, especially after the elimination of serfdom. The western regions of Germany, particularly the Ruhr-Rhine area, became major recipients of foreign and internal migrant workers.

Emigration to North America rose sharply from 1880 until the mid-1890s. This was the last of three main emigration waves in the nineteenth century: from 1846 to 1857, from 1864 to 1873, and from 1880 to 1893. The third period saw the largest numbers for the whole century; at its conclusion Germany ceased being a country of emigration (Bade 1987). German emigration was mostly directed to the United States where they came to be thirty percent of the foreign population in 1890; after that they declined to 18.5 percent in 1910 and 11.3 percent in 1930. Most emigrants in the late 1800s came from the agricultural areas of the northeast, with an enormous jump in 1880. It is at this particular period that the northeast emerges as the main sending area; in the two earlier waves it had been the southwest region in Germany where overseas migration originated.

Both regions had land ownership and inheritance patterns that resulted in diminishing opportunities for a land-based livelihood. Growing numbers of people had to leave the countryside. In the southwest continuous splitting of farms due to customs of equal land division among heirs made the plots less and less viable economically. In the northeast inheritance customs passed the land entirely to older sons, creating a growing mass of landless people; further, the large estates, which dominated agriculture here, employed contract and seasonal farm labor at extremely low wages. The formation of a vast poor landless class of workers was a factor feeding migration, particularly to the western areas of Germany in the case of the poorest. The shift to root crops concentrated much of the demand for labor on the summer and left little paid work for the winter. It seems that many left, both overseas and to other parts of Germany, in the hope of returning with enough money to buy sufficient land to live on. Also for those with land, it was impossible to find work paying reasonable wages to supplement their livelihood and maintain their land-based household because wages on large estates were extremely low.

Unlike some of the other European countries, the emerging German nation-state adopted a liberal stance toward emigration – though, as we shall see, it kept very tight controls over immigration already in the nineteenth century. After hot debate in the 1830s about the question of emigration, the Emigration Bill of 1849 was passed, an act which even considered setting up an office of emigration. At the Reich level, though, it was not until 1897, when mass emigration had ended, that the state implemented an emigration act. This act also was liberal, except for controls over the emigration of young men who might be escaping military duty.

The abrupt ending of emigration in the early 1890s has been explained in various ways. One explanation invokes Turner's famous "frontier thesis" about the Western United States: Turner argued that shifts in westward movement in the United States changed when the possibility of acquiring empty, cheap, and above all unregulated land evaporated in the late nineteenth century; the desire for such "free" land had certainly motivated earlier emigrants from East Prussia. Now, in the late 1800s, emigrant Germans in the United States wound up in cities: fifty-one percent of German-Americans were found by the census to reside in cities of 25,000 or more, compared with thirty-five percent in Germany. Further, the United States experienced a great economic depression in the early 1890s while Germany had an economic boom in the mid-1890s. This boom led to a situation of full employment and required, indeed, recruitment of foreign workers to fill demand.

In the early 1890s, when emigration dropped sharply, internal migration became the major flow. Internal migration to the rapidly industrializing areas in Germany, particularly in the west, replaced overseas emigration. During the 1880s and 1890s we see the emergence of long-distance internal migration, especially to the Ruhr district. Migrants from the northeast had first gone to Berlin, drawn to its industries. Later in the 1870s they started going to the industrial areas of central Germany. For some of the earlier migrants it was possible to take temporary industrial jobs and maintain a land-based household in the east. In some areas such as Mecklenburg there was a long tradition of both overseas emigration and of internal migration. The volume of internal migration was already exceeding overseas emigration in the 1880s.

In East Prussia, where farmers were the poorest and wages for farmworkers were the lowest, there was no overseas emigration. Emigration was not an option for the very poorest – a theme that recurs in the twentieth century. These poor farmers had no help to pay for the ticket overseas; they lacked transatlantic networks providing support and resources and thus could not make chain migrations. Instead, they had very high internal-migration levels to the western regions of Germany, and it was with these regions that they established networks (Bade 1980). By 1910 almost half a million Germans from East Prussia, West Prussia, and Posen were living in the western provinces (Bade 1980).

The migrations from the northeast in Germany to the western provinces consisted of many ethnic groups (Barfuss 1986; Benz 1985). Among these were "ethnic" Poles, who became isolated laborers in the so-called subculture of the Ruhrpolen (Crew 1979). They went to work in the coal mines beginning in the 1870s, foreign-speaking farmworkers entering all at once an industrial world. Many had gone with the idea of a temporary migration to earn enough money to go back and buy land in the east. For most, however, it became a permanent migration. There is a parallel here with many who had gone to the United States with the same intention yet never returned.

Like the migrants going overseas, these migrants going to a western economic "frontier" found that a foreign land awaited them. In the westward movement within Europe, as in America, the new migrants encountered problems of alienation and of integration, of strained bonds of dependance and mutual help among family and friends. By looking a little more closely at this westward thrust within Germany, we can understand better how the nation-state by the end of the nineteenth century pursued a policy of temporary migration as an ideal for Germany.

From 1880 to World War I, the northeastern region of Germany was drained by out-migrations of diverse kinds. Where urban employment was available nearby as in Brandenburg, or industrial employment as in upper Silesia, rural populations left rural jobs for these jobs even though they continued to reside in their rural areas–an instance of *berufliche Landflucht*, or occupational landflight (Quante 1933). The expansion of beet production, a labor-intensive crop, generated a whole new and vast demand for seasonal migrants, much larger than that in other regions of Germany. Opportunities elsewhere in the country, the development of mines and factories, the building of railroads and cities, all drew German people away from the northeast.

This labor vacuum was filled by a movement across the German border, from those who in turn lived further east in Europe (Benz 1985). Migrant farmworkers, including men, women and children from Central Poland (at the time under Russian control) and from Austrian Galicia, came to form an annual flow of a quarter million by the early 1900s (Bade 1980). Employers saw these desperately poor migrants, with no choice but to work at low wages as *willig und billig*. Over half of the Poles who migrated to Germany were women, and they were often preferred by employers who attributed to them great skill in digging roots, or greater docility and willingness to work for lower wages than men (Perkins 1981). One cannot help but notice the parallels with the assertions by employers of young women in today's export-production factories in Asia and Mexico. The Poles had in fact seen their livelihoods devastated by the elimination of serfdom in Russia and Austria (Morawska 1989). And the partitioning of Poland between Prussia, Russia, and Austria had transformed them into "minorities" in what had once been their own nation-state.

Jews also formed part of this east-to-west push through Germany. From 1880 to World War I, Germany served as a first stop for many Jews on their way to the United States: about 700,000 Jews entered Germany from the east from 1905 to 1914. These poor, premodern eastern Jews shocked and revolted many German Jews who had assimilated into Germany's professional and middle-class life. And though there was immense Christian hostility toward Jewish migrants, Germany never sealed its frontiers with Russia. Instead the German government encouraged poor Jews to leave and others with resources to stay. Though at times the government expelled some poor Jews back to Russia, most were sent to America; shipping companies worked with the government, and with Jewish relief agencies, to transport Jewish emigrants to the United States. By 1910 there were only about 70,000 East European Jews left in Germany.

To be sure, the flow from east to west was not the sole human stream which flowed through Germany. In the early 1900s in the whole of Germany, seasonal agricultural workers entered legally from Italy and Scandinavia, as well as from white Russia, complementing the dominant westward stream of Austrian and Russian Poles. In 1914 alone entrants numbered almost half a million.

How did the nation-state respond to this influx? The sheer importance of these migrant laborers for agriculture in East Prussia, for mining in upper Silesia, for the industrial districts of the Ruhr, was fully acknowledged in various statements by local authorities and employers associations. The Prussian administration conceded that the absence of foreign migrant workers "would almost mean the deathknell for agriculture;" the mining industry in upper Silesia asserted that the industry could "not continue to operate without foreign labor" (cited in Bade). Yet such acknowledgments did not mean that these immigrant workers received the same pay or treatment as native workers, nor that employers or the receiving authorities made any attempts toward their social integration. Long before any Turkish workers appeared on the German scene, these East European masses were treated as the nation's "guest workers."

Though Germany was liberal about emigration, its immigration policy tended toward curbing permanent immigration and promoting temporary migration. Unlike other European countries Germany already had a strict system of control over immigrant workers before World War I. Almost all the lander had introduced requirements for work permits for a particular job (called Legitimations Karten); a new card was required for a change of job. A foreign worker found without such a card, or looking for a job without a card which specified he had been dismissed by his prior employer, was expelled from the country. Originally meant for farmworkers, this system was eventually extended to all job categories. There was also mandatory identification (Legitimationszwang), a state control applied with particular rigor to the Polish workers who were half of the migrant workforce.

As a result Germany saw the formation of a highly mobile foreign workforce, controlled in terms of residence and work permits. Germany numbered a temporary migrant workforce of more than a million; between 1890 and 1910 the number of foreign residents tripled, from 430,000 to 1.26 million, about 200,000 of these had been born in Germany. Although less than the 3.5 million German emigrants at the turn of the century, it is a significant number. And this number does not include undocumented immigrants, who often became permanent residents against the will of the state.

In *Discipline and Punish*, the social philosopher Michel Foucault argued that the powers of the modern state developed partially through the identification of minority or deviant populations in modern societies, such as the enumeration and classification of prisoners or asylum inmates. Certainly this was also true of the treatment of migrants, though German state controls over migrants did not aim, and certainly did not encourage, integration of these minorities in German society. The division between state and society appeared most dramatically in the discourse about the "Polonization of the west" (Knoke 1911; Benz 1985). There are resonances here with later post-World War II conceptions of immigration in Germany.

The state apparatus distinguished between ethnic Poles, living on territory annexed by Germany, and foreign Poles, living on territory annexed by Russia and Austria. Foreign Poles were only allowed in as temporary workers by the German state. Foreign Poles were not allowed to settle, they were required to depart Germany by December 20 every year and not return until February 1, and they were allowed to go only to the eastern provinces. The state viewed these Poles as ineluctably alien, people who wanted to reconstitute Poland and whose presence in Germany threatened the state's eastern border. Yet the presence of Poles coming from territory which Germany controlled did not create a more receptive, integrative attitude. The state repressed or regulated the cultural life of ethnic Poles working in the western provinces; their press and organizations were monitored and censored, their national symbols not allowed (Crew 1979). These rules ensured that even permanent residents could not connect their cultural histories with the circumstances of their present lives; culture dwelt in an imposed silence, an unassimilable memory of elsewhere. Such views were signs of the state's belief in the ineluctable "foreignness," a belief which led logically to equating foreign workers with those who should have only temporary ties to Germany.

But because of the very centrality of *Polenpolitiek* in Germany's politics of nationality and citizenship, this attitude could not simply and mechanically be translated into practice; the divide between state control and social integration, the effort to maintain Poles in, as it were, a state of suspended animation during their German stay, proved more traumatic. The Polish population was a mobilized population with its own strong nationalistic sentiments and leaders. The state had at first attempted to make Poles "loyal" to the German state; the perceived failure of this project eventually led to the mass expulsions of 1885. Initially, while chiefly aimed at nationalist agitators among the immigrants, this policy became an indiscriminate expulsion of both foreign Poles and East European Jews. From 1885 to 1887 more than 30,000 Poles and Jews with Russian and Austrian citizenship were expelled (Neubach 1967).

In turn the government sought to replace Poles with Germans in the eastern frontier districts through a new settlement law. This was an internal colonization program inaugurated in 1886 which resulted in the settlement of 20,000 Germans, 120,000 with their families included. Yet this program, too, did not succeed. The Polish community had an effective cultural and nationalist organization which operated as a kind of colonization counter-program. Moreover, the western frontier within Germany continued its magnetic pull, causing more Germans to leave than to come to the eastern border districts. This failure led to even harsher measures. In 1904 a new law required local administrative permission for all new settlements. Though a 1898 law had made the furthering of *Deutschentum* a duty for administrative officials, the new 1904 law clearly discriminated against Polish settlement. A 1908 expropriation law permitted expropriation as a means to strengthen *Deutschentum* in West Prussia and Poznan, but the outrage inside Germany and abroad caused by this law meant that it was used only once.

Within Germany the state's efforts at regulation also wrinkled, due to the economic needs of agriculture and industry. Following the expulsions of 1885, for instance, new Polish immigration was banned. But labor shortages continued and intensified because of ongoing out-migration overseas and to the western districts. On the land the growth of beet crops demanded additional workers, for growing beets is more labor intensive than cultivating grains, and thus agrarian interests pushed for the reopening of Polish labor migration.

In 1890 after the fall of Bismarck a compromise was reached that allowed for the re-admission of Austrian and Russian Poles but under strict control to prevent their permanent settlement: only unmarried Poles, restricted to agricultural work in frontier districts, required to return to their home countries during the winter (Herbert 1986). There continued to be very strong opposition to Polish immigration even under these strict conditions. But nonetheless seasonal immigration continued to grow.

The condition of Prussia on the eve of World War I showed the result of the interplay of state and economic forces. Prussia accounted for about three fourths to four fifths of all foreign workers – in itself an interesting illustration of the patterning of migrations. About forty percent of foreign workers in Prussia in the early twentieth century were employed in agriculture, and of these about two thirds were Poles; by 1913 there were about 240,000 Polish seasonal workers employed in Prussian agriculture (Bade 1980). Poles were only five to ten percent of the larger number of immigrant workers in industry, mines and other sectors. Indeed, only about a third of all foreign workers in Germany were Poles, and a much smaller share of resident foreign workers were Poles because most Poles were seasonal. Yet the public discussion and debate about immigration was dominated by the imagery of "the alien Pole," and more generally by the idea of a massive invasion of Slavs and Jews from the east (Herbert 1986).

We would err greatly, however, in imagining that the xenophobia and the racism of the 1930s simply reflected the Germany of the 1880's and 1890's. Neither state nor nation reacted to all foreigners, such as the Swedes or the Italians, as they reacted to Poles; indeed, without the trigger of the Polish-eastern question, immigration in Imperial Germany was a rather invisible issue, receiving little attention from the general public. Moreover, "the state" of the 1880s and 1890s was not a single body. Different German Länder had rather divergent naturalization policies; thus Prussia was free to pursue, and pursued, a particularly restrictive policy, as did Bavaria and Saxony, the two other German states that were considered most vulnerable to immigration from the east. And it was in Prussia in early 1885 that Bismarck eventually forbade the naturalization of Russian subjects (almost all Poles or Jews), preceeding the mass expulsions of 1885 elswhere.

Moreover, the fear of invasion from the east met resistance

throughout certain sectors of German society, though it was an ambivalent resistance. Trade unions, for instance, were divided between a political attitude of internationalism and the immediate interests of the workplace. Labor unions in Germany tried to organize the migrant workforce but failed to get equal rights and benefits for them. At the same time the presence of foreign workers willing to work for lower wages and longer hours led to fights, criticisms, and name calling: the foreigners seemed to be inherently "strikebreakers," "wage cutters," etc.

World War I brought an end to these divisions, debates, and ambivalence. Society and the state now both sought to force migrant workers in the country to stay, especially those in agriculture, which still numbered 374,000 at the end of the war, and without whom there would have been an even greater labor shortage crisis. Prisoners of war, of whom there were about 900,000 by 1918, were also put to work in agriculture.

What the Polenpolitiek reveals about Germany generally was a certain conception of the nation itself, one based on the notion of jus sanguinis – a nation being formed by those sharing a common "blood," as though a nation were a biological inheritance rather than a cultural acquisition. In the nineteenth century, this was hardly a belief unique to Germany. Darwin flirted with the idea of jus sanguinis in *The Origin of Species*, arguing against Lamarkian notions of cultural and biological adaptation; Abraham Lincoln several times invoked it during the American Civil War, in arguing that America's North and South formed, by blood, inseparably one nation; Slavophiles made of "blood" a mystical connection binding together peoples dispersed among several arbitrarily separated territories.

Germany was distinctive in the ways it sought to enact that widely held belief in jus sanguinis into law. Germany legislated a strict conception of citizenship and nationhood embodied in jus sanguinis in a law of 1913, which allowed Germans residing abroad (*Auslandsdeutsche*) to retain their citizenship and to pass it on to their descendants. Before this law was passed, German citizenship was lost after a person had resided abroad for ten years, except if one followed elaborate registration procedures with a consulate. The 1913 law in turn rejected legal provisions associated with jus soli, that is, the principle that place of birth and residence determines citizenship. Indeed, before the new law, German citizenship law had fluctuated between ancien régime versions of jus solis, appropriate to residence in a territory which was a dynastic holding, and the nineteenth-century version of jus sanguinis, which emphasized the virtues of social bonds formed gradually over time among a community by descent, the community welded together by blood ties no matter what marriages, covenants, and legacies were made among princes.

A law of 1870 had declared the principle of jus sanguinis in the emerging nation-state without challenging solis. The economic situation of the country made it possible to do so; in 1871 there were only 200,000 permanent foreign residents in Germany out of a total population of forty million. There was high demographic growth and little expectation that more immigration would occur. By 1913 the demographic and economic changes surveyed above made it difficult for people to think of these two principles as coexisting (Brubaker 1992). The 1913 law not only privileged the community-of-descent criterion at the expense of residence, it also introduced two new criteria for having one's German citizenship taken away: taking another nationality and failing to do military service. There were multiple exceptions and qualifications. One of these concerned German emigrants in countries with citizenship laws based on jus soli, in which case they were allowed to keep their German citizenship as well. Notwithstanding exceptions, these two criteria made it difficult for many German emigrants to hang on to their German citizenship. In the end, the new law strove to facilitate the reacquisition of German citizenship by emigrants and their descendants, again reflecting a need for more Germans to make the new Germany work.

This citizenship law figures as a prime example of what Max Weber saw as the thrust toward bureaucratic rationalization in the modern state, and yet also shows the limits of the state's power to legislate citizenship according to a single principle. Jus solis could not be so easily banished. German Social Democrats made several proposals to liberalize naturalization so that it should be a matter of jus solis right for certain persons, notably for those born and raised in Germany. They were seconded by, among others, Poles. The Social Democrats, when accused of wanting to create an impure nation via jus solis, argued that almost all other major states, and notably France, had elements of jus solis.

Yet this appeal to the realities of contemporary international law ran counter to certain German memories. The ethnic frontier between Germans and Slavs, so basic to the German's state understanding of the German nation, derived from migrations of Germans eastward in the high Middle Ages, and then again from the sixteenth century onward. Those migrations east had created and maintained multiple German settlements throughout Eastern Europe and Russia (Hagen 1980). Some assimilation had occurred, yet the Germans had continued to identify themselves as German, maintaining their language and rituals in alien lands, even as in these territories, particulary Poland and Russia, contrary images of native culture grew stronger. A law based on blood seemed to make sense of this web of cultural separations, a cultural history transposed into biology, a biology rationalized by the state as the distinction between those who belong permanently and those who coexist temporarily together.

France showed a contrary effort to cope with the movements of people.

FRANCE:
THE MORE THE BETTER AND MAKE THEM ALL FRENCH

In the French tradition universal political values define membership rather than blood or descent. The state's institutional, imperial, and territorial framework provides the elements for a definition of the nation and of citizenship. Already in the ancien régime there was a political rather than a blood-based emphasis on the nation. A shared culture provided the experience through which nationhood could be constituted and assimilated.

This assimilation was facilitated by the gradual penetration of the central state into all parts of its territory through schools, public administration, the military, the infrastructure of communications. The internal Mission Civilisatrice in the late nineteenth century, carried out by the Third Republic's army of schoolteachers, was perhaps one of the sharpest formalizations of the assimilationist understanding of nationhood (Weber 1983). The right as well as liberals in France shared this sense of a mission civilisatrice, which included a concern for national grandeur and at various times was extended onto a broader imperial territory, both overseas and inside Europe. Indeed, these assimilationist policies vis á vis regional cultures inside France were often quasicolonial (Weber 1983)

This project of assimilation through a shared culture addressed both internal, provincial differences and the question of immigrants. This is reminiscent of France's particular mode of imperial expansion: the French mission liberatrice et civilisatrice, which institutionally went much further than British or German forms of the legal and political assimilation of metropolitan and overseas territories. In the 1880s the internal assimilation linked to reforms of primary education and military conscription created a context for a broad assimilationist reform of French citizenship law whose central provisions exist today. In spite of various xenophobic phases, including the anti-Semitism toward the end of the nineteenth century, the French maintained an essentially political conception of nationhood, one that overrode questions of race and language.[1]

One line of analysis (cf. Brubaker) posits that the introduction of jus soli was not as instrumental as is often claimed – that is, that its purpose was to increase population growth and to increase the pool of military recruits. There were larger political and ideological factors at work in these reforms. Brubaker argues that the 1851 liberalization of naturalization provisions was definitely not in response to military and demographic needs, because neither were an issue at that time.

Yet France's economic experience of migration complemented this political culture. It is as an immigration country that France reveals the most interesting and significant patterns. Throughout the nineteenth and much of the twentieth century France was Europe's main immigration country. Beyond the government's worries about stagnant demographic growth and insufficient supplies of young men for military conscription, immigration policy and practices were informed by a broader political understanding. The rational, state-centered, and assimilationist conception of nationhood that was implemented with the French Revolution – though there were elements of it already in the ancien régime – led to an inclusionary stance regarding foreigners who resided in France. In this regard France was quite different from Germany.

A major theme in French immigration during the nineteenth and well into the twentieth century was France's declining fertility. There was relative stagnation in the growth of the French population in the sixty years up to World War I when other European countries experienced rapid population growth (Dyer 1978; van de Walle 1974). There is considerable consensus that at least two other factors made immigration far more important in recent French history than emigration (Fohlen 1985, 11). First the pressure to leave the countryside because of periodic agricultural crises in the nineteenth century was balanced by the growth of French cities and the corresponding demand for labor. Foremost was Paris with its large growth during the second Empire. Second, in many areas rural industry and custom kept people attached to the countryside. France lacked the pressures to leave we see in Ireland at mid-century and in Italy or Northeastern Germany after the 1870s.

But, though French emigration levels were significantly smaller than those of other European countries, there was some emigration. According to Fouche (1985), the latent emigration potential in France throughout the nineteenth century was rather high: it could have reached massive levels, pushed by the periodic crises, including famines, in the French rural economy. But it did not–again showing us the extent to which migrations are patterned. Indeed, it was not the areas close to the large ports which contributed most of the emigrants, but rather areas in the interior where these crises took place.

Although the figures are not totally reliable, they suggest that the numbers of French nationals living outside France and outside its colonies rose from about 310,000 in 1861 to 600,000 in 1911. There was a rise in emigration in the 1880s and the decade before World War I (Chevalier 1958): in 1881 to 1886, 426,000 emigrated; in 1901, 495,000; and in 1911, 600,000 did so. This is a relatively small figure compared with Germany's 3.5 million at the turn of the century. Between forty and forty-five percent of French emigrants went overseas for much of the nineteenth century, until 1890. About twenty percent went to French colonies, and the remainder to other European countries. After 1890 there was a fall in overseas migration, with sharp fluctuations ranging from thirty percent to ten percent in the migrations to French colonies, and a steady increase in intra-European migration. In the 1901–1910 period French emigration to other European countries reached 54 percent of all emigrants.

In his detailed historical analysis of travel and other records covering the period of 1816 to 1889, Fouche (1985b) finds that the typical French emigrant was more likely to go to South America and the Caribbean than to North America, was male, young, came from the countryside of southwestern France, but had resided in Bordeaux and worked in commercial, maritime, or port activities. Once again, the

patterning in migrations stands out. Roudie (1985) working on records
for 1865 to 1920 also finds that Latin America was a stronger destination than North America. Guey (1980) describes a case of chain migration in the 1830s from the poor isolated Barcelonette Valley in the Alps
to Mexico.

In the late nineteenth century pronatalism was not unconnected to
broader colonization projects insofar as settling colonies with
Frenchmen would provide future generations of French with land
and opportunities. But only one fifth of French emigrants actually
went to French colonies from 1850 to 1925, a far smaller share compared with the English and the Dutch.

The colonization of North Africa began mostly after 1848. There
was an organized emigration which followed the decree establishing
forty-two agricultural colonies in three provinces of Algeria, with an
annual quota of emigrants from Paris fixed at 12,000 (Katan 1985).
While many of the Parisians returned, migration from southern
France continued to grow in response to local agricultural and commercial crises and in view of encouragement by the French government. As described in chapter 3, Algeria became the site for the
development of new vineyards in response to the phylloxera crisis.
Migration to North Africa was strongest from 1875 to 1890 when phylloxera was destroying the vineyards in the Mediterranean plain. The
numbers of French in Algeria rose from 66,050 in 1851 to 129,601 in
1872, 233,937 in 1881, and 271,101 in 1891 (Chevalier 1947, 167). By the late
1880s emigration to Latin America had declined and movement to the
North African colonies had grown, though it never reached the levels
of French emigration to other European countries, particularly Belgium, Switzerland, and Spain.

But France was principally an immigration country. Net immigration throughout this period played an important role in population
growth. It accounted for a third of such growth between 1851 and 1886.
From 1886 to 1891 it accounted for eighty percent of population growth
(Rabut 1974). The foreign population as counted by the census grew
from 100,000 in 1800 to 380,000 in 1857, to over one million in 1881, 1.2
million in 1911, and reached 2.7 million in 1931.

As with other countries the immigrant population in France was
becoming increasingly diversified even though it was always a limited number of nationalities that accounted for most of it. The largest
immigrant groups in 1896, according to the last census of the nine-

teenth century, were Italians and Belgians. Far smaller were the next groups, Germans, Spanish, and Swiss. Italians were the largest nationality group; they numbered 292,000 in 1896 and 419,000 by 1911. Other large groups also came from bordering countries: Belgium, Switzerland, Germany, Spain, and England. And they mostly settled in the border provinces, except for the Paris region which at 153,600 in 1907 was the second-largest concentration of foreigners (Didion 1911).

The geography of settlement also shaped the employment characteristics of the immigrant workforce and vice versa. Thus the Spanish and Italians were in agriculture in the south, and the Belgians, Germans, and Italians were in industry in the north and east. Immigrants were heavily concentrated in industry, where fifty percent of them were employed in 1891 and forty-three percent in 1911, compared with respectively twenty-six percent and thirty percent of French. About forty-five percent of the French on the other hand were in agriculture, compared with respectively, nineteen and twelve percent, respectively, of foreign workers (Mauco 1932, 48).

The precipitating issue in the 1889 liberalization was resentment at the exemption from military service for foreigners often long time settled. This resentment intensified in the 1870s as the military induction rate increased, and especially in the 1880s with the ascendance of Republican doctrines of universal and equal military service. The general context within which this is to be understood is one of reverence for the army as an incarnation and instrument of France's grandeur and a state-centered and assimilationist understanding of nationhood that would make naturalized immigrants into French men and women.

Opinion in France was divided between those who saw immigration as economically necessary and considered that immigrants could be made into Frenchmen and those who considered immigration a threat to the culture, economy, and society of France, the latter a familiar argument heard today in most immigration-receiving countries (Wihtol de Wenden 1988, Green 1985). Racism was not absent during this period. About fifty laws on immigration were proposed between 1883 and 1914 which aimed at taxing immigrants or their employers or restricting entries. They were seen as competing with French workers, as poor, as *malfaiteurs*. One law passed in 1899 limited the percentage of foreign workers in public-works projects. But almost all the fifty proposed laws were defeated. In practice the interests of firms in industry prevailed and there was a tacit encouragement and often active recruitment of immigrant workers before World War I.

It is quite clear that immigrant workers were not there for only demographic purposes. They were recruited for hard, dirty endless days of work in areas that were often quite unattractive. The story of Longwy illustrates this well (Noiriel 1984). In 1905 the Comité des Forges de l'Est began to recruit workers from Italy and later Poland for the mines and steel works of Longwy. Noiriel found that this was a flow of workers that actually was already underway in the 1880s. By the time of World War I this area had the largest concentration of immigrant workers in the whole of France. It was in many ways an immigrant frontier zone, a "far west" as Noiriel puts, with a far larger concentration of men than of women, high mortality rates, high levels of disease, and inadequate housing and services for the population. Some of these conditions were evident in many of the mining towns in Europe.

An event that took place in 1889 reveals something about the stance toward immigration at the time. During the 1889 World Fair held in Paris, there was an International Conference on Governmental Intervention with regard to Emigration and Immigration, with delegates from the old and the new worlds. There was intense discussion about the costs and benefits of each, and what governments should do, how migration should be regulated, and so on. In the end the delegates came back to the free market as the best regulator of state and individual interests and hence to a laissez-faire policy.

ITALY: THEY WORKED THE FIELDS AND MINES, BUILT THE RAILROADS FOR THE REST OF EUROPE

The major destination of Italians in their century of emigration from 1876 to 1976, was Europe (Rosoli 1978; Sori 1979). Almost 12.6 million Italians went to other European countries, a million more than went overseas. And although the United States was the single largest recipient country, with 5.7 million, France with 4.1 million was not that far behind given its far smaller size. Switzerland received almost four million, Germany 2.4 million, and Austria almost 1.2 million. Overseas, Argentina was the next-largest recipient after the United States, with 2.97 million and Brazil with 1.46 million; Australia received about 428,000 and Canada 650,000. There were smaller flows to other countries as well. Together the European and overseas countries received over twenty million Italian emigrants.

It was only at the turn of the century that Italian emigration was mostly directed overseas. But in the period after Italian unification in 1861 and then again after 1920 with the closure of U.S. immigration, Italians went largely to European countries.

There were clear patterns in terms of origins of the different flows. The north of Italy had had a long tradition of seasonal and temporary emigration to France and Switzerland, and when it entered its mass emigration phase, this European emigration continued to come largely from the north of Italy. The southern emigration was largely directed overseas. Once established these patterns reproduced themselves: chain migration meant that southern Italians who had gone overseas brought their kin overseas, while northerners brought theirs to other European countries. But there were also incidental factors shaping these streams. The sharp development differences that were emerging between the north, where Piedmont, Liguria, and Lombardy were becoming the most advanced regions in Italy, and the south may also have sharpened the differential patterning of emigration. Further, a fact such as the cost of travel may have played its own autonomous role initially: from southern Italy it was cheaper on average to go to New York than to northern Germany. The recruitment patterns of different countries may have initially contributed to the differential patterning and eventually reproduced it. After 1920 and ever since, Italian emigration gradually became more and more Europeanized.

This century of Italian emigration was a period where there was industrial growth and development in the country though characterized by considerable unevenness. The critical factor explaining the coexistence of industrial growth and emigration was the reorganization it brought about in agriculture including the proletarianization of erstwhile peasants and the radical transformation in economic organization brought about by the factory system of manufacturing, which expelled many people from rural cottage industry. Italy is in this regard not different from other European countries to the north, though the timing may be different. The 1880 agricultural crisis contributed to a sharp acceleration of Italian emigration in the same way that it did with German emigrants from the northeast. In addition implementation of a free trade policy hurt industry in the south, which had remained fairly backward under the prior protectionism. Further the need to meet monetary obligations in peasant economies that generated little money forced people into searching for wage labor. Finally the formation of an international labor market (cf. Rosoli 1985) was a crucial factor in the initiation and reproduction of these labor flows: the search for flexible, cheap labor supplies, especially in the face of growing trade unionism, all meant that contractors and employment agencies played a role in these migrations and immigrant workers were welcomed by firms.

Between 1876 and 1915, fourteen million Italians left their country. Each decade showed a higher total outflow than the preceding one, peaking in the 1906–1915 years with almost six million departures. For this whole period of four decades European countries received forty-four percent; the rest went overseas. The major European destinations were France, with almost 818,000; Austria-Hungary, with 600,400; Germany, with almost 354,000; and Switzerland with 327,000. They came mostly from northern regions. Emigration rates for major sending areas reached very high levels: in Veneto they reached a peak of forty per thousand in the 1880–91 period. This was almost exclusively a male emigration; women were seventeen percent in the first few years and twenty-five percent towards the end of the century. About forty percent of emigrants were agricultural laborers.

From 1901 to 1915 Italian mass emigration peaked. It reached such levels that it became destabilizing if not destructive of social and economic structures (Rosoli 1985, 101–2). A total of almost 8.8 million Italians left in this fifteen-year period, of whom about twenty percent were women. The share of agricultural workers in the outflow kept decreasing, falling from thirty-five percent to twenty-six percent. It is the period of growing proletarianization of the Italian, and European, population. Five million went to the Americas, mostly to the United States. In Europe, Switzerland, France, Germany, and Austria, respectively, were the main destinations. The main sending region within Italy was Sicily, which accounted for over 1.1 million emigrants in those fifteen years, and reached a rate of forty emigrants per 1,000 inhabitants in 1913. In view of today's fears of mass immigration, it is worth noting that even considered at this small regional scale, the "mass emigration" from Sicily reached four percent of the population.

The evidence on return migration is very partial. It covers only returns after 1905 and then only from overseas destinations. According to these figures from 1905 to 1915 about two million Italians returned home, of whom 1.2 million came from the United States, and hence returned mostly to the south. Data on return migrants from European countries only begin with 1921.

By the end of the nineteenth century Italians were the largest immigrant group in France (Bezza 1983; Wlocevski 1934). Their numbers rose from 63,300 in 1851, one sixth of all foreigners living in France, to 264,600 in 1886, one fourth of all foreigners, to over 414,200, more than a fourth of all foreigners. The 1906 census found that Italians were forty percent of the foreign workers in agriculture and forestry, and forty percent in manufacturing, two thirds in transportation, and one third in commerce. In some industries Italians represented significant shares of all workers in France, not only foreigners; they were eight percent of all chemical workers and seven percent of all quarry workers. These figures underestimate the presence of Italian workers in that they exclude many seasonal workers as described in earlier chapters (cf. Rosoli 1985).

There were also women and minors: the Italian community in Lyons consisted mostly of women and children (Bonnett 1977). The silk industry employed many Italian women, and the glassworks employed up to 4,000 Italian youngsters in jobs the French forbade their own minors from holding. Italian minors were contacted in Italy and initially walked over from Italy; later on they were transported by boat from Naples to Marseilles (Cafiero 1901; Schiaparelli, 1901). Marseilles had one of the largest concentrations of Italians, who held many of the hardest and lowest paid jobs in the harbor; most of the 2,400 fishermen in Marseilles were Italians. In addition they also worked in salt production, soapworks, highway construction.

Typically Italians were contacted directly in Italy by firms or employment agencies. In France Italians did the hardest jobs, lived in dreadful conditions, were paid less than the French, and were typically considered to be more docile than French workers. They played a crucial labor role in the development of mines, roads, railroads, and manufacturing. French workers and trade unionists did not look kindly on them, though there were times when they collaborated (Milza 1977; Bezza 1983). But there also were terrible incidents of violence; for instance, in 1893 French workers savagely attacked the Italians in the saltworks of Aigues Mortes, killing fifty and seriously wounding another 150 (Vertone 1977)

It was the construction of the Brenner railroad in the 1860s and the St. Gothard railroad that brought significant numbers of italians to Germany after 1860 (Jacini 1915; Knoke 1911; Sartorius von Walter-shausen 1903). The censuses, taken in December when many sea-sonal workers had returned home, do not give good figures on Italian migrants. It is estimated that in the period before World War I Italians numbered about 175,000 during the summer. Besides railroads, Ital-ians were concentrated in manufacturing, mining, and construction. By 1860 there were already several hundred Italians working in the mines of Westphalia. In southern Germany there were brass workers, chair weavers, travelling vendors from northern Italy, sellers of marble and alabaster statuettes from Lucca; they worked in the brick factories of Bavaria, Württemberg, and the Rhine-Palatinate (Rosoli 1985, 109). The 1906 census found that almost half of all foreign work-ers in construction were Italians, and that they were the third-largest immigrant group in manufacturing. Unlike Italian emigration to France during this period, Italians did not settle in Germany and they did not do farmwork.

The situation of Italian workers in Germany was one of hard work and low pay. For instance, in the brick factories of Bavaria Italians worked eleven to twelve hours per day without interruption, a far longer day than natives. The workforce included women and chil-dren who were used to clean the furnaces, to load and unload them, to move heavy trolleys and in night work. The silk, cotton, and jute industries also employed women and children.

Italians were recruited by German contractors or firms; they often travelled in special trains which took several days. The main destina-tion was in the West, where the largest iron and coal deposits of Eu-rope were being developed, in the Ruhr, Lorraine, and the Saar Basin.

Prejudice against Italians seems to have been rather strong and there was little integration into German society. Italians had low-paying jobs and little opportunity for advancement. High levels of illness, extremely unhealthy work environments, up to sixteen-hour workdays, overcrowded and unsanitary living conditions, all charac-terized the Italian migrant work experience in Germany. German workers and trade unions did not like the low wages accepted by Italians and saw them as weak and ineffective as workers and as trade unionists. Nonetheless it was in Germany where the local trade unions worked the hardest to organize Italians. By the nineteenth century the Central Federation of Trade Unions of Germany published a newspaper in Italian, *L'Operaio Italiano*. Union representatives also sought to organize inside Italy during the winter months.

Italians had been going to Switzerland for many decades, but it was not until the 1870s and the building of the St. Gothard Tunnel that significant emigration of Italian workers began (Amman 1917; de Michelis 1903; Bezza 1983). By 1880 there were 41,500, and by the end of the century 95,000. The 1910 census counted half a million foreigners in Switzerland, accounting for fifteen percent of the total population in the country, and up to thirty and forty percent in certain cantons. Germans and Italians together accounted for four fifths of the foreign population, about equally divided. Italians were six percent of the entire Swiss population, their highest incidence in any of the European countries, and this figure excludes Italian seasonal workers of which there were considerable numbers.

Italians in Switzerland held the most dangerous and heaviest jobs. They were crucial to the building of roads, tunnels and railroads: they worked on the Mont Cenis (1857–1871), St.Gothard, and the Alpine railroads of Rigi, Pilatus, Albula, including the Brig-Furka-Disentis railroad begun in 1914, the Simplon tunnel and later the Loetschberg railroad. By 1914 one third of all workers in construction were Italians. Italians also worked in the brick, silk, cotton, chocolate, footwear, and tobacco industries.

As in other countries Swiss workers and trade unionists saw the Italians as weakening their efforts and often called them scabs; violence also erupted, such as in Zurich in July of 1896 when Swiss workers attacked Italians. There were some Italian migrant worker unions, such as the Federazione Muraria Italiana, a union of Italian masons. Italians also set up quite a few mutual benefit societies. The Swiss generally were not interested in integrating Italians into Swiss society; there was considerable open contempt. Illness and poor health were common among the Italians given the severe work conditions and dismal housing.

CONCLUSION

Each of these countries represents a complex trajectory and no brief summary can do it justice. Here I just want to extricate a few elements that serve to illuminate some of the issues of concern in this book, notably issues present in current debates about immigration.

The case of Germany brings to the fore the fact that a relatively small number of immigrants can take over the public imaginary and come to be seen as representing a threat to the integrity of the "nation" and of the state. In the particular German situation, this representation of a threat was embedded in the "Polenpolitiek." Polish immigrant workers were not even a majority of all foreign workers, but it was their case which dominated the debates and the concerns, the fears and the aims of immigration policy in Germany in the late 1800s and into the early 1900s. We see here how a particular group of migrant workers can become the site for a larger state project of power and self-representation. In my reading, there are resonances here with current conditions in some of the European countries, as well as in the United States.

The case of France shows us that even a country that wanted immigrants as a way to increase its population and get men for its armies, can have an ambiguous relationship to its immigrants. They were paid less, they were treated badly, they were often hated. This is all the more revealing because France's was a republican project of making citizens out of those who lived in its territory, and it had fairly elaborate laws protecting the rights of people. Yet it allowed the recruitment of Italian minors to work in jobs and industries where French children were prohibited from working. Again, today we see that states determined to respect and strengthen the rule of law, can nonetheless accommodate considerable abuse of the civil and human rights of immigrants, including the extension of policing as a way of regulating immigration.

The case of Italy tells us something about the force of representation, no matter what the facts. The hundred years of Italian emigration stretching from 1876 to 1976 have largely been associated with the new world. In fact a majority of Italian emigrants went to European countries. They worked on the tunnels, the roads, the railroads, the cities in much of Europe. Further, while we think of Italian emigration as an indiscriminate flow out of poverty, there was in fact an enormous amount of patterning and only select areas of the country had strong emigration. Most emigrants came either from particular areas in the North and went to other European countries, or they came from particular areas in the South and went to the new World.

Each of these, then, captures a theme that is a challenge today in the making of immigration policy.

NOTE

1   The definition of French nationality was widened through the law of June 26, 1889, whose basic provisions remain in place today. It granted the French nationality to those born on French soil; children of immigrants born in France became French. This law also made naturalization easier, reducing the waiting period from five to three years. It could even be obtained after one year of exceptional service to France, including military service, or for the introduction of an industry, or for bringing distinguished talent to the country.

5

THE STATE AND THE FOREIGNER

Another history began to take shape in the 1880s, one which at times intersected and became part of the history of migrations: the history of mass refugee movements. What is remarkable from the particular vantage point of this book is the combination of two elements: the first, the extent to which the states of Western Europe had a relatively low level of involvement in regulating or controlling refugee flows until World War I, the second, how little impact these massive refugee flows taking place mostly in the eastern regions of Europe had in shaping interstate relations within Western Europe before World War I.

With World War I the modern European state strengthens its border-enforcement functions and sovereign control over its territories; passports are suddenly checked. The changes after World War I regarding both refugees and immigrants stand out sharply. We can see to what extent the contemporary debate about immigration and refugee control is a response to a rather new history for Europe, a history that began with World War I.

Between the early 1880s and World War I several massive refugee flows were initiated. About 2.5 million Jews left Eastern Europe. Hundreds of thousands of refugees were also created in the late 1800s and early 1900s by the gradual disintegration of the Ottoman Empire, and the savage nationalist battles that ensued. Of particular interest here is that the events of this time in the Balkans show us, without any ambiguities, how a different meaning of the notion of "foreigner" or "outsider" emerged, different from that which had prevailed for many

centuries in Western Europe, though it was also beginning to change
there toward the mid-1800s. Ethnicity becomes a marker of allegiance
as new states mobilized to secure independence and national cohesion.

In the case of the East European and Russian Jewish emigration,
European states basically did not have to adjust their immigration
policies, because there was America ready to receive this vast influx.
Nor did the refugee flows in the Balkans bring about a revision of
nineteenth-century notions about refugees.

It is only with World War I and the formation of the inter-state
system that large refugee flows would bring about a fundamental
change in the role of the state in population flows and a change in the
notion of the "foreigner." It would signal the beginning of the modern
notion of refugee "crisis" as we have come to understand this term
today. The strengthening of the interstate system in Western Europe
and the centrality of sovereignty and border control it entailed, the
rise of communism in Russia, and the closure of immigration in the
United States, created a confluence of conditions forcing European
states to address the matter of refugees coming from the east. They
could no longer be simply shipped to America. The fact itself of classification and identification of refugees in the context of the centrality
of border controls forced states to deal with one another on the refugee question.

The nationalism associated with states seeking sovereign control
over their territories and the strength of the interstate system transformed the whole notion of "foreigner," compared to its rather lighter
connotations in earlier centuries. Oppression by those with power
had been common in undemocratic political systems, and oppression
by "foreigners" had as well in situations of vast empires encompass-
ing several nations or multiple small provincial realms where any
outsider was a "foreigner." The coupling of state sovereignty and nationalism with border control made the "foreigner" an outsider. The
state was correspondingly able to define refugees as not belonging to
the national society, as not being entitled to the rights of citizens. Unlike the refugees of an earlier period who had been outsiders in the
same way the transients or vagabonds were, refugees in the twentieth
century were identified as a distinctive category; the state now had
the power and the institutional legitimacy to exclude refugees from
civil society (Arendt 1958).

What distinguishes Europe in the first quarter of the twentieth century is the combination of the formation of mass refugee movements and the participation of the state in their identification as refugees and in their regulation. In the past the receiving state was not an active party in the definition of arrivals as refugees and in the organizing of their settlement. The role of the state changed in a fundamental way when the state assumed control over borders and over a growing range of events in its territory. Refugee flows emerge as one such event. Further, refugee flows begin to affect the relations between states even as the interstate relations in turn produce some refugee flows.

It is in this context that the states of Western Europe confront the masses of refugees engendered by World War I and its aftermath. In response, the League of Nations established a High Commission for Refugees, marking the recognition by European states of an international refugee crisis. With it came governmental obligations toward a formally defined group of refugees.

The new role of the state and the interstate system also contributes to lengthen the duration of the status of refugee, one sometimes passed on to a second generation. This was and often continues to be partly due to the identification of refugees as a specific category; for example, one characterized by lack of nationality status or statelessness given the formation of new states and the elimination of some old ones. This was also partly due to the length of the procedures to obtain a new nationality; and partly due to the vast numbers involved. The internment of large numbers of civilians in refugee camps is one consequence of this combination of conditions, one unknown in earlier times.

Also their size made twentieth-century refugee flows different from any earlier flows. World War I and the subsequent interwar period brought massive refugee flows into existence. But even these were dwarfed by the aftermath of World War II, when it is estimated that sixty million European civilians had been forced to move (Marrus 1985). This is ten times more than the refugee mass created by World War I and its aftermath. This made Europe the continent of refugees, a title that has now passed to Africa and Asia.

THE JEWISH FLIGHT WEST

Between the early 1880s and World War I, the mass departure of 2.5 million Jews from Eastern Europe and Russia out of a total of 5.6

million resident Jews in the 1870s was in some ways the first modern mass refugee movement. Most Jewish emigrants came from tsarist Russia, particularly the Polish provinces, with much smaller numbers from Austrian Galicia and Rumania[1] There was growing official anti-Semitism as of 1863, and eventually in 1881 there was the first in a series of pogroms – collective attacks by the local population, typically abetted by the police, the military, and official representatives of government. As a result an average of 20,000 Jews left each year for America. After the Revolution of 1905 and up to 1910 there was a sharp increase, with an average of 82,000 Jews a year leaving for America. Russian Jews accounted for about half of all Russian emigrants to America.

And yet, notwithstanding extreme anti-Jewish sentiment, a mercantilist approach to population emerges. The obstacles to emigration in Russia were such that most Jews actually had to leave illegally, even after 1891 when some of these obstacles to departure were lifted. Marrus (1985: 28–34) argues that even though persecution played a role in Jewish emigration there was no concerted effort to force Jews out. There were other factors that fed the desire among Jews to leave besides persecution. The rapidly sharpening poverty in the Jewish community and the impossibility of overcoming this poverty particularly given persecution. All these factors made the trip to America look promising. Yet many Jews returned to their countries of origin, a feature not associated with refugee movements in the twentieth century. Recent scholarship has found that the return rate was about fifteen to twenty percent in the 1880s and 1890s, which is significantly higher than the five percent maximum long assumed to be the case (Sarna 1981).

In a way then this Jewish emigration was different from later twentieth-century mass refugee flows where there was no hope of return. And in this sense it was a premodern refugee flow.[2] For Marrus the Jewish mass migration from Eastern Europe had some elements of a mass refugee movement. But only some. There was no refugee "crisis" before World War I in that European states basically did not have to adjust their immigration policies and did not have to worry about refugee settlement. America was open to this vast influx, and America, it seems, was where most wanted to go. In this sense the East European Jewish migration did not bring about a revision of nineteenth-century notions about refugees.

There were no legal obstacles for Jews moving in other areas of Europe: within the Hapsburg Empire, in France, Belgium, Holland, Great Britain. There were significant numbers of Jewish emigrants throughout Western Europe: in Paris, Vienna, Amsterdam; in the waterfront districts of Hamburg and Bremen; at certain railway junctions and in certain frontier cities. By the end of the century opposition to the Jewish emigrants was widespread, anti-Semitism, xenophobia, prejudice, all were present. Yet Germany, a key transit point for Jews going to America, never closed its frontiers with Russia. The government encouraged some to leave and others with resources to stay. Shipping companies worked with the government to carry Jewish emigrants to America. At times the government returned some to Russia, but most were sent to America. By 1910 there were only about 70,000 East European Jews left in Germany.

Britain had an open-door policy that allowed any destitute alien to come without controls; in this Britain was different from all other countries in Europe at this time. Russian revolutionaries were free to enter and so were Jewish emigrants. This policy ended formally in 1905 with the Alien Act which set limits to unwanted immigration. This act made a distinction between refugees and immigrants; its perspective on refugees was one of political activists or revolutionaries suffering persecution, not masses of poor persecuted people. The Jews were not seen as refugees. In practice the new regulations were only sporadically enforced and did not make much difference. Jews were still free to come in, and did.

Established Jewish communities in the West, partly concerned about their fellow Jews from the East, and partly concerned about the vulnerability of their own newly acquired status in the West, organized various kinds of relief efforts that sought to facilitate the transatlantic emigration of Jews, to return Jews to Russia, or to keep them from trying to leave Russia.[3]

THE BALKANS AND EARLY VERSIONS OF ETHNIC CLEANSING

Another major process that contributed important elements to the modern conception of refugee movements took place in the Balkans. The history of the Balkans in the decades preceding World War I is extremely complex given the vast number of players and the often long-standing grievances and nationalist projects. It is impossible to do justice to this history here, and this is not the purpose of this book.

The Ottoman Empire, which at its height had run from Vienna to the Mediterranean and east to the steppes of Russia, began to lose control over its European territories as early as the eighteenth century. Not only the Russian and the Hapsburg empires made claims on the lands, but also numerous nationalist movements in the nineteenth century. The multiplicity of language, ethnic, and religious groups encompassed by the Ottoman Empire had often enjoyed considerable local administrative autonomy. The receding imperial structure reinforced prospects of autonomy and the claims to independence.[4]

These claims to independence were grounded on specific "national" identities. In the context of war such "national" identities could easily assume absolute and exclusionary forms and lead to what Lord Curzon called "the unmixing of people." Such conditions are likely to produce refugee flows. And they did. There were major flows of Christians going northward, away from Turkey, and of Muslims going toward Turkey. There were also a multiplicity of more local refugee flows as the unmixing proceeded. Refugees sought to go to the places where those of their "national" identity ruled. The savagery of the fighting and the massacres led refugees to desperate searches for sanctuary in friendly jurisdictions. The conflicts that were engendered by the Ottoman Empire's struggle to keep control over its erstwhile territories produced many refugees. But even larger were the refugee flows produced by the Balkan conflicts of 1912–13 and after, conflicts centered on nationalist claims, intra-Balkan antagonisms, and the worries of the Habsburg monarchy and Russian Empire. The savagery and the cruelty of these conflicts may well have been unprecedented in modern European history, though the destruction of Armenia by the Turks cannot have been far behind. The drive to exterminate the enemy was part of these conflicts. The fierce nationalism of the struggles for independence only added to these refugee flows. Marrus (1985) describes how this nationalism did not create sanctuaries for victims of Ottoman persecution; it created enclaves of supposedly "pure" ethnicities.

Because the unmixing could not be complete given the many interactions and intermarriages that had historically bound the different regional localities in the Balkans, nationhood based on distinct ethnic identities was perhaps doomed to ongoing armed conflict and impossible resolution. It would seem that peaceful coexistence in the region was only possible under a stronger overarching authority than each autonomous entity – whether the Ottoman Empire in its time of strength, or such supra-states as Yugoslavia under Tito. It is the impossibility of a resolution based on the exclusion of all outsiders, or "foreigners," that is crucial here, and that reveals the mythical nature of the "national" identities on which claims to independence were made (Sennett 1993).

The refugee movements in the Balkans were part of state-building processes. Zolberg (1983) speaks of "integration crises" as important factors in triggering refugee flows in the modern period, particularly where ethnicity emerged as a marker of national identity. This seems to have given the conflicts among Balkan States a particular ferocity, according to observers of the time. Toynbee referred to "the chaotic, unneighborly races of southeastern Europe." He was not alone in this perception. Marrus (1985) notes that much of Western Europe saw the entire region as barbaric and not really part of Europe, not capable of the standards for state conduct expected from western states.

In this same spirit the vast movements of desperate refugees criss-crossing the region in all directions had little impact on Western European politics of the time. The West could still regard mass refugee movements, whether the Jews from Eastern Europe or the refugees of the Balkans, as types of events that were not part of the Western European interstate system, or perhaps even more broadly, of Europe. World Wars I and II were going to reveal other truths about the nature of the state and about mass refugee movements.

WORLD WAR I AND ITS AFTERMATH

World War I marks the beginning of a period when the modern European state and its politico-military project create the setting for massive refugee movements on a scale hitherto not seen. The mechanisms which engender these state capacities for the "production" of refugees are the state-building process, which assumes a new intensity in this period, and correspondingly, the new role and importance of the interstate system, which crystallizes with the formation of the League of Nations. State-building processes contribute to mass flight and mass expulsions. And the emergent interstate system was the key to the creation of the stateless person, the identification of refugees as such, and their regulation or control.

With World War I the state emerges as the most powerful and organized machine for death and destruction. Together, the European states put seventy-four million men under arms, killed between ten and thirteen million combatants, wounded another twenty million, and destroyed cities, factories, and agriculture on a scale never seen before (Best 1980). The bureaucratic machinery of the state was put to the use of maximum possible destruction of the enemy.

The results? One of them was an estimated 9.5 million refugees in the decade following the war. These refugees included those escaping revolutionary upheavals and persecution and those expelled for having the wrong "nationality" or ethnicity in still fragile nation-states that sought to establish themselves in terms of a national identity. To a large extent these masses of refugees were on their own. Every now and then the governments involved in the peace treaty in Paris introduced some provisions to address the most extreme instances of persecution and expulsion. The League of Nations created the Office of High Commissioner of Refugees and appointed Fridtjof Nansen, the highly regarded scientist and explorer, who became a major force supporting the cause of the refugees. But in the end the refugees of this period were "the people left out of the settlements of 1919, those whom the treaties failed satisfactorily to address, whom the Great Powers considered of secondary importance if they thought of them at all" (Marrus 1985, 52–53).

The process of state building was strongest in the East, with the collapse of the four major dynastic empires that had dominated Eastern Europe–the Ottoman, the Romanov, the Hapsburg, and the Hohenzollern (Zolberg 1983). And so was the formation of mass refugee movements during and after the war. The nationalism that imbued the war meant persecution during the war of populations whose identity could not be assumed to assure loyalty: besides Poles and Jews, by then long-standing incarnations of "the foreigner" that could not be trusted, there were now ethnic Germans. All three groups were forced out of much of Eastern Europe and Russia. In addition there were multiple expulsions in the Balkan States of those whose nationalities did not "belong." One of the most tragic of these flights was the famous trek to the Adriatic by 500,000 Serb civilians and soldiers ravaged by war and disease after the onslaught by armies of the central powers. It has been estimated that ten percent of the Serbian population was rounded up and sent to camps in Hungary or Bulgaria, often as forced laborers.

Russia accounted for a large share of refugee flows. When the Russian army had to retreat in mid-1915, whole villages were uprooted, forced to leave as the army followed a scorched-earth policy. Ethnic Germans were deported en masse, carried in sealed cattle trains to Siberia and Central Asia (Koch 1977).[5] By December 1915, Russia counted 2.7 million refugees (Kulischer 1948). The numbers kept growing and the tsarist government did not do anything about it. The arrival of masses of exhausted and starving refugees in cities and villages often created clashes and riots. One estimate has it that by early 1916 there were as many as five million refugees adrift in Russia. Aristocratic ladies charities worked with government committees and municipal organizations to help refugees.[6] Freezing and starvation were constant threats to life. Many of these refugees were still not settled by the time of the 1917 revolutionary events. In the early stages of the revolution a whole new emigration occurred – old elites, of whom some went abroad, and many others to the edges of the new Russia. And when terror and repression were used to ensure the new regime, yet another new emigration ensued. Refugees went to Finland and the former Baltic provinces, to Poland, to Ukraine. Multiple battle fields emerged as the antirevolutionary forces sought control over various areas. Refugee flows were going in opposite directions, those escaping the Bolsheviks and those escaping the counterrevolutionaries.

Poland was another major site of conflict and the formation of refugee flows. The 1918 collapse of Russia, Germany, and Austria lifted the partitioning of the Polish territories. Yet Poland had to fight with its neighbors to establish her borders, and it was not until the 1921 Treaty of Riga that the frontiers were set and the organized move of displaced persons among various countries could take place. Returning displaced Poles, who came mostly from the east, entered a completely devastated land, particularly on the eastern side. In some regions there was hardly any human life or agriculture. An Australian relief worker described hills covered with skeletons of Russian soldiers who had been killed years before and who still lay as they had fallen (Marrus 1985, 57–58). According to Polish authorities by 1920 over 1.25 million Poles had returned (de Bryas 1926, 56). There are many tragic accounts of the hardships experienced by the repatriates. One describes a train that at origin had 1,948 persons; coming from Kazan on the Volga this train had travelled 1,700 kilometers, at a slow pace, and had taken three months, with hardly any food. Only 649 arrived alive; the other 1,299 died of exhaustion, privation, and disease. This appears to be a fairly common description of what repatriates went through (de Bryas 1926, 21).

The high point of devastation and refugee crisis was reached with the 1921 famine in Russia. It is estimated to have killed over five million people, making it probably the worst famine in European history. Orphans were estimated to number 1.5 million in famine areas, with thousands dying of famine and disease by the roadside or in streets (Nansen 1923). Together with civil war, political upheaval, repression, and generalized economic crisis, it unleashed yet another refugee movement. Large numbers left and there were several evacuations.[7] By the early 1920s there were over one million Russian refugees abroad. In addition the Soviet government initiated the practice of exiling unwanted people, mostly intellectuals, professionals, and politicians. Many went east. Shanghai was a key center for Russian emigrés in the East, with about 60,000 of them in China by 1924. They went to Manchuria and Mongolia, to Syria and Palestine. The largest concentration of Russian refugees was the half million in Germany; next was France with 400.000. Paris was the political capital of the refugees (Nansen 1923).[8] By the late 1920s these figures had fallen considerably because of deaths, returns, and settlement in foreign countries.

According to Marrus (1985, 61) Jews in Eastern Europe and Russia had the bloodiest experience they had had until then in Europe in modern times. They were attacked on both sides of the armed conflict. Systematic persecution of Jews on the western borderlands of Russia, battles over the Pale Settlement, where Jews had been for a century, and pogroms in Russia, Poland, Hungary, and Ukraine created the displacement of hundreds of thousands of Jews. The Russian army began to deport Jews in 1914 and soon a policy of widespread eviction was implemented (Marrus 1985, 61–63). These evictions were mostly on twenty-four-hour notice and they were brutal, forcing Jewish families onto the street, with vandals immediately setting on to their properties. Thousands of Jews could be seen in railway stations, by roadsides, dying of cold, hunger, and exhaustion. About 600,000 Jews were thus uprooted, with thousands kept as hostages by the army and many others attacked by rampaging troops. Jews in Austria also fled westward driven by the fear of falling under Russian control as its army advanced onto Austria. As they advanced eastward German troops raided Jewish population centers in Lodz, Vilna, Warsaw for laborers, and forced loans. About 35,000 Jewish farm and factory workers were deported to Germany from Poland and western Russia (Tartakower and Grossman 1944).

After the war, hostilities against Jews broke out everywhere in disorganized fashion. According to one estimate, from 1917 to 1921 there were more than 2,000 anti-Jewish riots in Eastern Europe. Half a million Jews were made homeless by this violence in Russia and Ukraine. Jews were killed and their homes destroyed by Russians, Ukrainians, Poles, and Austrians. Jews were caught in the civil war in the Soviet Union and in the Polish-Russian War, and the notion was always the same – "all Jews are traitors." In countries such as Austria and Hungary, where in the past there had been some support of Jews, now anti-Semitism became common, repeating the patterns of Eastern Europe. By the early 1920s Jews were on the move throughout Eastern Europe, moving mostly westward. Agents of western shipping companies would organize transport of Jews in Warsaw and Kovno and send them directly to the docks in Hamburg, Bremen, Rotterdam, and Antwerp to go eventually to America.

It was only when North America closed its borders to immigration, which included a disproportionate share of Jewish refugees, that the Western European states experienced the refugee crisis as a crisis, one that affected the interstate system. Until then the mass of refugees had been safely shipped to North America. The Johnson Act in the United States in 1924, and a similar act in Canada in 1923, had closed both countries to most transatlantic migration. Many Jews in Poland, under threat of deportation by the government, pleaded with the U.S. embassy to give them permission to immigrate to the United States. About 100,000 succeeded, but many more did not. European countries began to close their frontiers to Jewish in-migrants and to deport Jews.

The combination of rising numbers of refugees and closed borders made it clear to the League of Nations and to individual governments that there was a refugee crisis, and that it was an international problem that affected interstate relations. But the League of Nations lacked the capabilities to handle the material and organizational needs engendered by this crisis. Before the Office of the High Commissioner was set up in 1921, private charities were mainly in charge of helping the refugees and coordinating international relief. They negotiated with consular offices and politicians, and took on efforts that governments would not touch. It was more than a dozen Jewish societies operating internationally that organized relief operations for the Jewish refugees. They had offices throughout Eastern and Western Europe and organized the emigration as well as repatriation of Jews, and offered elementary assistance.

There were other refugees besides the Jewish ones. Notwithstanding the great care taken by the Paris drafters of the Treaty of Versailles to ensure that people living under "alien" rule could choose to obtain and were meant to be granted the nationality of their original country, the treaty left many issues uncovered. There were large numbers of people who did not fit in the legal and political categories designed by the treaty. And there were many who did not want to take the "nationality" they were supposed to according to the treaty, because it was the nationality of their oppressors. We can see how the rules of the treaty and the geopolitics of the time combined to produce a large number of "stateless" people. To be "stateless" was not an advantage in an emergent interstate system which had almost absolute control over the territory of the continent (and, through colonialism, much of the world) and in which states are the source of most rights and entitlements. Further, territorial changes in Central Europe, particularly the partitioning of a large part of German territory, created refugee flows.

Germans had to leave the former German territories now divided among the victorious allies. Germans, often settled for generations, were forced to leave various eastern countries. The German government aided German refugees in territories of the former Russian empire which had become newly formed states with strong nationalist and anti-German orientations. German aid to these refugees (*Flüchtlingsfürsorge*) was a major effort and represented state involvement with refugee issues on an unprecedented scale (Marrus 1985, 71). The German government set up camps and placement offices, took care of the refugees and their eventual resettlement in Germany. In addition the government had to take care of the repatriation of two million prisoners of war coming from Allied countries and hundreds of thousands of forced laborers who had been deported to Germany during the war (Kulischer 1948).[9] This signals a new level of government intervention in refugee crises and operational practices which begin to resemble contemporary ones.

There were many other sites in Europe where refugee issues assumed central importance in the aftermath of World War I and into the 1920s. There was above all the massacre of about one million Armenians by the Turkish government. By several estimates this represented about two thirds of the Armenian population. By August 1915, the Turkish interior minister had delivered himself of the by now well-known phrase "The Armenian question no longer exists," thereafter a marker in the history of genocide (Chaliand and Ternon 1980, 41–42). By 1919 flight from the massacres had put hundreds of thousands of surviving Armenian refugees on the road.

Large-scale warfare and refugee flows continued in Turkey and in much of the Balkan region long after World War I ended, producing masses of refugees. One line of negotiation to settle the various refugee issues was to organize orderly population exchanges. Christians were to leave Turkey, Muslims were to leave Christian-dominated areas, and various other particular exchanges among Balkan neighbors. The U.N. Commissioner of Refugees got Turkey and Greece, and Bulgaria and Greece to sign two separate agreements in the mid-1920s toward the orderly population exchange of two million refugees.[10] Greece received the largest share of these refugees. A poor country of five million people, Greece suddenly had to absorb over one million mostly destitute refugees. It was overwhelmed, with refugees camping everywhere, ill-fed, starving, and with extremely high mortality rates. The conventions of the exchange agreements did not work well for Greece; the League of Nations took special measures and set up an international relief effort to feed and house the destitute refugees in Greece, an effort that probably set a precedent and that overall was considered to have worked very well (Macartney 1934).

By the mid-1920s there was a generalized sense in Europe that a more stable period had begun. The League of Nations considered the efforts on the refugee front through the High Commissioner to have been a success and the High Commissioner himself asserted that refugee problems were finite and could be resolved through international organizations. There was reduced activity regarding refugee flows. Emigration to the United States had been a key part of the solution. About one million Europeans migrated overseas annually in the early 1920s. Closing immigration in Canada and the United States required solving remaining refugee problems in Europe itself, because South America and other emigration destinations were insufficient and had high return rates.

France emerged as the main immigration country in Europe, second only to the United States in the world.[11] France had lost 1.5 million young men in the war and had suffered the highest incidence of casualties of all the major European countries. About seven percent of its entire male population was dead. Another large share was crippled. After World War I, securing foreign workers became critical and the open immigration policy was seen as insufficient: the government signed bilateral treaties with Poland, Czechoslovakia, and Italy in 1919 and 1920 to import labor (Cross 1983). The Société Generale d'Immigration played an important role in organizing immigration of foreign workers (Noiriel 1984). France also continued to encourage immigration as a demographic measure (Mauco, 1932). They also recruited refugees. French recruiters actually went to trouble spots where there were refugees. For instance they went to Constantinople to recruit Greeks and put them on ships to Marseilles, where they were then put in camps and deployed to various work sites throughout the country (Pluyette 1930). It is also after World War I that a number of important refugee communities are formed. The Jewish Spanish community begins its life in Paris, in the eleventh arrondissement, as refugees from the Ottoman Empire, escaping from Turkey, Greece, and Bulgaria (Benveniste 1989). By the end of the decade about 1.5 million foreign workers had immigrated to France, among them a large proportion of refugees.

TOWARD WORLD WAR II

In the interwar period two new refugee flows emerged: Italians in flight from Fascism in the 1920s and Germans in flight from Nazism in the 1930s. Initially they were political elites; eventually they became mass refugee flows. Shortly before the outbreak of World War II Franco's coming to power in Spain led hundreds of thousands of Republicans to flee into France. In addition there were hundreds of thousands of other refugees, largely Eastern European Jews. There were other refugees in Europe from various countries where dictatorship or support of Nazism was spreading and persecution of Social Democrats and anti-Nazis became ugly and murderous.

Over 1.5 million Italians emigrated during the first five years of Fascism mostly for economic reasons. This is a considerable number even for an emigration country, which amounted to a significant share of the 9.2 million Italians living outside Italy by 1927 (Cannistrano and Rosoli 1979). Mussolini implemented controls over emigration after 1926. Frontier guards were to shoot anyone attempting to leave without permission. All passports were annulled and government permission was required to leave the country. The imposition of legalized terror produced new refugees; eventually about 10,000 left Italy, mostly for France where there already was a large Italian immigrant community of about 900,000 in the mid-1920s. Mussolini put repeated pressure on the French government to stop taking in the refugees, whom he referred to as "fuoriusciti." The French government refused; further, the government allowed anti-fascist activity to take place in France, where several organizations were set up. These Italian refugees had it well compared with the refugees of World War I.

The story of refugees from Nazism is well known in all its detailed horrors. From the first wave of exiles including prominent Germans, to the beginning of the terror-driven flight of Jews in 1933, even through 1935, after the elimination of civil rights for Jews, there was a generalized impression among Jews and among European observers that this was a temporary, disorganized violence that would cease and that Nazism would not last. Indeed, tens of thousands of Jews actually returned after 1933. Economic growth in Germany due to rearmament contrasted sharply with the severe depression in other countries, and thus may have been a factor for some. It is sobering to see how a wide spectrum of people and organizations failed to read properly what was lying ahead. Germany's attempt to be a good neighbor in the year before the Olympics must have contributed to the deception as well. It was not until all these processes culminated in the extreme forms of persecution and repression of 1938 that mass flight began. But the acts of violence, legal repression, what we would today think of as serious violations of the human rights of Jews, and the systematic attempts to drain Jews from all their resources and properties–were perhaps still of another order than the organized genocide of the war years. This book, however, is not the place to address the controversy as to whether there is or is not continuity from prewar practices and the political culture of Deutschtum dis-cussed briefly in chapter 4, and the regime implemented during World War II.

There was at that point no particular will it seems either in the League of Nations or in individual states, to address this refugee crisis effectively. Less was done than in the World War I aftermath. Partly it may have had to do with the slow spread of Fascism and the fact that it elicited considerable admiration as a system throughout Europe. Thus refugees from Fascism were not necessarily looked on with kindness or admiration, even though persecution of non-Fascists in Italy became increasingly violent and murderous.

One key factor playing into state politics regarding refugee admis-sions was the economic crisis of the 1930s. After the financial crisis of 1931, depression was a fact in all European countries west of Russia. Massive failures and mass unemployment did not create a climate propitious to receiving immigrants and refugees. It was the massive unemployment–six million–in Weimar Germany that brought the republic down and brought the Nazis to power. The solutions envis-aged in Europe at the time were protectionism, preventing growth of the labor supply, reducing government expenditures. The problem for refugees was that receiving governments did not want to add to their populations; the mechanism for regulating refugee flows was to prevent refugees from acquiring permanent residence rights. Much of the discussion in European governments about refugees had to do with the fact that they would add to the labor force and hence to unemployment. The discussions were not political, it was not the is-sue of the "Jew as traitor" as had been so common in World War I; it was economics. The notion was that as soon as countries had been able to absorb their labor forces there would be room for refugees.

This depoliticized approach to the refugee crisis also became the norm in states that had historically been the most liberal: France, the Netherlands, Belgium. Eventually the governments instituted checks to ensure that refugees would not become burdens; this also happened in the United States after 1929. The United States every year failed to fill the quota of 26,000 German immigrants that had been set in the 1920s. In 1935, in response to pressure from Jewish leaders, Roosevelt allowed greater numbers to come in, mostly Jews. The numbers remained very small, between 4,000 and 6,000 a year, up to 1936 and then up to 10,000 in 1937 and 1938.

Concern about Jews centered more on Eastern Europe, with a total of about 4.3 million Jews than on Germany's 525,000.[12] Further, German Jews were fairly prosperous and well integrated while those in Eastern Europe remained poor and culturally distinct. The conditions in Eastern Europe worried the governments in the West in the sense that encouraging Jewish flight from Nazism might open the floodgates of massive flight from the East. Eastern European governments in fact made repeated calls for organized mass evacuations of Jews from their countries. In the meantime the economic situation of Jews in Eastern Europe deteriorated sharply and the level of anti-Semitism and persecution rose, as exemplified in the "war against Jews" in Poland from 1935 to 1939, involving economic boycotts, segregation, exclusion, and pogroms. But the West closed its doors; even the most liberal countries did. None wanted to take Jewish refugees. Nor did they formally accept to take in Jewish refugees from Nazi Germany after the fact of extreme persecution was evident.

The case of France, long the main immigration country in Europe and a haven for exiles and refugees, illustrates some of these issues. Throughout the interwar period France was the main country receiving refugees from Fascism: almost half a million Spanish Republicans were taken in as were Italian anti-Fascists. In the 1920s France was the only European country with a positive immigration balance and a further opening in its immigration refugee policy. The need for labor was such that France's enlightened social policies (the prohibition of child labor in the nineteenth century, and later the legalization of the eight-hour workday in 1919) were criticized for reducing the labor supply in France. France's recruitment of foreign workers from Poland, Belgium, Italy, and other countries raised its immigrant population to almost three million by 1931.

But the economic crisis changed matters, and it did so fast. France in the interwar period was characterized by massive recruitment of unskilled workers, the growth of Italians as the main foreign nationality group, and the recruitment of new workers from Central Europe, particularly Poles (Girard and Steotzel 1953; Noiriel 1984). The onset of the economic depression in 1931 raised the levels of xenophobia and underlined the Italian and Polish presence in the immigrant workforce. Earlier prewar immigrant groups had become fairly assimilated, including older Italian and Spanish immigrant groups. Discriminatory legislation was passed in the early 1930s aimed at the new immigrants: Italians, Poles, and Polish Jews. (Eventually these immigrants would of course become assimilated and xenophobia would be addressed to the "new" immigrants of the post-World War II period.) Business and politicians called for a revision of immigration policy when economic depression hit France after 1931, and resulted in more than 250,000 unemployed by 1934. There were growing demands to tighten immigration, to send foreigners home, and to get rid of the notion that foreigners contributed to the strength of France.

The question of the value of "foreigners" thus was already emerging in France before Hitler's policies produced new waves of refugees. The first wave of refugees from Nazism going to France in 1933 was allowed to enter without any constraints and received a lot of sympathy. This lasted for six months, and then restrictions were implemented. By the end of 1933 conditions for entry were tightened; some of the refugees from Germany were even turned back and in other cases bureaucratic obstructionism was used to delay acceptance. In France refugees found it difficult to obtain work permits, and those who had entered illegally were expelled. Yet France all along maintained a nominal policy of granting asylum to victims of persecution and had indeed accepted more refugees than any other country in Europe. But pronounced changes were under way: opposition to the French policy of asylum, xenophobia, anti-Semitism, and opposition to liberal democracy all grew in the context of severe economic depression and mass unemployment (Bonnet 1976; Schor 1985). A phrase that rings with contemporary meaning was increasingly heard: that refugees were taking away the jobs of Frenchmen and undermining France's cultural purity.

The Socialist Popular Front government of Leon Blum in 1936 brought about an easing of the restrictions on entry and a sharp fall in the numbers of expulsions which had peaked in 1934–35 (Livian 1982). The Ministry of Labor supported the issuing of work permits to refugees already in France. But France's popular sentiment remained opposed to immigration and in fear of a massive invasion of refugees. The Socialist Party did not change French immigration policy as such; it made a change on operational aspects, facilitating and speeding up admissions procedures. It was ultimately opposed to new arrivals given the economic crisis and the position of trade unions.

The economic crisis brought down the government in 1938 and brought in a strong antiimmigration regime, which was also an anti-trade union one. Even temporary residence permits for refugees were made difficult to obtain. France's position to the world was that it was "saturated" with refugees. Marrus (1985) notes that this was probably an exaggeration, that the number of Central Europeans in France was not that large. Further, at any given moment after 1933 there probably were no more than 30,000, and probably more like 10,000, illegal refugees from Nazi Germany. These figures are small compared with the total foreign population of 2.5 million that resided in France.

England had no policy of asylum and no liberal immigration policy. If it admitted refugees it was more on the basis of individual rights than a policy of admitting people in flight. Mass unemployment in 1933 reached 2.5 million. Strict controls on entry were possible because of being an island. If England admitted refugees it was conditionally. Entrants needed a visa to another country because Britain did not want permanent settlers, it considered itself too overcrowded and with too many unemployed. Jews from Germany were admitted when the English Jewish community assumed all the costs of receiving and supporting these refugees; further, they were expecting only 3,000 to 4,000 refugees, a misreading they shared with many others. Few German refugees actually wanted to go to Britain. The refugee question never became an issue in parliament. The growing numbers of refugees after Germany's Anschluss in 1938 led public opinion to become critical of the government's increasingly restrictive admissions policy in Britain. In 1939 the government lifted restrictions and helped fund refugee trips to Britain. This was a time when most other governments were tightening their admissions.

The real crux for Britain was Palestine, and its concern to keep good terms with Palestine's Arab population made Britain reluctant to allow much Jewish immigration into the area. By the mid-1930s Pal-

estine had a Jewish population of about 400,000, one third of the total
population, and was thriving economically. Polish and German refugees had been going in increasing numbers. Britain decided to clamp
down on Jewish immigration precisely when the need to find asylum
was most extreme given mounting violence against Jews in Germany
and Eastern Europe, and the closing of most Western European countries to Jewish immigration. It reduced an annual quota of only 10,000
Jews into Palestine over the next five years, significantly down from
the 60,000 that had entered in 1935. Illegal immigration became a
common practice after this.

It is worth noting how these multiple efforts towards closing Western Europe to immigration and refugee flows from the East presages
the issues today in many European countries; but the general
economic-political context is a very different one. In the 1930s these
economies closed up and sought stability rather than expansion. Today these economies seek to be as internationalized as is possible and
expansion is a key aspect of economic policy.

CONCLUSION

A combination of conditions by the early twentieth century altered
the place of and the perception about refugees in Europe. It is the
beginning of modern refugee history. Refugee history, which today we
think of as primarily embedded in Africa and Asia, is actually a profoundly European product. Its genesis lies in the distinctive organization of the state in Europe in the early twentieth century. The history
of mass refugees is the other side, the lesser-known side, of the history of the state and interstate relations in the Europe of the twentieth
century. The rising importance of borders and of sovereignty over
national territories, the increasingly long arm of the state, and the
ascendance of variously conceived constructions of national identities as part of the nation-state, all these specify a distinctly novel
phase in the history of the European state. They are the fertile soil in
which the production of mass refugee movements can thrive. It is
difficult to imagine one without the other. It is in this regard that we
can say that the modern refugee is a European product in the same
way that the state we see emerging in the twentieth century is a European product

NOTES

1 Most Eastern European Jews lived in the Russian Empire in the nineteenth century and up to World War I. In the 1870s about four million Jews lived in the western part of the empire in what was known as the Pale Settlement; about 750,000 in the Hapsburg lands of Galicia and Bukovina; about 700,000 in Hungary, and 200,000 in Rumania.

2 Marrus (1985, 32–33) also argues that the Jewish emigration from Austrian Galicia was not primarily driven by persecution but by the extreme poverty of the region. The emigration of Jews from Rumania was probably the most strongly shaped by persecution, even though there was also abject poverty and survival was not ensured.

3 Marrus notes that according to the historian of the Jewish Board of Guardians, an entity in charge of coordinating London's Jewish charities, the board sent about 50,000 Jews back to Russia between 1880 and 1914. But he notes that out of this at times not so charitable relief effort came a network of refugee-assistance organizations that became of enormous value later on.

4 Greece in 1832 was the first to claim independence from Turkey, after a decade of warfare. Serbia, Moldavia, Walachia followed. Montenegro, Bosnia, Herzegovina struggled to achieve independence, with the Russians and Austrians increasingly involved. By the outbreak of World War I Turkey had lost control over all its European territories, except for eastern Thrace.

5 Koch notes the horror of this experience: "an entire train with its human cargo got shunted onto a railway siding and was forgotten for days because of locomotive priorities, chaos, traffic management, or simply the indifference of slovenly Russian train crews who functioned best or only through bribery. When the doors of the wheeled cages were finally opened, they yielded the tortured living and the rigid dead who had succumbed to hunger, thirst, disease, freezing, or heat prostration."

6 One of these headed by Countess Tolstoy organized automobile patrols to rescue infants abandoned at roadside; four hundred such infants had been collected by early 1916 (Marrus 1985, 54–55).

7 The best known of these was Wrangel's army – the remaining soldiers of one of the anti-Bolshevik armies. In late 1940 over 130,000 soldiers and their dependents were evacuated by boat from Crimea to Constantinople, at that time under the control of Allied troops who provided emergency support. It became a scandal because the arriving refugees swamped and overwhelmed the facilities. Insufficient food, shelter, and medicines left many of these Russians starving in the streets of Constantinople. And these were after all allies of the Allied troops, enemies of the Bolsheviks. This group received an unusual amount of attention from the international community, perhaps presaging the eventual conception of refugee as someone escaping communism.

8 Although subsequent analyses of the data suggest that Nansen's figures may have been an overestimate, it seems clear that at the highest point there were about one million Russian refugees.

9 The Weimar Republic saw a fall in the numbers of foreign workers. This was partly because the borders were moved west, and many Poles returned to or found themselves in the new Poland; some Poles left for France. And it was partly because of mass unemployment in Germany. Mandatory identification was expanded to all foreign workers in the form of a yearly work permit (*Genehmigungspflicht*). Such permits were restricted only to cases where unavailability of a native had been established. The foreign workforce was highly controlled. The depression of the 1930s further reduced the foreign workforce in Germany. Those who re-

mained were largely of German descent or had been in Germany for a long time; in both cases the restrictive regulations on foreign workers ceased to apply.

10   The Convention of Adrianople between Bulgaria and Turkey in November 1913 is considered to be the first interstate treaty on the exchange of population in modern history. The exchanges it prescribed, however, had already taken place: Turks were to leave Bulgaria, Bulgarians were to leave Turkey. But it codified procedures for the organization of such exchanges and the requirements for resettlement (Schechtman, 1946).

11   We see here the lasting impact of the 1889 legislation discussed in the preceding chapter. Major revisions to this law in 1927, 1945, 1973 had the overall effect of further expanding the inclusionary nature of the law. The 1927 reform sharply expanded the provisions for naturalization; it permitted French women marrying a foreigner to remain French citizens and attributed citizenship to the children of such marriages if born in France.

12   Poland had three million Jews, Rumania, 750,000 Jews, and Hungary, almost a half million.

6

PATTERNS, RIGHTS, REGULATIONS

After World War II and into the 1950s, the vast numbers of refugees, displaced persons, and returnees from the colonies wound up providing a needed additional labor supply to the European economies which were in full reconstruction. The capacity of the economic system to absorb these millions of people is a sharp contrast to the configuration of only a decade earlier, the 1930s. Most remarkable was West Germany, which absorbed fourteen million people from 1945 to 1988. In the period of decolonization, which varied from country to country, there were "white" colonists and colonial officers who returned; several of the European countries had also granted citizenship or some other forms of status facilitating migration to residents of their former colonies. The battle for independence in Algiers, from 1954 to 1962, brought more than one million French settlers back to France. Algeria had actually been providing France on and off with foreign workers since after World War I. Indonesians came to the Netherlands in the 1950s and people from Surinam and the Antilles came in the 1970s. Portugal received returnees and immigrants from its former colonies in Africa.

This capacity for absorption in major European countries represents a remarkable shift over a very brief period of time: a shift from feeling invaded by foreign workers in the 1930s to a overwhelming and it seemed insatiable demand for them in the 1950s and 1960s. Indeed the need for additional foreign workers led to the active organized recruitment of foreign workers. In the 1950s Italy was the main European labor-sending country. West Germany, France, and Switzerland were the main countries recruiting Italians. In the 1960s Spain and Portugal became the main sending countries, followed by Greece and Yugoslavia. Several of these countries had had significant overseas emigration until the 1960s. Algeria, India, Pakistan, and the Caribbean emerged as the main non-European labor-sending countries in the 1950s and into the 1960s. In the 1970s Turkey, Morocco and Tunisia emerged as important labor-supplying countries.

In the late 1980s refugees, resettlers, and asylum seekers once again became a significant factor in Western Europe. In the early 1980s asylum seekers in fourteen OECD countries were fewer than 100,000, a number that increased manifold by the early 1990s. Germany emerged once again as a major destination for resettlers and asylum seekers. By the mid-1990s the overall numbers had fallen as most of these countries, and particularly Germany, tightened their entry policies.

The share of foreign workers in Western Europe's labor force peaked in the early 1970s. And then, as rapidly as had happened in the past, came yet another sharp shift: between 1973 and 1974 most of Europe's labor-importing countries closed immigration and attempted to repatriate foreign workers. By the mid-1980s antiimmigrant sentiments and fears of invasion were once again voiced even in relatively liberal countries such as France. One cannot help but notice the rapidity and the intensity of each shift, and what would seem their almost cyclical character.

Today a key new era has been set by the combination of three processes. One is the expansion of the geography of migrations to include new flows from North and West Africa as well as Eastern Europe and the former Soviet Union. This new geography of migrations also includes new destinations: countries such as Italy, Spain, and Greece, long-time labor exporters, have now also become receiving areas; and some of the more prosperous countries in Central Europe where significant emigrations have originated have now in turn become major new receiving areas: Poland, the Czech Republic, and Hungary.

A second major process is the transformation of what was until the 1970s largely represented as a foreign workforce into immigrant and or ethnic communities, with families and neighborhood institutions, with political actors and aspirations. Family reunion and natural growth in the foreign-resident population have contributed to the ongoing expansion in the foreign-resident population notwithstanding closure of immigration. The formation of communities has contributed to a politics of social issues and political claims going far beyond the question of jobs and wages which dominated in the 1960s when immigrants were constituted as a foreign workforce. The coming of age of a second generation has further contributed to this marked transformation.

A third process is the implementation of the Maastricht provisions for the European Union (EU), which will take freedom of circulation inside the latter to a new level. This raises a number of issues regarding broader trends toward transnationalization of economic activity on the one hand, and attempts to control the flow of immigrants on the other. Such controls concern various categories of immigrants, notably non-EU immigrants seeking entry into the EU, and non-EU immigrants who have the right to reside in one of the member countries but are not as of yet free to circulate within the EU. The larger questions raised by this juxtaposition of regimes is whether it is viable to a) neutralize borders when it comes to the circulation of capital and EU nationals, and b) strengthen those same borders when it comes to the circulation of non-EU resident immigrants. Further, is such a dual-policy regime viable when it comes to access to the EU: on the one hand, lifting multiple restrictions on access by non-EU firms, investment capital and goods in the context of WTO, and the general opening of financial markets in the European economies, and on the other, building a Fortress Europe when it comes to immigrants and refugees.

This chapter first examines the basic trends in the history of immigration and asylum seekers over the last several decades. Next come sections that focus in greater detail on some of the major developments beginning in the late 1980s with the disintegration of the socialist bloc to the east. Subsequent sections examine the politics of immigration, including citizenship law, and the intersection of EC regulations and national governments in the field of migration policy. There is a vast literature for most of the countries discussed in this chapter; it is impossible to do justice to many of the important details contained in this literature. The effort is toward presenting basic empirical trends and policies in order to lay the groundwork for the more explorative concluding chapter of the book. (An appendix contains tables presenting additional numbers).

IMMIGRATION

In 1950, before widespread recruitment of foreign workers began, the total foreign-resident population in the eighteen present-day EU and EFTA (European Free Trade Association) member countries was 5.1 million.[1] France alone had 1.7 million foreign residents, a third of the total. In Germany foreign residents numbered only 568,000, a figure that excludes the millions of ethnic Germans it took in after the war. The numbers were small in most countries.[2] Between 1960 and 1973, the year immigration was closed in most of these countries, the number of foreign workers in the group of the then twelve doubled from 3.3 million to 6.6 million, that is from three percent of the workforce to six percent.[3] For instance, Germany's foreign workforce went from 461,000 in 1960 to 2.5 million in 1973, that is from two percent to eleven percent; and France's, from 1.3 million in 1960 to 1.9 million in 1973, that is from six percent to eleven percent.

In the early 1970s most West European countries stopped labor immigration. This was partly due to the recessionary impact of the oil price crisis of the early 1970s, and the reduced need for foreign workers once post-World War II reconstruction had been fully accomplished and deindustrialization was hitting a growing number of regions. The total number of foreign workers declined to different extents in different countries. In each Germany and France the number of foreign workers fell by less than half a million from 1973 to 1980, to 2.1 million in Germany, and to 1.5 million in France. But in Belgium, Luxembourg, and the Netherlands, the share of foreign workers never stopped growing from the 1960s onwards.

The main labor-sending countries for the six main labor-importing countries in Europe (Germany, France, Sweden, Belgium, Switzerland, and Austria) in 1970 were Italy with 820,000, Turkey with 770,000, Yugoslavia with 540,000, Algeria with 390,000, and Spain with 320,000. These figures exclude undocumented workers of whom there appeared to be growing numbers in several countries.

After the closure of immigration in all the major receiving countries in Western Europe, the foreign population stock kept growing through natural increases, family reunification, and ongoing inflows of new foreign workers who came in under one or another regime. In the major receiving countries the foreign population grew significantly in the 1980s and 1990s (See Tables 1, 2, 3, 4).[4] The actual migration figures would be higher if all foreign-born residents had been counted: naturalized foreigners, returnees, which may include descendants of emigrants, immigrants from former colonies who had the right to come as citizens.[5] Even in countries where the stock of foreign population declined in the years after 1973, Switzerland and Sweden, it eventually grew again in the 1980s and 1990s.[6] By 1990 Western European countries had a total foreign population of fifteen million, mostly from other European countries. In the broader area of the EC and EFTA countries it had reached eighteen million by 1990, of which eight million were foreign workers.

Most of these countries had declining annual entries of non-EC workers for much of the 1980s, and significant increases beginning in 1989. (See Table 5) (The following figures exclude EC residents.) Excluding ethnic Germans and those coming from the GDR, Germany registered about 83,000 entries of foreign workers in 1980, a level which fell to 20,000 or 30,000 annually in subsequent years, then rose to 60,000 in 1988, 139,000 in 1990 and 262,000 in 1996. France registered 17,000 entries in 1980, a level that climbed in the early 1980s, then fell and rose again in 1993 to 46,000 in 1992, to fall again to 16,000 in 1996; the United Kingdom registered about 19,000 in 1980, with falling levels in the ensuing years and increases to 35,000 in 1990 and 37,700 in 1996; Switzerland and Austria had similar trajectories, with Austria showing an enormous increase to 103,000 by 1990 from a level of 44,000 in 1980, and sharp declines during the 1980s, down to 16,000 in 1996.[7] (See also Table 7).

When it comes to seasonal and frontier workers, the best data and the highest levels are recorded in Switzerland, with about 110,000 seasonal workers and 100,000 frontier workers in 1980, going up to respectively 153.6 thousand and 180.6 thousand by 1990 and sharp declines in the 1990s. France registered over 120,000 seasonal workers in 1980, a figure that went down to 58,000 by 1990; and Luxembourg registerd 12,000 frontier workers in 1980, and 34,000 in 1990.

Although there is immense cross-country variation in the occupational/industrial distribution of workers in Western Europe, it is clear that a majority of immigrants were and are employed in low-wage jobs no matter what the country. The labor force participation of women in Western Europe is overall low at thirty-two percent compared with thirty-nine percent in Japan and forty-two percent in the

United States; yet this does not seem to have improved the work opportunities of immigrant women. There is an enormous literature documenting the labor market situation of immigrant men and women.. The evidence shows that as early as the 1880s immigrants were disproportionately concentrated in sectors such as construction, assembly production, agriculture, and low-level service jobs. They are there today as well.

ILLEGAL IMMIGRATION

Illegal immigration, a fact in all migration processes, has emerged as a major issue in the last few years. The closure of labor immigration and most recently the tightening of asylum provisions are assumed to have contributed to an increase in illegal immigration. The International Labor Organization estimated for 1991 that there were 2.6 million illegal residents representing some fourteen percent of the total foreign population (Böhning 1991). Italy is thought to have one of the highest numbers, with 600,000 estimated in 1991 compared to 200,000 in France. Germany is estimated to have 350,000 illegal immigrants, to which should be added an estimated 300,000 illegal refugees. By 1993 some estimates put the illegal immigrant population to between four and five million. It is impossible to know what the validity of these figures is. We do know in the United States through the indirect measures obtained with the regularization program of the 1986 Immigration Reform and Control Act, that the common estimate of about five to six million illegal immigrants in the United States was found to be far too high. Whether we are seeing inflation of estimates in Europe today in a context of growing anxiety about massive floods of immigrants is difficult to establish but is certainly a possibility.

European states have basically developed two types of policy responses: regularization of the illegal population, predicated on a series of conditions to be met by the immigrant; and punitive responses, including deportation of illegal immigrants and penalties for employers of such immigrants.[8] Most European countries had adopted employers sanctions by 1980; there is an excellent literature examining the successes and failures of governmental attempts to control illegal immigration (Weil 1991; Wihtol de Wenden 1990). And most have enacted regularization programs between 1971 and 1991; Germany is not one of them, arguing that it would only encourage such immigration (Castles and Miller 1993, 90–96).

The Mediterranean region is seen as one of the major sites for illegal immigration. Here illegal immigration is partly a function of the following conditions. First, firms that used to employ foreign workers, including illegal ones, before the closure of immigration, kept employing such workers, often with the tacit acknowledgment of local authorities and notwithstanding various sanctions against such employment. Second, the continuing search for flexibility among firms under pressure from international competition is likely to lead some firms to avoid the costs of employment regulations associated with regular full time jobs. Third, the fact of a partial articulation of illegal immigration to the informal economy is likely to facilitate the absorption of illegal immigrants. This combination of conditions along with geographic location have made the Mediterranean region a key site for illegal immigration. Italy, Spain, Portugal, and Greece, all once labor-exporting countries have highly accessible borders and lack the control capacities for tight border surveillance. Further, various geopolitical factors and judicial powers that can defend the rights of individuals constitute constraints on too brutal an apprehension and deportation policy. The rise of fundamentalism may bring additional humanitarian considerations into play. It is likely that for diplomatic and economic reasons the response to this growth in illegal immigration from North and West Africa might be a series of regularization campaigns.

The estimates about the size of this population in the Mediterranean countries ranges from between 1 and 1.5 million, though there are multiple estimates which cover a far wider range, including some that put the illegal population in Italy alone at about that level. By 1990 it was estimated that the North African component of the illegal population was sixty percent in France, thirty percent in Italy, forty percent in Spain, fifteen percent in Portugal and less than five percent in Greece. This amounts to 536,000 illegal immigrants from Maghreb in these countries, with the largest contingent, in Italy (255,000), followed by France (150,000) and Spain (117,000) (Khader 1991, 42–43).

As a consequence of various efforts by EU states to control illegal immigration, to harmonize policies, and particularly in the context of the so-called Schengen Agreement, the Mediterranean countries strengthened their efforts toward this end. In 1991 Spain instituted a visa requirement for the estimated one million annual visitors from the Maghreb, most of whom are Moroccans coming for seasonal work. The Italian government made efforts to reduce the illegal immigrant population through an amnesty (Veuglers 1994). The Portuguese government withdrew the automatic right of Brazilians to become Portuguese citizens and hence to EU-wide rights. All these southern countries have increased the policing of their external frontiers.

A second major site for illegal immigration has emerged in the context of the new east-to-west migrations. Prominent in this development is Germany's tightening of its asylum policy in 1993. Perhaps another consequence of Germany's new policy is a growth in illegal entries into Germany, particularly across the Czech-German border. In 1992 apprehensions reached 12,000 and those sent back (which includes those apprehended after entering Germany) numbered 16,000 on the Czech-German border; these categories numbered, respectively, 2,617 and 12,000 on the Polish-German border. According to newspaper accounts, every night hundreds of persons from the poorer Eastern European countries and non-European countries are caught by the German border police. Finally the tightening border has engendered what we see at many other borders: people who charge up to several thousand dollars to get others illegally over the border. They have received various not so endearing names in different parts of the world – coyotes, snakes – which have become part of migration mythology. In the early 1990s Rumanians were a majority of the apprehended and expelled on all major borders: they were sixty-four percent on the Polish and over fifty percent on the Hungarian borders (Okolski 1992). It should be added that a good part of the Rumanian migrating population are ethnically Gypsies, or Roma people. Insofar as they are a long persecuted people, without a land of their own, their level of migration cannot be used as an indication of foreseeable emigration from the Eastern European countries. They are estimated at between 2.5 and 4 million, a majority of whom are in Rumania, Hungary, and the territories of the former Czechoslovakia and Yugoslavia; there are very few in Poland.

ASYLUM SEEKERS AND REFUGEES

Another major trend that takes on a whole new shape in the late 1980s is the inflow of asylum seekers, which reached a high of 700,000 in

1992 alone. Although there were strong fluctuations in the numbers reflecting particular refugee crises or policy changes, overall their numbers grew sharply toward the end of the 1980. (See Table 8.) Most Western European countries saw up to five-fold increases from 1980 to 1991. After 1992 most of the fows declined. Germany was by far the largest recipient in these years, with 256,100 entries of asylum seekers in 1991, and over 400,000 in 1992, almost four times the level in 1980. In 1991 the United Kingdom was the second-largest recipient, with an inflow of 73,000 asylum seekers, a seven-fold increase over the 9,900 received in 1981 and for much of the 1980s. France was next with 61,400 in 1989, three times the 18,800 received in 1980 and in most years for the decade. Switzerland reached its highest numbers in 1991 with 41,600 asylum seekers, an enormous increase over the 6,100 received in 1980. Among the sharpest increases was the inflow of 31,400 into Italy in 1991, and the 84,000 into Sweden in 1992.

As discussed in a later section, the policy changes in Western Europe regarding third countries of asylum have brought about a change in the numbers of applicants and raised the numbers in several of the Central European countries, particularly the numbers of those coming from the former Soviet Union and the poorer countries in Eastern Europe. Policy changes in particular countries have also reduced the inflow of asylum seekers from outside Europe; this has especially been the case for Germany, which until recently had probably the most liberal asylum policy on the continent.

Indeed, even before reunification Germany was receiving more asylum seekers than the whole of the EC. After the collapse of the socialist bloc and with the wars in former Yugoslavia, all countries received significant numbers. Only in Germany and Sweden did the numbers continue to increase through 1992. In 1990 Germany received forty-four percent of all asylum requests in Europe coming from East Europeans. In France entries of asylum seekers declined after 1989, in Spain after 1990, and in the United Kingdom, Austria, and Italy, after 1991. The declines are generally the consequence of policy changes aimed at restricting the inflow and access to refugee status.

Germany's tightening of its asylum policy, which made it impossible to request asylum in Germany if a person was already in a safe country, has had signficant impacts on Central European countries. Considerable pressure was put on the latter to assist in restricting the flow of refugees and asylum seekers into Western Europe. Poland signed a treaty of re-admission in May 1993 thereby committing to re-admit up to 10,000 persons a year. It should be added that reaching this agreement was arduous and included financial aid of DM120 million. There is now considerable convergence on retaining asylum seekers in their first country of admission if this is a safe country.

Refugees and asylum seekers remain a small group in Central Europe. But the numbers are growing. By 1990 Hungary had 3,000 asylum seekers.[9] The United Nations High Commissioner for Refugees reported an estimate of 29,000 Yugoslav war refugees in 1992, with some estimates ranging from 50,000 to 100,000. Poland expects to receive up to 50,000 asylum seekers a year from various countries; but current refugees in Poland tend to leave for other countries (for instance, Yugoslavs who were offered a sort of refugee status went on to Denmark, Finland, Germany, and Sweden). The Czech Republic is seeking to put a ceiling of 12,000 annually, but actual entries are far lower—for instance, there were about 1,200 asylum seekers in 1991; and most of the refugees in the country leave after short stays.

West European governments have sought to restrict entries of asylum seekers and refugees and to harmonize policy on the matter. They have done so largely through intergovernmental agreements and to a much lesser extent through EC institutions. The Schengen Treaty and the Dublin Convention include many of the legal and administrative procedures aimed at greater control.[10] A meeting of EC ministers and officials held in London in November-December 1992 produced agreements among the EC12 group on the handling of unfounded applications for asylum and on asylum applications from host third countries which asylum seekers have left unlawfully (Butt Philip 1994). This particular group, the Working Group on Immigration, is developing a "no serious risk of persecution" test which would automatically refuse applications from an individual residing in a country considered to be safe by the EC. These efforts toward concerted action have had some effects. Thus the German government and parliament actually amended Article 16 of the Basic Law to restrict the almost unlimited right of asylum; a much more restrictive asylum regime was introduced in July 1993.

The available information also points to more restrictive practices. Data for 1992 from the US Committee for Refugees shows declining rates of recognition of refugees in EU states. In 1992 these rates ranged from twenty-eight percent in France, 6.5 percent in Spain, 4.5 percent for Italy and Germany, to 3.2 percent for the United Kingdom. In Europe there have been proportionately higher rates of recognition for lower types of formal status: such as humanitarian status, or "exceptional leave to remain" as in the United Kingdom. These are statuses that fall outside the UN Convention on Refugees and provide far fewer rights than full refugee status.

But these governmental efforts to restrict entries by refugees and asylum seekers are also running into a new set of constraints, notably courts defending the universality of certain rights. For instance, in August 1993 the French Constitutional Council challenged a core presumption of the Dublin and Schengen accords by ruling that legislation that would prevent asylum seekers from entering the country was in violation of both the Geneva Accords on refugees as well as the French Constitution, specifically the Rights of Man. Eight of the fifty-one articles of the new immigration law were censured. Two rulings by the German Constitutional Court in September 1993 attacked another core presumption of the Dublin and Schengen agreements, by refusing to consider Greece a "safe third country" for asylum seekers and authorizing the applications of the particular plaintiffs bringing the case to be made in Germany. Even though Greece is a signatory to the European Convention on Human Rights, and to Dublin and Schengen, the court considered that human rights could not be guaranteed.

We see then on the one hand a sharp tightening in asylum and refugee policy and, on the other, a multiplication of legal instruments and court decisions that aim at protecting and enhancing the rights of asylum seekers and refugees.

NEW MIGRATORY PATTERNS

Toward the late 1980s a set of new labor migrations became evident: erstwhile major labor-exporting countries had become labor-receiving ones. (See Tables 1 and 2). In 1981 Italy had 211,000 foreign residents; by 1996 this number had increased to over one million. It is estimated that with the inclusion of undocumented immigrants, Italy may today well have up to two million foreign residents. In 1982 Spain had 201,000 foreign residents; by 1996 there were half a million. Though the numbers are smaller, Portugal and Greece have also become immigrant-receiving countries. Besides the transformation in the numbers, there has been a sharp transformation in the composition. A good share among earlier foreign residents consisted of high-level professional workers and their families. Spain received many highly educated refugees from the dictatorships in Argentina, Chile, and Uruguay during the 1970s. Italy has long had a highly educated foreign population of artists and intellectuals. In the late 1980s the composition of the foreign-resident population, including undocumented, consisted of a growing number of people who found employment as laborers, for instance agricultural workers in southern Italy, miners in northern Spain, domestic workers in all these countries. Many come from poor countries, with a rapidly growing share from Africa.

There are at least three other major new patterns that have developed since the late 1980s. One of these formed when former labor-exporting countries, Spain and Portugal, became members of the EC. The right to free movement in the EU led many Spanish, Italians and Portuguese to retun home from Germany, France, and the Benelux.[11] It raises the broader issue of free circulation within the EU and the possibility that we may see the growth of commuting and seasonal migration to replace some of the more long-term and permanent flows of the past.

The other two patterns involve the new and renewed East-West migrations after the lifting of restrictions on travel and more generally the changes in political regimes, and the growing migration flow from the East into several of the more prosperous Central European countries. The next sections discuss these two patterns in more detail, beginning with East-West migrations.

THE NEW AND RENEWED EAST-WEST MIGRATIONS

The fall of the Berlin Wall and the general dismantling of restrictions on emigration and travel from the former Soviet Bloc produced sharp increases in the foreign population of several West European countries after 1989. In the first eighteen months after the fall of the wall, about 1.6 million people left the region. Before the opening only about 100,000 left per year from the COMECON area, an insignificant number for a population of about 400 million.

For no country was this truer than for Germany.[12] In 1989–90 Germany admitted almost 1.5 million people from the Warsaw Pact countries, including East Germans. This is almost twice the entries for 1980–88. In 1989 Germany registered a net increase of 977,000 immigrants, including workers and family members. About two thirds claimed to be of German nationality; 377,000 ethnic Germans from Poland, Rumania, and the Soviet Union; 120,000 refugees, asylum seekers, and relatives of already legally present aliens; and 383,500 from the former German Democratic Republic (Statistisches Bundesamt 1992, 91). These numbers are far higher than what had been the levels of East-West migration. From 1963 to 1987 the average entry level from the GDR to West Germany was about 13,000 per year (OECD 1990, 21 ff.) It began to rise in the 1980s reaching 43,300 in 1987. Migration from East to West Germany grew consistently over 1990 and 1991, from 129,000 in the first quarter of 1990 to 382,000 in the fourth quarter of 1991. Entries from the former East Germany are no longer counted in immigration figures.

Both ethnic Germans and Germans from the former GDR are very special types of inflows happening under very special circumstances. Both these groups have the right to permanent citizenship, unlike all other immigrant groups in Germany. However, the privileges of ethnic Germans (but not of the former GDR Germans) have been altered somewhat, making it more difficult for them to enter Germany.[13]

These developments brought about a dramatic recomposition in immigration flows to Germany. Up until then the old labor-exporting countries, mostly from the Mediterranean region, had accounted for a majority of all foreign workers; in 1989 their share fell to less than a third, while that of East and Southeastern European immigration rose to forty-four percent; of these Polish workers were the largest group, accounting for a third.

It should be noted that a large number of East Germans had left their country before unification, mostly but not exclusively for West Germany. Thus from 1971 to 1981 about 910,000 left. Since the formation of the GDR and up to its demise a total of about 3.9 million left. The largest departures were after World War II as part of the mass flows of refugees and of displaced persons discussed in the preceding chapter. Much emigration from the GDR in the 1980s was directed to the FRG. Thus in 1986, of the 55,000 who emigrated, 25,400 went to the FRG; of the 77,600 who left in 1988, 40,400 went to the FRG (Central Department of Statistics of the GDR, 1990, 2).

Before the fall of the Berlin Wall, in September 1989, Hungary and

Chekoslovakia had lifted multiple restrictions and made travel to the West for those departing from these two countries (even if not originating there) rather easy. This shows in the figures for the few months preceding the fall of the wall. In November 1989, after Honecker's forced resignation in October, the GDR government opened its borders under sharp pressure. It is in this month that the highest levels of emigration from East to West Germany were registered for a single month in that year, about 80,000. In the first year after the economic, monetary and social union of the two Germanies, from July 1990 to July 1991, another 240,000 persons migrated to the West. After this the movement was no longer registered as immigration and became part of internal migration.

After reunification we see the emergence of a significant level of commuters, Germans whose homes remained in the eastern part but commuted to jobs in the western part. The German Bundesamt für Arbeit has a survey that monitors labor market developments in the "neue Bundesländer". One of the findings is that by July 1991 the number of commuters had grown to 446,000 persons, from about 200,000 in July 1990.[14] During this same period of time total employment in the former GDR fell from eight million to under 7.5 million. Over fifty percent of commuters require over an hour of travel to work, and twenty-five percent of all commuters cannot return to their homes every day.

In 1991 average wage levels in the former eastern territories were sixty percent of the western level, and if we consider actual wages received, they were fifty percent. Commuters to the West raise their income on average by fifty to sixty percent compared to those in the East. In addition the share of commuters that reached above average eastern wage levels rose from sixty-eight percent to eighty-two percent. In July 1991, the sector employment distribution of commuters in the west showed about one third were employed in manufacturing, fifteen percent in the construction sector, and forty-eight percent in the services sector as a whole, including a nineteen percent share in trading. There was a large incidence of temporary jobs in these three sectors, a fact that might explain ease of access by eastern commuters. On the question of actually migrating to the West, about sixty percent of commuters compared with thirty-five percent of the East German population said they would consider or would like doing so.

The new migrations from the East while going largely to Germany, are also directed to Austria, Scandinavia, and several Central European countries. Scandinavia is likely to receive new migrations from the northwestern part of Russia because of old ethnic and economic linkages. Further, Poland, the Czech Republic, Slovakia, and Hungary are expected to receive growing numbers of immigrants from the former Soviet Union, a subject discussed in the next section.

CENTRAL EUROPE AS A RECEIVING AREA

Long a sending area, today Central and East Europe reveal a multiplicity of patterns. (See Tables 1, 2, 4, 7 and 8 for some additional numbers) The major Central European countries all send and receive immigrants, asylum seekers, illegal workers, "tourists" who work as petty peddlers.

They share a common concern about massive inflows from Rumania and the states of the former Soviet Union. After the passing of new regulations in May 20, 1991, in the Soviet Union about the movement of people, and their implementation in Russia in January 1993, Russian citizens were free to leave and reenter the country. The more prosperous Central European countries – Poland, the Czech Republic, Hungary – feared that millions of "tourists" would arrive from the former Soviet Union and stay. Further, migrants from third countries intending to go to the West and finding it increasingly difficult to do so, are remaining "stranded" in these four major receiving countries.[15] Changes in policy have contributed to this: in exchange for lifting visa requirements for their citizens in Western Europe, these countries have accepted to re-admit third-country aliens who were in transit through these countries and were refused admission into Western Europe. These countries are facing difficult policy questions and challenges, including mutual cooperation on these issues.

In addition there were fears about the possible return of the millions of Eastern Europeans who, often against their will, were "repatriated" or "resettled" in the Soviet Union after World War II, a subject discussed in chapter 5. Poles are the largest single group, with 1.2 million counted in the 1989 Soviet census but estimated to be twice that and up to four million according to various estimates.[16] Then there are people of Hungarian, Bulgarian, and other Central European descent. Significant shares of these groups declared their language of origin as their mother tongue, a fact which could be interpreted as indicating a proclivity to emigrate.

From 1987 to 1991 about one million people left the Soviet Union. This is extremely high compared with the preceding four decades when total emigration was below the level for 1990 alone. But it is far from the figures of five to ten million that have been asserted would be coming. Further, a very small minority of this one million actually stayed in Central Europe; most went on west to Germany, Israel and the United States. Ethnic Germans and Jews have been major components of this emigration. Once again this shows us the extent of patterning in migrations. It is also worth noting that after the coup in August 1991 only a few Soviet citizens left. Several hundred visiting in Poland at the time sought asylum. But only fifty of the 20,000 commuters who were in Poland for their jobs asked for asylum; the rest went on with their routines and returned home (*Wall Steet Journal*, 21 August 1991). A survey done in March 1991 in Mosocow reported in *Liberation* (25–26 May 1991) found that only six percent of those surveyed said that if they left they would choose a Central European country as their destination.

Other potential emigrant populations such as the ethnic minorities described above have not shown much impetus to migrate, perhaps with the exception of the 35,000-strong Hungarian ethnic minority in Rumania. One exception is Rumania where the International Organization for Migration (1993) found that up to thirty percent were interested in leaving. IOM obtained similar responses in a 1992 survey in Russia, Ukraine, Albania, and Bulgaria. There is considerable evidence showing that many citizens of the former Soviet Union indicate that they would like to go abroad but very few want to leave for good (IOM 1993; de Tinguy 1991; Brym 1992).

According to several analysts (See Morokvasic and de Tinguy 1993) the most important migration impact for Central Europe resulting from the political changes and the economic restructuring in the former Soviet Union has been the development of circular-migration streams, including commuting. This has been facilitated by the possibility of easy exit and reentry to home countries in the region. In the past departure was a once and for all decision. A common pattern in the 1990s is to come as "tourists" and stay for a few hours, a few days, or several months, for small-scale trading and peddling. Though it has been going on for many years, the numbers have risen sharply since the opening of borders.

A few figures will illustrate this. The numbers for Soviet tourists give an indication of what the increase might be, though they encompass several categories of tourists, many having nothing to do with work. Thus there were 720,000 Soviet tourists in Poland in 1980, and 1.74 million in 1988, three million in 1989, and well over five million by early 1992. Again their stays range from a few hours to several months and the total may include several counts of the same person. Many are tourists or visitors of various sorts. Many are small, informal traders and peddlers: they sell on street markets and street corners, on trains; they sell Russian made goods such as cigarettes, toys, clothes, food, alcohol, crafts. A similar pattern has emerged in the Czech Republic where tens of thousands of citizens from the former Soviet Union enter every day to engage in petty trading. In Poland it is estimated that there were between 50,000 and 70,000 Rumanians in early 1991. There were also estimated to be up to 300,000 workers from Russia, Belorussia and Ukraine in Poland; they worked in construction, in mines, agriculture, and as taxi drivers. These undocumented workers are known to get wages lower than those of citizens, but they are still higher than those they could get in their home countries. In Hungary there were estimated to be up to 100,000 illegal workers by 1992 from other Eastern European countries, from China, and the Middle East.

There are also criminal and semicriminal forms of economic activity that involve migration. Well-known criminal gangs are operating out of Poland and the Czech Republic, and now increasingly connect to Chicago and New York in the United States. There are illegal markets for cross-national trading in arms and prostitutes. There is by now considerable information about the prostitute trade in Eastern European and Russian women throughout Western Europe and beyond. Within Central Europe there are women from the former Soviet Union, mostly from Russia and Ukraine, and from Rumania and Yugoslavia. For example, one estimate has it there were 3,000 prostitutes from the former Soviet Union in Warsaw alone by the early 1990s (Morokvasic and Tinguy 1993).

The main challenge for these countries are refugee flows and illegal migration. These four major central European countries have held multiple meetings to strategize how best to achieve control over their borders. In the Czech Republic asylum seekers have to declare their intentions on the border and cannot enter until the Ministry of the Interior accepts them. In addition border patrols and deployment of military have been increased to gain more control over migrant flows. Similar measures have been taken in the other Central European countries. The tightening of asylum requests, the increased requirements of visas, the increase in border patrols and military deployment on the border, all these are aimed at gaining control over who enters. As a result between the end of 1991 and April 1993, 1.3 million persons were refused entrance to Hungary, for instance (Larrabbe 1992).

Also a regional policy has emerged. Hungary has made agreements with Austria, Slovenia, Croatia and Rumania on re-admission of undocumented migrants. So have Poland and the Czech Republic. Ministers of the interior of Poland, Hungary, the Czech Republic, Slovakia, Austria, and Slovenia met in March of 1993 to pursue further regional efforts on border-control matters. These governments have also actively sought the collaboration of the West, both in terms of technical assistance and economic and social aid. In their view the migration and refugee events taking place on their territories are part of a broader European process.

The association agreements betweeen the EC and these four countries do not entail full free-movement rights for persons, even though visa requirements have been lifted. There is already cooperation on border and migration matters and bilateral deals between Germany and Poland, and Germany and the Czech Republic; economic aid from Germany is conditioned on such cooperation. Germany is offering financial and practical assistance in exchange for tighter border controls and tougher rules on asylum. It is expected that this will lead to an increase in illegal immigration from Poland to Germany.

From a Cold War position demanding the right of persons in the East to cross borders, the West Europeans are now asking Central Europe to police its borders to the East and the West, to retain asylum seekers, to re- admit those who were incorrectly allowed to go to the West.

THE POLITICAL RIGHTS OF IMMIGRANTS

Since the 1970s policies concerning immigrants have become increasingly similar throughout Western Europe and across the political spectrum: strict limits on further immigration, encouragement of voluntary return migration, integration of permanent and second-generation immigrants, and with the exception of France, liberalization of naturalization laws. Most countries have passed legislation that gives more rights to resident immigrants as well as policies for the provision of housing and education to aid their integration. This convergence has taken place notwithstanding sharp differences in immigration histories, in colonial links to migration, in policies regarding asylum, and in the particular sectors of the immigrant and refugee populations emerging as the "source" of concern in each of the West European countries – from Germany's worry about asylum seekers to France's concern with undocumented immigrants. Converging immigration policies have also taken place notwithstanding sharply differing citizenship and naturalization politics, the central subject of this section.

The general direction of most immigrant-receiving countries in Western Europe during the 1980s was toward liberalization and the granting of various kinds of rights, including local voting rights, to settled immigrants and their families. Sweden, the Netherlands, Belgium, and, to a lesser extent, France have been most liberal. In Sweden and the Netherlands the government funds immigrant associations, facilitates learning one's mother tongue, promotes equal opportunities in the labor market, and allows immigrants to vote in local elections. Most Western European countries liberalized their naturalization law in the mid-1980s and then again in the early 1990s, often in contested legislative battles. In this context Britain is the exception, moving from a broad imperial-based notion of citizenship to a more restrictive one; the liberal definition of British subject could not be maintained as pressure grew inside Britain for greater immigration controls against British subjects.

Simplifying matters, it can be said that most political systems in Europe fall either under a regime where citizenship is acquired by birthplace (jus soli) or by descent (jus sanguinis). In fact most European countries have elements of both though one or the other may be dominant. Jus soli is dominant in the United Kingdom, Netherlands, France, and Belgium. Acquisition of citizenship is direct at majority for aliens born in the country or in the form of double jus soli for children born in the country with one parent who is also born in the

country. Jus sanguinis is dominant in Sweden, Germany and Switzerland: the children of foreigners, even if born in the country, have no
way of acquiring citizenship except by prior naturalization. However,
a given regime of jus sanguinis or jus soli can incorporate different
types of law. To take the case of jus sanguinis, Sweden, where aliens
born in the country have the option to register for naturalization, is
very open compared to Germany and Switzerland where naturalization is extremely difficult to obtain.

In all these countries a resident alien meeting certain conditions
can request citizenship from the public authorities which then have
the right to decide, though often the applicant lacks the right to appeal
the decision. There are differences in the conditions legally imposed
for obtaining citizenship through naturalization. For instance, one
must renounce one's prior nationality in Germany but not in France.
And within a given regime there can be sharp differences: thus Sweden requires renunciation of one's prior nationality but increasingly
tolerates dual nationality in most cases; Germany does not.

And then there are more general differences.[17] Thus Germany
lacks a general culture of support of naturalization and its administrative rules on naturalization assert that Germany is not a country of
immigration. In France it is anomalous for immigrants not to naturalize; as noted in earlier chapters, France is the only country in continental Europe with a tradition of immigration for settlement and the
desirability of naturalization (Brubaker 1992; Wihtol de Wenden 1988;
Weil 1991). In Germany's conception one cannot join the nation-state
by voluntary adhesion, as in the North American model, or through
state-sponsored assimilation as in the French model (Kohn 1967; but
see also Hoffmann 1990; Oberndörfer 1991.

In 1980, before several countries implemented significant revisions,
naturalization rates per 100 resident aliens (mostly for the same year)
ranged from 0.3 percent in Germany and one percent in Belgium to
3.5 percent in Sweden, five percent in the Netherlands and 3.4 percent
in France. These figures are not strictly comparable and there are
different counts in certain cases depending on the source and what is
included; for example, inclusion of citizenship acquisition by ethnic
Germans would raise the figure for Germany and inclusion of automatic attribution of citizenship would raise the figures for France. By
1991, after significant liberalization in most countries, naturalization
rates were 2.5 percent in Austria, 0.9 in Belgium,[18] 0.8 percent in Swit-

zerland, 0.5 percent in Germany (excluding Ethnic Germans, "aussiedler," with whom it was 2.4 percent), two percent in France (but 2.7 percent including estimated automatic acquisition at majority for children born in France) 4.2 percent in the Netherlands, 5.7 percent in Sweden, 3.4 percent in the United Kingdom (See Table 9; see also Baubock and Cinar, 1994). By 1996 there were marked increases in Germany and the Netherlands.

Rath (1990) in a detailed comparison of seven major nationality groups represented in six major immigrant-receiving countries in Western Europe in the mid-1980s found that the rates of citizenship acquisition varied more across countries than across nationality groups within countries. This suggests that the citizenship law in a country is more significant than the imputed propensity to naturalize of particular nationality groups. Sweden and Germany were the two extremes: none of the groups considered had lower percentages than 1.8 percent in Sweden, and none had higher rates than 0.6 percent in Germany.

The importance of citizenship law is also underlined comparing two such contrasting countries as France, where there was automatic attribution of citizenship until the changes in 1993 for second-generation immigrants, and Germany where this is not the case. The overall rate of civic incorporation for immigrants and their descendants is ten times higher in France than in Germany. France now has a growing population of second generation Franco-Portuguese, Franco-Maghrebiens, and so forth who are French citizens. But half a million second-generation Turkish immigrants born and raised in Germany are not citizens. This sharp difference happens in an economic context where the employment facts for immigrants are very similar since the 1960s. Yet we can see convergence. The 1993 change to the nationality code in France requires a declaration of intent at majority to acquire citizenship where before it was automatic. And the 1990 Foreigners Law in Germany eases the process of naturalization for the second generation (Faist 1994): it gives a claim to naturalization for all foreigners who have lived in Germany for ten years; further, young foreigners aged sixteen to twenty-three can be naturalized if they have attended four years of school in Germany. The convergence continues to strengthen in the late 1990s in the renewed liberalization instituted by the new Socialist government in France and by the new Social Democratic government in Germany.

However, what is perhaps most remarkable is how marginal all these rates are once we exclude automatic attribution of citizenship. The sharpest differences are revealed when comparing given nationalities across countries. Taking Germany and Sweden, for instance, we see that Moroccans had a rate of 0.1 percent in Germany and 20 percent in Sweden for a ratio of 1:200, one of the highest ratios for all the countries and nationalities covered by the study. Other sharp differences were found among Greeks, with a 0.1 percent rate in Germany and 10.5 percent in Sweden; among Turks, with respectively 0.1 percent and 6 percent; among Spaniards, 0.2 percent and 7.4 percent; among Italians, 0.2 percent and 2.2 percent; among Yugoslavs, 0.6 percent and 1.8 percent. Although these differences move within fairly narrow ranges, a country's citizenship law does matter: thus, there were four-fold and five-fold increases in naturalizations among several national groups in the Netherlands after the new Nationality Act of 1985.

Many factors influence these rates: proximity to country of origin, whether one's country of origin is a member of the EU or is soon to be one, citizenship policy in country of origin – for example, Morocco and Greece do not allow renunciation of their citizenship.

By the late 1980s the distinctions among countries were in broad terms as follows. Sweden, Britain, and France have liberal policies. All three impose modest conditions for the acquisition of citizenship by resident foreigners: automatic or optional citizenship for children born in the country, five years or less residence, no or modest cost for the application procedure, limited conditions of good conduct, and a simple application procedure (Rath 1990). The Netherlands and Belgium have recently liberalized their procedures, but they are still more demanding about establishing the applicant's will to integrate in the receiving society and require an investigation by authorities which entails more complex procedures. Germany and Switzerland impose numerous and demanding conditions for naturalization. There is no facilitated procedure for descendants of immigrants, a ten to twelve year residence requirement, high fees, complex and discretionary procedures to prove that the applicant is well integrated into the society. In Germany and Switzerland naturalization is seen as the final stage of assimilation.

A somewhat more detailed description of the policies of the United Kingdom and Switzerland serves to illustrate, respectively a so-called liberal and one of the least liberal procedures. What is perhaps most remarkable is the gradual tightening of the more liberal regime and the gradual, if ever so mild, loosening of the conservative regime. These are some of the elements we are seeing in many of the West European countries which have as an overall outcome a growing similarity in immigration and refugee policy, no matter how radical the original and ongoing differences in naturalization and citizenship law.

The United Kingdom has traditionally been a jus soli system: all persons born in any British territory in any part of the world could claim British citizenship, even if their parents were not British. Even when after World War II countries in the British Commonwealth began enacting their own citizenship legislation, their citizens continued to be British as well. Immigration controls were introduced in the 1960s and 1970s which began to undermine this broad definition of citizenship in that they restricted the right of citizens to enter and settle. Eventually this was formalized in a narrower definition of citizenship in the British Nationality Act of 1981. By this act a person born in the United Kingdom is a British citizen if at the time of birth the father or mother is a British citizen or is settled in the United Kingdom. A person born outside the United Kingdom is a British citizen if at the time of birth the father or the mother is a British citizen other than by descent, or if one parent is serving in the armed forces, or in some other government entity or is serving in an EC institution. A person born in the United Kingdom who does not qualify at birth for British citizenship is entitled to be registered as such after the age of ten providing he or she has not been absent for more than ninety days in the first ten years of life. There were also a variety of transitional arrangements through which citizenship could be obtained; these were ended on December 31, 1987. Under various conditions, including three to five years of residence, it is possible to apply for naturalization; but it is the Home Secretary's prerogative to decide on the application, and no reason for refusal needs to be given.[19]

In Switzerland citizenship is constituted at three autonomous levels: the confederation, the canton, and the commune (commune d'origine), where a citizen has a hereditary "right of city" even if he or she has never lived there. An applicant for naturalization needs to be accepted at each of these levels. Thus rates of naturalization vary considerably by canton and commune. The Federal Nationality Act of

1952 was revised in 1984 but remains firmly grounded in jus sanguinis. Citizenship is automatic only by marriage (to a Swiss man) and by descent. Otherwise prior naturalization is required. At the federal level it is conditioned, with some exceptions, on twelve years residence and "aptitude for naturalization." The latter is a complicated procedure that seeks to establish the aptitude of the applicant and his family for the Swiss way of life and it requires approval at all three levels. At the cantonal and communal levels the decision is often made through a legislative body or even assembly of citizens and often depends on the political climate.

Various referendums on naturalization policy reduced some of the restrictions: 1983 saw the implementation of equality of men and women in the capacity to transmit citizenship to their children and a 1987 provision extended this capacity to spouses. Naturalization policy came under severe attack from the antiimmigrant party National Action Against Overforeignization of People and Fatherland, which sought to limit naturalizations to 4,000 a year through an amendment of the constitution. Put to the vote in 1977 it was rejected by a majority of two to one.

An instance of a far more sweeping atempt at liberalizing a system that puts quite a bit of responsibility on the immigrant's capacity to "integrate," is that of the Netherlands. The new Dutch Nationality Act of 1985 which replaced the rather recent law of 1982, allows foreigners aged eighteen to twenty-five years residing in the country since birth to acquire Dutch citizenship by option. It is a simple declaration. For a transitional period which ended in 1987, the foreign children of Dutch mothers could also use this option; it was widely used. Dual citizenship is accepted. A person whose father or mother is Dutch has the Dutch citizenship. The children of aliens born in the Netherlands are Dutch citizens if they were born in the Netherlands, too. Other aliens must first naturalize. Naturalization requires five years of prior residence, eighteen years of age or more, absence of a certain type of criminal record and the ability to converse in simple Dutch. It is possible to appeal if one's naturalization application is refused.

The main changes in this law were provisions giving equality to men and women in acquiring or transmitting citizenship, provisions for the appeal of refusals of naturalization, and the substitution of a legislative procedure with an administrative one. This new act is part of the Dutch "ethnic minority policy" which combines strict control over admissions and a liberal naturalization regime. It recognizes that the cultural identity of foreign citizens and residents should be respected and hence establishes minimum "integration" criteria for naturalization.

In the early 1990s, confronted with major pressure to control what was seen as a flood of immigrants and refugees, some European countries implemented changes that amounted to a more restrictive set of rules for entry and also raised the convergence of policies across Western Europe. Some liberal countries, such as France, implemented greater restrictions on access to citizenship and naturalization (cf. the New Nationality Code of 1993), while others, notably Germany, loosened the conditions for naturalization, a necessary step toward citizenship. Switzerland has amended its citzenship law and now allows retaining one's prior nationality in naturalization. In the Netherlands renunciation of former nationality is no longer necessary. This brings these two states closer to major immigration countries such as the United States, Canada and Australia, and to the United Kingdom and France, countries that have allowed more than one nationality. Germany, Austria, and Luxembourg now remain as countries requiring renunciation of prior citizenship, since Sweden tolerates dual nationality in most cases (Baubock and Cinar 1994). In Germany the development of "social citizenship" has expanded the political opportunities of immigrants, and there is a broad campaign demanding some elements of jus soli and dual citizenship. At the same time Germany made its asylum law far more restrictive in 1993. The convergence in migration and asylum policies is certainly one of the objectives in the formation of a European Union. The Council of Europe Convention of 1963 which aimed at reducing multiple nationalities has been made less restrictive through a second protocol that is up for ratification, and more substantial changes are expected in the near future.

These are extremely brief and simplified descriptions of the rules in these countries. Such descriptions leave out the whole realm of practice in the implementation of procedures and controls, and it leaves out the broader issues of how "immigrants" are represented as a sociopolitical category in the law and in political practice; how immigrants, indeed different sectors of the immigrant population, represent themselves; the redefinition of the immigrant question in

Western Europe from a labor market to an identity issue and the racializing of immigrants and refugees (Schnapper 1991; Wihtol de
Wenden 1988; Faist 1994; Weil 1991; Miles and Phizacklea 1984).[20]
These are issues that tend to mobilize popular sentiment. I return to
some of these in chapter 7.

IMMIGRATION AND FREEDOM OF CIRCULATION

The formation of the European Union requires harmonization of policies on immigration controls, on recognition of political refugees, the
handling of illegal immigrants, and the status of foreign residents.
The aboliton of frontiers inside the EU will also call for harmonization of general rules concerning housing, stays, visas, access to jobs,
criminality. One of the major issues confronting policy makers is the
current distinction built into much policy and law between two
classes of immigrants: those belonging to EU member states and
those from outside the EU. The former have gradually been granted a
number of rights. Further, the development of supranational forms of
"citizenship" as symbolized by the current EU passport may sharpen
the differences in the regimes covering different categories of residents, notably EU nationals and non-EU nationals. Maastricht, by giving new strength to the development of EU- wide citizenship rights,
including voting rights across the EU, has brought to the front the
matter of immigrants and refugees and what is entailed by their naturalization.

What brought the issue of immigration to the forefront in the early
1990s in discussions about harmonization of policies was on the one
hand, the provisions on the free movement of persons as a key aspect
of a single European market, and on the other, the great increase in
the foreign-resident population, illegal immigration, and asylum
seekers. The immigrant population had increased sharply through
family reunification, natural growth, and the new migrations from
the East. Illegal immigration was estimated at about 2.6 million by
1991 and between four to five million by 1993. Asylum seekers and
refugees had quadrupled in numbers in only a few years, with
700,000 arriving in 1992 alone – about a quarter of the total immigration inflow to the EU.

By 1991 there was growing concern about many refugees and asylum seekers actually being economic migrants who used the asylum
option because it made entry easier given closure of labor immigra-

tion. There was also mounting concern and criticism about the slowness of applications processing which often led and continues to lead to asylum seekers suffering great hardship if not allowed to work until their status is confirmed, or, where that is the case, costly welfare benefits to support asylum seekers until their status is confirmed. To these concerns was eventually added the worry of massive refugee flows escaping the wars in former Yugoslavia. Indeed concerted efforts were made to stop refugees from leaving the country, to keep these refugees "as close to their home areas as possible," and within the confines of the former Yugoslavia.

As for the principle of free movement of persons in the EU, it has long been a subject of contention, including contention about the right of EU nationals, let alone non-EU immigrants. Thus free movement for Greek citizens was not established until 1988, and for Spanish and Portuguese citizens not until 1992.

In principle, initiatives taken by member countries on these subjects (TREVI Group, Schengen Agreement, etc.) do not tend to exclude nonmember country nationals explicitly. But the national state remains the sovereign arbiter in these matters, even though its power to excercise this sovereignty has been eroding as a consequence of a whole configuration of rights and institutions that can override a state's decision. This is a subject I return to in chapter 7.

In this context the regulations implemented concerning immigrants are focused on restricting the issuance of work permits, apprehending and returning undocumented workers, and promoting voluntary return to home countries for those who have lost their jobs. The purpose is to give priority of employment opportunities to workers of member countries. This tightening of employment practices has hurt immigrant workers because they often lack training and professional background.[21]

EU member states could grant the same rights of circulation to legal immigrant residents from nonmember countries as those enjoyed by nationals of members states. The Netherlands has considered this for all immigrants with at least five years of residence in the country. It would also be possible, in principle, to sign bi-and trilateral treaties covering particular nationalities: thus France, Belgium, and the Netherlands all have significant populations of Moroccans and might conceivably benefit from their freedom of circulation, for example, to facilitate a more efficient labor allocation given differential unemployment conditions in these three countries. But how would the cutoff line in terms of nationalities and group size be established?

At least some have argued that such agreements for free circulation among signatory countries should concern all nationalities in these countries to avoid new types of differentiation. This would, conceivably, be a way of addressing the reluctance of states that might not want to open their doors to any national groups, or national groups not present as of now in their territory. Such partial spaces for free circulation would strengthen the current geograpahy of immigrant nationalities, reproducing the concentration of particular national groups in a specific set of countries.

What we see emerging out of the confluence of the single European-market project and the changing immigration and refugee reality is a greater involvement of EC institutions in immigration and refugee policy than could actually have been expected only a few years ago. This has happened even though national governments have long been unwilling to relinquish even an inch of their sovereignty in this arena, and EC institutions in many ways lacked competence in these matters. And it has taken some time. Thus at Maastricht, EU governments did not give EC treaty-based institutions the lead on immigration issues, except for visa policy. As a result individual states had to act in concert to put in place effective policies and procedures and to avoid exporting problems into neighboring countries. National governments set up intergovernmental agreements and working groups to keep control over EU-wide policy making and EC institutions gradually developed an interest and expertise in immigration and refugee matters. (Voisard and Ducastelle 1988).

Intergovernmental agreements have a long history among EC member states.[22] Already in the 1970s we see the formation of various intergovernmental groups, mostly concerning foreign policy. Thus there was nothing particularly unusual about the European Council setting up an ad hoc working group on immigration in 1986; it grew out of the work by the TREVI Group and out of a growing recognition that the single European market would bring to the fore immigration issues which could be resolved through intergovernmental efforts.[23] Indeed, since the Hanover European Council of June 1988 addressed immigration issues, almost every EC summit meeting has had to do so. The main products coming out of the intergovernmental work on the free movement of people since the ratification of the SEA (Single European Act) have been the Dublin Convention on Asylum in 1990 and the External Frontiers Convention initialled in 1991, both of which carry implications for migration and immigration (Butt Philip 1994).[24]

More broadly, several EC states sought to address the formation of a frontier-free area within Europe through the Schengen Agreement of 1985, signed by the national governments of France, Germany, and the Benelux. The five Schengen states were not able to sign a second agreement in November 1989 as planned in order to deliver a frontier-free Schengen area by January 1, 1990. This inability centered on issues such as bank secrecy, drugs, and data protection, besides the declared problem of external frontiers control with the fall of the Berlin Wall. The second Schengen Agreement was eventually signed in June 1990. But many of the problems remained and implementation dates kept being postponed: January 1, 1992; December 1, 1993, February 1, 1994. The difficulties were partly a result of the need for EC-wide institutions to handle some of the matters. On the other hand, the United Kingdom has claimed that the difficulties in implementing freedom of circulation and the fact that EC institutions have competence in only some of the necessary procedures underlines the state's unrestricted competence to deal with terrorism, immigration, and nationality matters.

Schengen showed both the limits and the possibilities of such intergovernmental agreements in immigration matters. The Schengen Agreement was strengthened by the addition of Italy, Spain, Portugal, and Greece, and their decision to impose stronger external border controls in the context of Schengen. A Schengen Information System was developed, and eventually located in Strassbourg. At the same time, Schengen represents an intergovernmental effort toward the dismantling of internal border controls (see Spencer 1990).

In 1990 and 1991 it became clear that both the intergovernmental structure and the EC structure faced similar hurdles. From that period onwards there have been various motions toward greater burden sharing on refugees and asylum seekers, especially because a few countries receive most of them; visa policy has become part of the competence of the EC institutions; and intergovernmental cooperation on asylum, refugee, and immigration issues has been included in the so-called third pillar of the Maastricht Treaty. EC institutions have increased their involvement with immigration and border-control issues generally. By 1991 the EC was making a call for common immigration rules and policies, not simply immigration as a by-product of border control issues. Illegal immigration, a matter of central concern to such intergovernmental bodies as the Working Group on Immigration, will require EC-wide action as will efforts to facilitate deportation.

Growing recognition of the centrality of immigration and refugee policy for a free-movement area, along with increased expertise both in EC and intergovernmental institutions, has produced a long list of items on which work is being done. A common list of "undesirable aliens" is being prepared for circulation among enforcement agencies, common training of officials in various border-control matters, and a new center for information exchange on border crossings and immigration is to be set up; finally, further work is being done on harmonizing family reunion rules. More work along these lines was carried out at the Copenhagen meeting of the WGI (Working Group on Immigration) of June 1993, including a call for more internal checks on non-EC nationals and the formulation of clear criteria for expulsion.[25]

On the agenda for the WGI lie various issues ranging from short-term contracts for third-country nationals, especially from Eastern Europe, to the position of long-term resident immigrants in the EU who have not acquired the nationality of a member state. The latter is part of a broader discussion about nationality policy in the EC, because the granting of nationality by one EC state gives EC-wide rights to the recipient. At the same time, the refusal of citizenship to long-term residents is increasingly seen as problematic, unsustainable, and not desirable in that it prevents immigrant integration into the host society, now recognized as essential. Even Germany, the most restrictive country in this regard, is open to revise its position and recognizes the difficulties some of its policies create for the EC.[26]

The difficulties entailed by harmonization of rules are underlined by the debate around family reunion rules, a principle about which there is no disagreement and on which there is considerable convergence among all countries. This policy is grounded in Article 8 of the European Convention of the Rights of Man which asserts the right to lead a normal life and the notion that the family is the natural and fundamental building bloc of society and hence deserves the protection of the state and of society.[27] According to this an immigrant has the right to bring his or her family if s/he has sufficient income, has adequate housing, and his or her request is considered acceptable—

which makes it a somewhat conditioned right. Even so, it is a center-piece in Western thinking about rights. Thus when France and Germany tried to limit family reunification, they were blocked by administrative and constitutional courts on the grounds that such restrictions would violate international agreements. In France, the Council of State struck down attempts by the government to inhibit family reunification in the late 1970s (Weil 1991).

There is considerable variation in the specifics of this policy in different countries. For instance, immigrants from the Maghrebian countries are more penalized by the regulations for family reunion in part because of their poor housing conditions and in part because they are far more vulnerable to unemployment given their position in the labor market (Khader 1991).

Harmonization of regulations in the EC should, according to many, entail a liberalization of these conditions. But there is fear that this will further raise the numbers coming in through family reunion. Yet according to some (cf. Khader 1991) a massive influx of relatives is unlikely for several reasons: it is not certain that a large share of those now living separately would bring in relatives given the cost of living in European countries and the difficulty of finding adequate housing for a family, given the desire to maintain connected to country of origin, the desire to have children educated in the country of origin, unlikelihood of uprooting older parents or children from their country of origin, generalized acceptance that in a labor migration there is going to be some amount of family separation. There is also the ongoing hope among many of returning to their home country after a few years of work in the immigration country.

There is still no EC immigration policy as such, nor a EC citizenship policy. The EC is acquiring authority and competence in these matters in a somewhat ad hoc way. It shares institutional responsibility with national governments, and most of this institutional responsibility is in fact intergovernmental rather than EC based. EC institutions are not subject to democratic controls, which contributes to limit their authority in many ways. This becomes evident in particularly sensititve areas where they have been challenged, for instance, in the courts regarding individual civil liberties. This has also meant that EC policies have often difficulty being accepted for consideration and confirmation in national parliaments. Yet the new confluence of con-

ditions which has engaged national governments and the EC in a
joint effort to harmonize migration and asylum policies in the EU
represents a remarkable change compared to only a few years ago.

NOTES

1   See Tables in Appendix for more detailed quantitative descriptions of various aspects of immi-
    gration and asylum seeking.

2   Belgium had 368,000 foreign residents; Switzerland, 285,000; Austria, 323,000, which included
    numbers of refugees from Eastern Europe. In the other countries it was slightly above 100,000,
    as in the Netherlands, Spain, and Sweden, or ranged from 3,000 in Liechtenstein to 47,000 in
    Italy.

3   Collecting data on foreign workers is complicated by the differences in immigration policy and
    in the provisions on access to the labor market; these differences reduce the comparability of
    the data somewhat.

4   The sharp differences in the ease of obtaining naturalization has an impact on the figures for
    the total foreign stock. Thus in France or Belgium, where it is relatively easy, the naturalized
    foreign-born population and natural increase show up as increases in the indigenous popula-
    tion; in Germany or Switzerland, where it is very difficult, such increases show up mostly as
    increases in the foreign population. For instance, France's 1982 census counted six million
    foreign-born but only 3.68 million foreigners (see SOPEMI 1992, 126).

5   On the other side of the balance sheet, the actual migration flow figures do not factor in
    migrants who returned to their countries of origins, migrants who moved on and left Europe,
    or those who died in the host countries.

6   The reductions in Switzerland and Sweden were achieved mostly by not granting work per-
    mits. In all the other countries the foreign population increased notwithstanding various in-
    centives to get people to return to their home countries.

7   After 1986 Austria changed its manner of counting; but the shift happened after this change.

8   In several countries the illegal immigrant has no right to appeal the decision of being expelled.
    For an appeal procedure to be effective it requires that the administrative decision regarding
    expulsion be made public and available to the immigrant; this is not the case in Germany for
    example. Other illegal entry control measures include carrier liability whereby airlines are
    fined for bringing passengers to EU countries without proper documentation.

9   Hungary was the first of the Eastern Bloc countries to sign the 1951 Geneva Convention on
    Refugees. Poland signed in September 1991.

10 For a brief description of the Schengen Treaty see later section in this chapter. The Dublin
    Convention is designed to prevent multiple or successive applications for asylum in EU mem-
    ber states, and to ensure that the decision on asylum should be made by the first country of
    application without other signatories to the convention having to re-examine identical appli-
    cations. This agreement is not without problems for particular countries. Both agreements
    present problems for one or another of the signatory countries. See also note 24 in this chapter
    on the External Frontiers Agreement.

11 With the implementation of the 1986 IRCA (Immigration Reform and Control Act) in the U.S.,
    we see a similar pattern after the legalization of undocumented Mexicans, particularly those
    residing close to the frontier with Mexico: having gained the right to live and work in the
    United States they felt freer to go back to Mexico, where the cost of living is much lower and

where they were likely to have a more satisfactory community life; the notion is that now that they can come in without restrictions they can do so when it makes sense rather than feeling the need to maximize their stay after an arduous, costly, and often extremely dangerous illegal crossing.

12   For instance, France has received sixty times fewer emigrants from East Germany than West Germany over a period of ten years 1980 to 1990. In 1990 the total influx from the East to France was ten percent of all immigrant entries to France. There is also an economically oriented Polish migration to France, in spite of the closure of labor migration. It consists of the organized recruitment of seasonal workers for agriculture and is operated through the International Office for Migration (OIM) which has opened a recruitment office in Warsaw for such workers.

13   From 1967 to 1990 there was a separate East German citizenship in the Democratic Republic. But from the perspective of the Federal Republic of Germany there was only one citizenship and it always included the citizens of the Democratic Republic. Thus after 1989 all citizens from East Germany had the right to reside, work, and have access to all citizen's rights in the West. Concerning ethnic Germans, the legal definition as a German rests on German *Volkszugehörigkeit* and on status as *Vertrieben*, that is a person driven out of Eastern Europe or the former Soviet Union because of their German ethnicity. Originally defined in terms of ethnic Germans physically driven out after World War II, eventually it was broadened to include de facto all ethnic Germans from Eastern Europe and the former Soviet Union. The large numbers who made use of this after 1989 (coming particularly from Poland, Rumania, and the Soviet Union), with over one million arriving from 1989 to 1991 alone, has led to a revision of the automatic definiton as Vertrieben and hence has made it less automatic for ethnic Germans to become citizens.

14   There was little if any variation in the following characteristics of the flow between the two points in time of the survey. About one third of the commuters went to West Berlin; less than a fourth originated from East Berlin, and about twenty percent in Thuringen. About eighty percent were men, a much larger share than their fifty-five percent in the labor force of the former GDR; half of all commuters were between twenty-five and thirty-nine years of age, also a far larger share than this age group has in the former GDR workforce; and fifty-nine percent were married, below the seventy-one percent in the former GDR workforce. Finally, commuters were found to have a higher level of education than the average employed person in the former GDR, though their job qualification showed no significant difference. The evidence suggests that commuters hold jobs in the West that require fewer qualification than they have.

15   The impossibility of effectively controlling Poland's 1,000 kilometer long border with the former Soviet Union is a source of great concern to the Central European countries. These countries fear they will become a final destination for emigrants and refugees from the East who are not accepted by the West.

16   In Poland repatriation was not seen as a desirable or economically viable option, although it is not known how many would want to go back to Poland. It was estimated that the integration of one million ethnic Poles over a period of five years would cost over two billion dollars; fewer than 1,000 persons were repatriated in 1991, the year after the opening (Morokvasic and Tinguy 1993). The policy adopted has been one of supporting Polish populations abroad, ensuring they can stay and have minority rights, and can protect their ethnic identity. To that end Poland signed friendship treaties with Ukraine in 1990 and with Belorussia in 1991. Hungary has followed a similar strategy of supporting and keeping Hungarian communities in place, thereby dissuading repatriation. It signed a friendship treaty with Ukraine; this was not without controversy because Hungary's acceptance of the existing borders was seen by some as a betrayal of the Hungarian community in Ukraine. On the other hand, the government has encouraged repatriation of Hungarians from Rumania (Sik 1990).

17 Most generally one would have to examine broad models of integration that organize a nation-state. Castles and Miller (1993) find that there are four possible models of incorporation: multi-ethnic empires with dominance by one group; an ethnic model dominated by common descent (Jus sanguinis); a republicn model – the nation as a political community (Jus soli or citizenship by birthplace); and a multicultural model: a new model which is a modified republican model but with recognition of cultural and ethnic differences. Baubock (1994) has examined the different possibilities for citizenship, including some version of a transnational citizenship corresponding to an increasingly mobile workforce.

18 But it should be noted that the new law of 1992 made for a six-fold increase from 1991, up to almost 46,500 naturalizations in 1992.

19 Also in France naturalization is ultimately a discretionary decision of the state. But it is rarely refused: one estimate is that only from ten to twelve percent of applications are refused and many of these are accepted in second attempts (Costa-Lascoux 1987). Another estimate, by CIMADE, an organization suppporting immigrant workers, estimates refusal rates at thirty percent of applications.

20 The importance and complexity of this other immigration policy reality is illustrated by Wischenbart's (1994) argument that immigration policy in Austria has meant a reworking of the cultural heritage of the Austrio-Hungarian Empire (see also Fassman 1985).

21 This is particularly so with North African immigrants, eighty-five percent of whom reside in France. National governments and EC institutions need to implement policies that support immigrants besides tightening control over immigrant workers. A good example is France's circular no. 84 – 05 of February 1, 1984, which implemented important measures about providing training to immigrant workers who lose their jobs.

22 Intergovernmental agreements allow individual states to pursue matters they would rather not pursue within the EC framework, including matters over which the EC has competence. Such agreements are governed by international law rather than EC institutions. The European Council, whose powers and functions are not defined by the EC treaties, provides the broad institutional umbrella for intergovernmental agreements. Intergovernmental resolutions, such as the 1993 resolution on family reunification, have no standing under international or EC law.

23 The TREVI Group, formed in 1975 – 7, made it possible for officials and ministers from the interior and justice ministries to handle matters demanding cooperation between governments and enforcement agencies for internal security and criminal activities.

24 The Dublin Convention is briefly described earlier in this chapter. The External Frontiers Convention provides for the mutual recognition of national visas for non-EC nationals; it abolishes the need for non-EC nationals residing legally in one EC member state to secure a visa to enter another EC state for a period shorter than three months, provided the purpose is not employment.

25 Regarding undocumented immigration governments have been urged from various quarters not to follow a policy of every now and then launching a regularization when things have gotten out of hand, but to coordinate the actions of the governments of sending and receiving countries, and set up a quota system to absorb the most determined pent-up demand.

26 Possible options would be for the EU to address nationality policy jointly, and to establish ceilings on the annual granting of new citizenship EU wide; essential would also be to consult before large-scale repatriations of third countries are authorized if these have naturalization and citizenship rights. In brief, what needs to be addressed is the fact that different citizenship regimes have EU-wide impacts.

27 Also the ILO Convention No. 143 on migrant workers signed in 1975 recognizes that family reunion satisfies a need for humanitarian and social integration.

7

MAKING IMMIGRATION POLICY TODAY

This chapter uses the history told in this book to develop several themes which are, in my reading, important if we are to advance our understanding, and the politics, of immigration. The first theme is that these flows are bounded in space, time, and scale. In the collective imagination of receiving societies, or some very vocal sectors of it, the imagery is one of floods of immigrants and refugees, coming from everywhere, with no end in sight. But this is not the case today, nor was it in the past when there were no border controls. A second theme is the growing transnationalizing in policy making around immigration and refugees, in a mirroring of other processes of transnationalization – economic, political, cultural. National governments still have sovereignty over many matters, but they are increasingly part of a web of rights and regulations that are embedded in other entities – from EC institutions to courts defending the human rights of refugees. A third theme is that there is only one enlightened road to take for Europe today: that is to work with settled immigrants and refugees toward their full integration, and to do so through frameworks that ensure cultural and religious diversity will be part of civil society, that is, part of what binds us rather than what segregates us.

Refugees are also, partly, encompassed by these themes. Once settled they are often subject to the same conditions as immigrants. At the same time there is a distinct specificity to the condition of refuge seeker that needs to be maintained; current conditions will require a revision of the Geneva Convention definition of refugee that came out of the aftermath of World War I. It is essential to ensure that those escaping persecution have a chance to make their case. This chapter addresses the refugee question, but only insofar as it is encompassed by conditions which immigrants and refugees share.

LABOR MIGRATION AS EMBEDDED PROCESS

The evidence for the last two centuries shows that labor migrations are patterned in terms of geography and duration. It is not an irreversible flow that only keeps growing. It is highly modulated. Similarly in terms of notions of mass invasion, it is important to note that even though migrants came largely from poorer areas, they were typically only a section of the population, and never could one see something akin to a massive flood. Nor does "invasion" seem to have happened. It was a minority of a region's or country's people that migrated even when the state had not yet gained full control over the borders, when the state lacked the technical and bureaucratic capacities to do so.

When there were so many poor in some regions, when there was inequality in wages and work opportunities between regions, and when there were no border controls, why did not all the poor, or the vast majority of them, migrate to the sites of prosperity?

Labor migrations took place within systemic settings and there appear to have been multiple mechanisms contributing to their size, geography, and duration. From a macrosocietal perspective these can be seen as a type of equilibrating mechanisms. It could be argued that precisely because labor migrations never became mass invasions, they are parts of a system, and are conditioned by the latter's characteristics. Enormous long-term excess inflows by immigrants are not part of the history of labor migrations in Europe.

The importance of recruitment and networks, often spatially circumscribed networks, the frequency of circular migrations that connected specific places of origin with specific destinations over long periods of time, all of these signal the extent to which migrations were embedded in and shaped by specific systems. This was the case long before states were able to control their borders; the shaping effect is, thus, not simply a consequence of immigration policy as such. There typically is something in addition to the will of individual migrants that contributes to form and sustain migratory flows. Very often it is the existence of one or another kind of geopolitically specified system.

Such systems can be characterized in a multiplicity of ways: economic (e.g., the Atlantic economy of the 1800s, the EEC, NAFTA); politico-military (the colonial systems of several European countries, U.S. involvement in Central America); transnational war zones (e.g., formation of massive refugee flows as a result of major European wars); cultural-ideological zones (e.g., impact in socialist countries of the image of Western democracies as offering the "good life" to each and all).

Yet notwithstanding this systemic shaping of the geography, duration, and size of labor migrations, and notwithstanding the fact that population growth was slow, mortality high, and labor shortages acute, immigrant workers were discriminated against already in the nineteenth century, were seen as undesirable by many sectors of the larger society. Today the argument may be centered on questions of race and culture, but in fact they are new contents for an old passion: the racializing of the outsider, of the "other." Today the "other" is represented, stereotyped as from a different race and culture. In fact, also when from the same phenotype and, broadly speaking European culture, immigrants were marked as "the other." Migration is typically a move between two worlds, even if it is in a single region, or country – such as East Germans moving to West Germany.

Although immigrants and refugees at various times reached significant numbers and were seen as "others" even if European, the experience of "invasion" and flows that are out of control does not seem to have been dominant images until the aftermath of World War I. The formation and strengthening of the interstate system brought to the fore questions of border control and nationality. The definition of "refugee" that comes out of the aftermath of World War I is centered on this interstate system and only weakly connected to broader notions of human rights and the right to asylum as a universal human right.

For much of the nineteenth-century "immigrant" was a category that was constituted differently from today because the question of border control was less central to state sovereignty than it became with World War I. Similarly, the category "refugee" was constituted differently even at the beginnings of mass refugee movements in the 1880s. The centrality of border control emerges partly as a function of the development of state capacities for full border control and generally control over its territory. The will to regulate and to "nationalize" all spheres of activity marks this new era in the history of the state. The other side of this coin was the strenghtening of the interstate system.

Today, with the emergence of EC-wide institutions, the associated changes in the interstate system, and the end of the Cold War, immigrants and refugees coming from poorer countries are once again conflated as one broad category of people coming from the East and the South, basically driven by economic need. The current experience and perception is probably closer to that of the nineteenth century than it is to the period spanning the two wars and much of the Cold War.

Establishing whether labor migration is an integral part of how an economic and social system operates and evolves is, in my view, critical. The logic of this argument is, put simply, as follows: If immigration is thought of as the result of the aggregation of individuals in search of a better life, immigration is, from the perspective of the receiving country, an exogenous process, one formed and shaped by conditions outside the receiving country. The receiving country is then saddled with the task of accommodating this population. If poverty and overpopulation grow, such a view would posit a parallell growth in emigration, at least potentially. The receiving country's experience is understood to be that of a passive bystander to processes outside its domain and control, and hence with few options but tight closing of frontiers if it is to avoid an "invasion."

If, on the other hand, immigration is conditioned on the operation of the economic system in receiving countries, including direct recruitment, then the receiving country cannot consider itself a mere, passive, bystander to the whole matter. Immigration emerges as an integral part of the spaces and periods of growth of the receiving economy, or, in certain cases. of particular phases of decline and reorganization—as is the case in the United States when sweatshops replaced unionized jobs during deindustrialization in the 1970s and 1980s. Immigration happens in a context of inequality between countries, but inequality by itself is not enough (see Sassen 1988; 1998 chap 2). This inequality needs to be activated as a migration push factor— through organized recruitment, neocolonial bonds, etc. The economic, political, and social conditions in the receiving country set the parameters for immigration flows. Immigration flows may take a while to adjust to changes in levels of labor demand or to saturation of opportunities, but eventually they always have tended to adjust to the conditions in receiving countries, even if these adjustments are imperfect. Thus there was a decline in the rate of growth of Polish immigration into Germany in the early 1990s once it was clear that the opportunities were not as plentiful, and a replacement of permanent by circular migration in many east-to-west flows, including from the former East Germany to West Germany. The size and duration of flows is shaped by these conditions: it is not an exogenous process that is only shaped by poverty and population growth elsewhere and hence is autonomous from the accommodation capacities of receiving countries.

If size and duration are overall shaped by conditions in receiving countries then the possibility of reasonably effective immigration policies also exists. Managing a patterned and conditioned flow of immigrants is a rather different matter from controlling an "invasion." Implementation of an effective policy does not necessarily mean perfect synchronization between conditions in the receiving country and immigrant inflow and settlement. This will never be the case: immigration is a process constituted by human beings with will and agency and with multiple identities and life trajectories beyond the fact of being seen, defined, categorized as immigrants for the purposes of the receiving polity, economy, and society. There is no definitive proof in this matter. But there are patterns, and there are past patterns, that have lived their full life. And they can tell us something about the extent to which immigration has consisted of a series of bounded events, with beginnings and endings, and specific geographies – all conditioned largely by the operation and organization of receiving economies, polities, and societies.

THE GEOPOLITICS OF MIGRATION

The mechanisms binding immigration countries to emigration countries can, in principle, assume many forms. But two appear to be dominant and account for most of the initiation of flows. One is past colonial and current neo- or quasicolonial bonds. The other is the launching of organized recruitment either directly by the government or in the framework of a government-supported initiative by em-

ployers. Such recruitment often overlaps with the first type of situation. Eventually most migration flows gain a certain autonomy from
organized recruitment mechanisms. While organized recruitment,
and therewith the constitution of certain countries as labor-exporting
countries, is in many ways radically different from the migrations
engendered by erstwhile colonial bonds, there are also similarities. In
many ways the labor-exporting country is put in a subordinate position, and keeps being represented in the media and in political discourse as a labor-exporting country. This was also the case last
century when some labor-exporting areas existed in conditions of
economic subordination and often also quasipolitical subordination.
The former Polish territories partitioned off to Germany were such a
region, a region which generated significant migration of "ethnic"
Poles to Western Germany and beyond. It is the case of the Irish in
England, and of Italy, which kept reproducing itself as a labor sup-
plier for the rest of Europe.

The fact that there is a geopolitics of migration is suggested by what
must be familiar facts to many. Sixty percent of the foreign residents
in Great Britain are from Asian or African countries which were
former dominions or colonies; European immigration is rather low,
and almost three fourths of these come from Ireland, also once a
"colony." There are almost no immigrants from such countries as
Turkey or Yugoslavia, which provide the largest share to Germany,
for instance. Almost all immigrants from the Indian subcontinent and
from the English Caribbean residing in Europe are in Great Britain.

Continuing along these lines, in the first ten years after World War
II, the vast majority of "immigrants" to Germany were the eight million displaced ethnic Germans that resettled there. Another major
group were the three million who came from the GDR before the
Berlin Wall was erected in 1961. Almost all ethnic Germans went to
Germany, and those that did not go to Germany went overseas. But
also eighty-six percent of Greek immigrants in Europe reside in Germany, almost eighty percent of Turks, and seventy-six percent of Yugoslavs. More recently also Germany has expanded its labor
recruitment or sourcing area to include Portugal, Algeria, Morocco,
and Tunisia, even though the vast majority of immigrants from these
countries reside in France. In brief, what we see in the case of Germany is first a large migration rooted in a long history of domination
over the eastern region, then an immigration originating in less-

developed countries following a by now classical dynamic of labor-import labor-export countries.

France, for long Europe's main immigration country, is since the late 1960s its second largest, after Germany. Decolonization brought about the return of two million French from overseas. During the period of sharp postwar growth a whole new migration developed originating in France's former zone of influence in North Africa. Almost all Algerians residing in Europe are in France; and so are eighty-six percent of Tunisians and sixty-one percent of Moroccans. Almost all immigrants in Europe from overseas territories still under French control—such as the French Antilles, Tahiti, and French Guyana—reside in France. But so do eighty-four percent of Portuguese and of Spaniards residing in Europe outside their country. As noted in earlier chapters, France also had an old history of recruiting migrant workers from Italy and Belgium.

The Netherlands and Belgium both received significant numbers of people from their former colonial empires. They also received foreign workers from labor-exporting countries, such as Italy, Morocco, and Turkey. Switzerland similarly receives workers from traditional labor-exporting countries: Italy, Spain, Portugal, Yugoslavia, and Turkey. All three countries have organized recruitment of these workers, until eventually a somewhat autonomous set of flows was in place. Sweden receives ninety-three percent of Finnish immigrants. Also here as in the other countries, there is a large expansion of the recruitment area to include workers from the traditional labor-exporting countries on the Mediterranean.

As a given labor migration flow ages, it tends to become more diversified in terms of destination. It suggests that a certain autonomy from older colonial and neocolonial bonds sets in. Immigrants from Italy and Spain, by now a largely long-standing resident population are now distributed among several countries. Among Italian immigrants in Europe one third reside in Germany, twenty-seven percent in France, twenty-four percent in Switzerland, and fifteen percent in Belgium. The fact that it is still a limited diversity of destinations can be seen as signaling the evolution of these flows into migration systems. On the other hand, more recent labor migrations reveal very high levels of geographic concentration, a pattern more typical of the initiation of flows. The largest immigrant group in any of Europe's labor-receiving countries today are the Turks, with 1.5 million in Germany.

It does seem, and the history of economic development supports this, that once an area becomes a significant emigration region it does not easily catch up in terms of development with those areas that emerge as labor-importing areas, precisely because the latter have high growth, or at least relatively high growth, it seems that there is an accumulation of advantage. History suggests that this is an advantage which labor-sending areas either a) cannot catch up with, and/or b) are structurally not going to be part of because the spatialization of growth is precisely characterized by this type of uneven development. History suggests it takes several major economic phases to overcome the accumulation of disadvantage and exclusion from the dynamics of growth. One cannot be too rigid and mechanical about these generalizations. But it is clear that for Italy and Ireland, even if now they receive immigrants, the fact of two centuries of labor exporting was not a macroeconomic advantage. Only some individuals and localities may have benefitted. Today when a whole new economic era is afoot, Italy and Ireland have become part of the new growth dynamics – each in its own specific manner.

In brief, analytically we could argue that as today's labor-receiving countries grew richer and more developed they kept expanding their zone of recruitment/influence covering a larger set of countries and including a variety of emigration-immigration dynamics, some rooted in past imperial conditions, others in the newer development asymmetries that underlie much migration today. There is a dynamic of inequality within which labor migrations are embedded that keeps on marking regions as labor sending and labor receiving, notwithstanding a blurring in the definitions as is evident with Central Europe, Ireland, and Italy, which are now also receiving immigrants.

CROSS-COUNTRY REGULARITIES

The two centuries covered here and the vast scholarly literature on immigration in Western Europe, as well as on the United States, points to a number of cross-country regularities. The purpose here is to establish whether immigration flows today have geographic, temporal, and institutional boundaries that point to a definition of the where, when, and who of immigration. These cross-country regularities contribute to a far more qualified understanding of immigration and, hence, of policy options.

1. *Emigration always encompasses a small share of a country's population.* Except for terror-driven refugees, we now know that most people are quite reluctant to leave their home villages or towns. Most people in Mexico have not gone to the United States and most people in Poland are not going to try to move to Germany. Thus most emigrants from Eastern Europe to Germany at the end of the 1980s were Gypsies (Roma people) from Rumania, and ethnic Germans, two populations with very specific reasons for migrating. There is a minority who are determined (pent-up demand) and will move no matter what; then there is a gray area of potential emigrants who may or may not leave, depending on pull factors. But the vast mass of people in a poor country are not likely to consider emigration.

This was already the case in the nineteenth century when borders were not controlled and the state in fact lacked the technical and bureaucratic capacities to do so. Also then emigration was confined to a minority of people. This holds even when we consider subnational regions. For instance, some of the historically highest emigration levels were reached in several southern Italian districts; when we specify such districts on a small geographic scale we find that even so the highest rates were 40 per 1,000 at the height of mass emigration from Italy to the Americas.

And it is the case today within the EU where EU nationals can easily move to another country and there is still considerable variation in earnings levels among different member states. Recent EU figures show little cross-border mobility among EU residents. About fifteen million EU residents out of a total population of 344 million are working in a country which is not their state of citizenship. A large majority of these are non-EU nationals, thus this may actually be their only country of residence in the EU. Only five million EU nationals are working in an EU country that is not their country of citizenship.

2. *Immigrants always are a minority of a country's population.* Immigrants are under five percent of the EU population. Out of the fifteen million immigrants, five million (or 36.4 percent) are from member countries and the remaining from third countries. Third country immigrants are under three percent of the total European population. For instance, the eight major EU countries have a total

immigrant population from the Maghreb, a group that has engendered considerable debate around questions of cultural and religious obstacles to incorporation, of two million. This is 14.5 percent of the total immigrant population in the EU, 21.2 percent of the non-EU immigrant population, and a mere 0.62 percent of the total European population. Even if we were to double the total Maghreb population by estimating undocumented and naturalized components, they would not reach more than 1.3 percent of the total EU population. Similar concern has been raised about Turks: yet, even though the vast majority of all Turkish immigrants in the EU are in Germany, they represent less than two percent of the German population.

More generally, except for Luxembourg, no EU state has over ten percent nonnationals in its resident population. For instance, ninety-three percent of residents both in Germany and in France are nationals; the share rises to ninety-nine percent for Spain, Portugal, Greece; most remaining countries lie somewhere between these two levels.

3. *There is considerable return migration* except when the military-political situation in countries of origin makes this unfeasible. For example, we now know that about sixty percent of Italians who left for the United States around the turn of the century returned to Italy. More recently, the incidence of cross-border residence by nationals of one EU state in another has declined since 1970, partly a function of the return of Italian, Spanish, and Portuguese immigrant workers to their home countries. We are seeing generally more and more circular migration in the Mediterranean but also in the Americas. This all suggests that the fact of return migration may become a different phenomenon. It calls for considering the sending and receiving areas as part of a single economic, social, political system. It is within this system that immigrants make their own individual decisions about migrating.

4. *One important tendency is toward the formation of permanent settlements* for a variable share of immigrants, but never all. This tendency is likely even when there are high return rates and even when a country's policies seek to prevent permanent settlement. We see this happening in all countries receiving immigrants, including such extremely closed countries as Japan (cf. the new illegal immigration from Philippines, Thailand, and other Asian countries) and Saudi Arabia, as well as in the more liberal Western nations.

European countries have diverged considerably in their understanding of this process. Thus Britain's policy makers recognized from the earliest phase of immigration that settlement would be taking place, unlike the gastarbeiter conception prevalent among Germany's policy-makers. But regardless of policies, all these countries now have a settled immigrant population, many born there. Whether simply permanent residents or citizens by virtue of birth, most of them are seen as "aliens" in one way or another. In France they are referred to as immigrés even when they have become French. In the Netherlands, Sweden, and Belgium most immigrants are described as minorities; in Britain as ethnic minorities, even though the United Kingdom has its own British ethnic minorities: Scotts, Welsh, and Irish, besides "alien" ethnic minorities.

5. No matter what the political culture and the particular migration policies of a country, *illegal immigration has emerged as a generalized fact in all Western economies in the post-World War II era,* including Japan. This has raised a whole set of questions about the need to rethink regulatory enforcement and the sites for such enforcement. (For a discussion see Sassen 1996, chapter 3). Although the fact of such illegal immigration suggests that it is possible to enter these countries no matter what policies are in place, the available evidence makes it clear that the majority of illegal immigrants are from the same nationality groups as the legal population and they typically are fewer in number than the legal population. Again, this signals a measure of boundedness in the process of illegal immigration, and the possibility that it is shaped by similar systemic conditions as the legal population, and is thereby similarly limited in its scope and scale.

6. *Immigration is a highly differentiated process*: it includes people seeking permanent settlement and those seeking temporary employment who want to circulate back and forth. The two major patterns that are emerging today are circular migration and permanent settlement. Circular migration was a key pattern in the nineteenth century before border controls were instituted in any systematic way. We also know that there was a significant increase in the permanent foreign-resident population when borders were closed in 1973–74, suggesting some of this growth might not have occurred if the option of circular migration had existed. Much migration has to do with supplementing household income in countries of origin; given enormous earnings differentials, a limited stay in a high-wage country is sufficient.

One important question is whether recognizing these differences might facilitate the formulation of policy today. There is a growing presence of immigrants who are not searching for a new home in a new country; they think of themselves as moving in a cross-border and even global labor market. We know that when illegal immigrants are regularized, they often establish permanent residence in their country of origin and work a few months in the immigration country, an option that becomes available when they can circulate more freely. We know that some of the Polish women who now work as cleaners in Germany only want (and feel they financially need) to do this work for three or four months a year and then want to live mostly in their home towns. This is also the case with some of the African migrants in Italy. The share and numbers of those who seek to become permanent residents seems to be considerably smaller than the numbers of the total foreign-resident population suggest.

FROM FOREIGN WORKERS TO SETTLERS

The shift in the 1970s from foreign workforce to immigrant or ethnic community made existing mechanisms for incorporation inadequate. This clash became the subject of much conflict at the national and local levels in the major immigration countries. In France, the Communist Party and trade unions could no longer effectively integrate foreign workers because their own institutions had been weakened by unemployment, deindustrialization, and political losses; and the French school system had become an increasingly weak instrument for cultural and economic integration (Schain 1985). The guest-worker approach in Germany explicitly excluded integration, and thus entered in conflict with family reunification and the growth of the permanent foreign-resident immigrant population, including a second generation that was reaching school age. For Britain, citizenship in the empire entered in conflict with the fact that growing numbers were using this to enter the United Kingdom, an unexpected turn of events from the government's perspective.

In the 1950s and 1960s when immigrants had been mostly a workforce, and one quite regulated, they had been automatically integrated in their employment situation. This was labor demand driven immigration. With family reunification and the coming of age of a second generation, housing, schools, neighborhood associations, became crucial institutional arenas.

Changes in EC institutions also gave immigrants another arena from which to make claims, beyond the institutions of nation-states. And eventually immigrants themselves became political actors and politicians (cf. Withol de Wenden 1994; Body-Gendrot 1993). Questions of incorporation were no longer confined to the workplace and the bases from which to make claims were sharply expanded.

There is considerable agreement that the only reasonable policy is to coordinate and to ensure the stabilization and full integration of current residents. The precariousness of the immigrant population is not good; it will lead to discrimination and anger (Body-Gendrot 1993). There is evidence showing that encouraging immigrant associations and cultural activities, for example, is an aid to integration; this represents a different form of integration from that presumed in the notion of a rational abstract nationhood to which immigrants are to assimilate, as in the original French conception.

Even in Germany some recognition is emerging about the lasting nature of dependence on some foreign labor and of a permanent community of foreign residents; the term ausländische Mitbürger – a form of denizenship – is increasingly being used to denote a certain type of membership in the German polity – in contrast to the origianl notion of Gastarbeiter. Local authorities in many German towns with large immigrant populations have often opposed local voting rights for immigrants because it is thought to provoke extreme popular hostility; instead German migrants have been encouraged to elect local advisory boards with which local authorities can consult. Yet also in Germany we can detect the general trend toward greater liberalization: thus Schleswig-Holstein and Hamburg sought to grant local voting rights to immigrants, though these were not implemented (see also Hoffmann 1990; Oberndörfer 1989).

Yet voting rights by themselves are, clearly, far from enough to aid and push toward integration. For instance, Commonwealth and Irish immigrants in Britain have full political rights and a high share have registered as citizens. Yet they are disproportionately concentrated in lower paying jobs. De jure rights do not necessarily eliminate racism against Afro-Caribbeans nor take away their feelings of injustice (cf. Wrench, Brar, and Martin 1993).

The limitations of purely legal instruments are evident in the fact that the second generation in two countries as diverse as Germany and France are not doing well in school and in the labor market (Wilpert 1988; Body-Gendrot 1993). And even in Sweden, where immigrants have long had local voting rights, young immigrants feel discriminated against (Drobnic 1988).

Most European countries have antiimmigrant, racist parties (Husbands 1988), regardless of ease of citizenship acquisition: France produced Le Pen's National Front and his victory of 14.4 percent of the vote in the first round of the 1988 presidential election;[1] Germany saw the successes of the Republican Party in West Berlin and the National Democratic Party in Hesse in 1989. Strong antiimmigrant feelings have been evident even in Sweden, when the proposal to extend the right to vote in national elections was defeated. In Switzerland, the Schwarzenbach initiatives in the 1970s aimed at limiting the size of the foreign workforce and population because of concern with *Überfremdung*; and in 1981 an initiative to improve the position of foreigners in Switzerland was defeated by eighty-four percent (Hoffman-Nowotny 1985).

There is some survey evidence which suggests that a majority of immigrants do not intend to acquire the citizenship of their country of residence even after twenty years of residence.[2] Hammar (1985) found low propensity for naturalization among immigrants. Identity, loyalty to the country of origin, hope to return, all these contribute to this reluctance. This seems to hold even when return is not being actively considered, as is the case with many of the second generation.

Given major changes under way and given limited interest in naturalization among immigrants it may be questioned whether citizenship is the final and most effective form of civic incorporation of immigrants. Hammar (1990) and Layton-Henry (1990) have suggested that "denizenship" might be a way of giving immigrants the full range of rights without the necessity to acquire a new citizenship. This would allow migrants to become significant collective actors.[3] In naturalization there are two sets of changes: a change in the status as formal members of political communities, and a change in the set of rights enjoyed in two different states. Immigrants are often reluctant to give up their rights in countries of origin (such as returning, owning property, inheriting property, participating in national elections), but do want full integration in countries of residence. Further, naturalization is often loaded with symbolic questions of identity and loyalty that immigrants may not be ready to take on. Denizenship would give full rights (to employment, residence, social rights) but not participation in national elections nor access to public office.

Notwithstanding limitations in the direct impact of legislation on integration, the low propensity among second-generation immigrants to naturalize needs to be addressed. All West European countries today are seeing a growing portion of their population who are not full participants in political democratic processes. There is growing recognition that it is important to liberalize naturalization procedures and to allow dual citizenship. There is also growing interest in granting full political rights even for those not willing to naturalize as long as they reside in what is their country of birth and upbringing. Another concept is that of the new citizenship, referring not necessarily to membership via naturalization but via participation and residence in a community (Wihtol de Wenden 1994).

Economic integration is of crucial importance. Overall high unemployment levels and higher than average unemployment levels among immigrants easily lead to the notion that the immigrant population is a surplus population. But this needs to be put in perspective. Taking account of labor-market organization and structural conditions in the economy allows us to read the evidence along different lines. The actual effective labor supply for a good share of the jobs held by immigrants is far smaller than unemployment levels would suggest; the effective labor supply for such jobs does encompass a variable number of nationals who once held such jobs or are ready to take on such jobs, but their numbers are far smaller than the number of unemployed. On the other hand, immigrants in higher-level, better paid, white-collar jobs may indeed be competing with nationals for the same jobs.

Most of us who work at desks or counters have never known what it feels like to work a whole day on a construction site or a whole night cleaning offices. We lack the physical experience of absolute fatigue, continuous dull muscle pain, often danger and high levels of workplace injuries. Nor do we know what it means to undergo this day after day, year after year for a lifetime, with typically low wages, pronounced deterioration of our bodies, almost no advancement opportunities and very little respect from the general "culture" of advanced societies fixated as it is on expertise and professions. There are very good reasons why all advanced economies, and now even Japan, have a permanent foreign workforce (Sassen 1998, chapter 4). Having such a workforce is a systemic condition produced by the combination of at least two major processes in advanced economies: the ongoing need for such jobs and a culture which proclaims that high levels of education is what an advanced economy is all about.

In terms of structural conditions in the economy, we need to recognize that fluctuations in labor demand are evident throughout much of Europe's last two centuries. For much of the 1970s and 1980s there were extremely high unemployment levels and low net job growth. From 1975 to 1985 the EC lost a net of one million jobs while Japan added six million and the United States twenty-one million; many of these however were low-paying part-time jobs. After 1985 the job situation improved somewhat, with a growth of 4 percent in employment from 1985 to 1988, for a net increase of 4.8 million jobs. The new jobs did not go primarily to the unemployed but to women, who took 2.8 million jobs, and new young entrants. The 1990 EEC Report on Employment points to labor shortages. Growth of service jobs will demand unskilled workers willing to work at low wages. It will also demand highly qualified workers. Europe has a shortage of both.

The demographic structure of the EU points to considerable aging of the population and a shrinking in the share of the young workforce and new entrants. In the EU 220 million, or almost sixty-nine percent, are of working age out of a total population of 340 million. Youth aged fifteen to twenty-four were twenty-three percent of the active population in 1990; in 2025 they will be eighteen percent if current trends (including closure of immigration) remain in place. The aging reduces the labor supply and creates social costs; the shrinking of the youthful workforce reduces the supply of newcomers with potentially new skills and willingness to learn on the job and to get additional training.

The total population in Central and Eastern Europe in 1990 was 140 million. Of these ninety-three million, about sixty-five percent, were of working age, and sixty million were in the workforce, partly due to a sixty percent female labor force participation rate. Also here we see an aging of the population and workforce: only twenty-two percent of the population is under twenty-five years of age.

This similarity in demographic structure between the East and the West suggests that there might be limits to emigration given that what the West will need might not be easily met by migration from the East. Thus sooner than might now seem possible there might again be a tightening in the labor market which will require immigrant workers willing to do low-wage jobs as well as highly qualified jobs. The history of Western Europe is strongly marked by cycles of labor need and labor surplus. But when a continent is in the midst of high unemployment it is difficult to make sense out of the current situation by remembering the past. The possibility that structurally and organizationally determined labor shortages might re-appear seems untenable. Yet Western Europe has been there before.

There is considerable consensus in the scholarly literature that it will become increasingly important to make distinctions between different types of migrations, contingent versus permanent, and to recognize the great diversity of educational backgrounds of immigrants. Recognition of a permanent immigrant population has underlined the importance of both full integration of permanent immigrants and the facilitation of contingent migration for those who prefer to reside in their countries of origin. What has generally come to be seen as destructive in the immigrant question is their creation as a separate class, one represented as not belonging to the country of residence. Such conditions can indeed produce feelings of being "invaded" by the "other."

THE TRANSNATIONALIZING OF IMMIGRATION POLICY

There is a fundamental framework that roots all the country-specific policies of the developed world in a common set of conceptions about immigration and the role of the nation- state and of borders (Sassen 1996 chapter 3). The purpose here is not to minimize the many differences in national policies discussed in the preceding chapter. Some countries, such as Germany, have immigration policies based on jus sanguinis, while in others, such as France, it is based on jus solis. Some countries, such as Sweden, facilitate citizenship acquisition while others, such as Switzerland, do not. Some, for example, Germany and France, have instituted explicit return-migration policies, including monetary incentives, while other countries, notably the

United States, hardly register the fact of return migration. In some countries, such as Canada and the United States, there is a political culture and identity formation that incorporates the fact of immigration, while in others, notably Germany and Japan, this is not the case whatsoever.

Yet with all these differences immigration policy and the attendant operational apparatus in all these countries reveal a fundamental convergence regarding immigration. The sovereignty of the state and border control, whether land borders or airports, lie at the heart of the regulatory effort. Further, immigration policy is shaped by an understanding of immigration as the consequence of the individual actions of emigrants; the receiving country is taken as a passive agent, one not implicated in the process of migration.

But there is a geopolitics of migration. And the state has typically been involved long before the moment of border control presents itself as is suggested by the colonial and neocolonial bonds discussed earlier. And there is a broader web of transactions and rights that transcends the national-state and confines its sovereignty in matters of border control and immigration. The globalization of economic activity, the formation of EC-wide institutions, and the struggle around human and civil rights are three of the most outstanding instances. They are the subject of this section.

The 1980s saw a major shift in the global economy. During that decade deregulation and internationalization of a growing range of economic activities and markets became hallmarks of economic policy in all highly developed countries. Global economic trends engendered a new framework for national economic policy making. As well as more open national economic policies, this new framework is also evident in the strengthening of the single European market and the formation of regional trading blocks such as NAFTA and those being formed in Southeast Asia. At the heart of this framework is a new conception of the role of national borders: borders no longer are sites for imposing levies, but rather transmitting membranes guaranteeing the free flow of goods, capital, and information. Eighteenth-century concepts of free trade supposed freedom of movement between distinct national economies. Twenty-first-century economics is about an economy which is itself trans-national, and about governments which coordinate rather than contain economic activities. In my readings, these policies amount to a partial "denationalizing" of national territory when it comes to the flow of capital and certain sectors of the workforce (see Sassen 1996).

To be sure, neither the old border wall nor the nation-state have disappeared. The difficulties and complexities involved in this transformation are evident in the many obstacles to the ratification of the Uruguay Round of the GATT talks, one aimed at further opening economies to the circulation of services. But the relentless effort to overcome these difficulties also signals the economic pressure on governments around the world to depart from an old conception of national economic policy and the emergence of a new conception of how economic activity is to be maximized and governed.

The framework for immigration policy in the highly developed countries, on the other hand, is rooted in the past: immigration policy has yet to address the changed role of borders and governments in economic integration as we move into the twenty-first century.[4] Border control remains the basic mechanism for regulating immigration. Moreover, the policy framework for immigration treats the flow of labor as the result of individual actions. The receiving country is represented as a passive agent; the causes for immigration appear to lie outside the control or domain of receiving countries; immigration policy becomes a decision to be more or less benevolent in admitting immigrants.

Absent from this understanding is the notion that the international activities of the governments or firms of receiving countries may have contributed to the formation of economic linkages with emigration countries, linkages that may function as bridges not only for capital and politics but also for migration flows (Sassen 1988). That older view emphasizes individual push factors and neglects systemic linkages. The worldwide evidence shows rather clearly that there is considerable patterning in the geography of migrations, and that the major receiving countries tend to get immigrants from their zones of influence. This holds for countries as diverse as the United States, France, or Japan. Today we can see clearly that the colonial empires of the past created bridges. We have far more difficulty seeing how current forms of transnational economic activity are also creating bridges.

Economic transnationalization suggests that the responsibility for immigration may not be exclusively the immigrant's. Refugee policy in some countries does lift the burden of immigration from the immigrant's shoulders. At one time or another, all the former European colonial powers have shown special treatment to immigrants or refugees from their former colonies. U.S. refugee policy, particularly for the case of Indochinese immigrants, does acknowledge partial responsibility on the part of the government for the creation of this flow. Clearly, in the case of economic migrations, such responsibility is far more difficult to establish than in war-induced refugee flows, and by its nature far more indirect. As governments increasingly coordinate rather than contain economic activity, their role in immigration policy, as in other aspects of political economy, becomes more ambiguous.

Far from being wide open, a more comprehensive approach can provide more analytic and empirical closure. The various transnational economic, cultural, political systems now evident in the EU tend to have very specific geographies. They occur in the relation of cities to cities, or in production chains linking factories and distribution centers across borders, or in transnational cultural and political sub-communities. Considerable migration flows within these new geographies for transactions. This should help governments address the growing range of trans-national economic, cultural and political systems they have to deal with. Gradually immigration in the EU may evolve into such a cross-border system.

The single-market program has had a powerful impact in raising the prominence of various issues associated with free circulation of people as an essential element in creating a frontier-free community; EC institutions lacked the legal competence to deal with many of these issues but had to begin to address them. Gradually EC institutions have wound up more deeply involved with such issues as visa policy, family reunification, and migration policy – all formerly exclusively in the domain of the individual national states. National governments resisted EC involvement in these once exclusively national domains. But now both legal and practical issues have made such involvement acceptable and inevitable, notwithstanding many public pronouncements to the contrary. The national political representation is still that immigration policy is firmly in the hands of individual governments, a matter of the sovereignty of the state. Similarly the political representation continues to be that EU states are not immigration countries.

It is becoming evident that many aspects of immigration and refugee policy intersect with EC legal competence. A key nexus here is the free movement of persons and attendant social rights as part of the formation of a single market. In practice the EC is assuming an increasingly important role and the fact that these are immigration countries is slowly being acknowledged. The monetary and economic union would require greater flexibility in movement of workers and their families and thereby pose increasing problems for current national immigration laws regarding non-EU nationals in EU member states. This is precisely the category that has grown rapidly since the late 1980s and the one that lacks the right to move to another EU country either as a visitor or as a worker. According to current policy it would mean border controls within the territory of the EU, the proclaimed "area without frontiers" implied by the Single European Act of 1986 that was to be implemented by December 31, 1992.[5] It would also require strengthening of outside borders. There is now growing recognition for the need of an EU-wide immigration policy, something denied for a long time by individual states. This has become even more urgent with the collapse of the Soviet Bloc, and the rapid increase in refugees. Though very slowly the general direction has been toward a closer union of member states' immigration policies.

It is not only national governments such as those of the United Kingdom or Denmark that have resisted the dismantling of internal borders. There is concern that this dismantling would strengthen the role of identity controls on immigrants and ethnic minorities. Further, organizations representing refugees and asylum seekers believe that this dismantling will make it more difficult for them to obtain asylum or refuge, because of the associated strengthening of external border control – the Fortress Europe syndrome. Ethnic minorities are concerned about the impact of additional checks on their identities and greater difficulty in family reunification as member states harmonize their policies possibly to the lower end common denominator.

But there is yet another way in which immigration policy making can no longer be confined to national governments. The state finds itself caught in a broader web of rights and actors that hem in its sovereignty in decisions about immigrants (Hollifield 1992). The political actors involved in policy debates and policy making are far more numerous than they were two decades ago: EC institutions, antiimmigrant parties, a vast network of organizations that often represent immigrants, or claim to do so, and struggle for immigrant rights, immigrant associations, and immigrant politicians, especially in the second generation. Coming from a totally different angle, members of national parliaments are increasingly upset by the secrecy and lack of democratic controls in intergovernmental agreements and in EC procedures. This may carry over to some aspects of immigration policy making. In brief, the policy process for immigration is no longer confined to a narrow governmental range of ministerial and administrative interaction. Public opinion and public political debate have become part of the arena wherein immigration policy is shaped. Whole parties position themselves politically in terms of their stand on immigration.

Further, there is by now a set of international agreements that have the effect of limiting state sovereignty in controlling immigration (Hollifield 1992; Jacobson 1996). And there is a set of rights of resident immigrants widely upheld by legal authorities. There is an emerging de facto regime, often centered in international agreements and conventions as well as in various rights gained by immigrants, that is limiting the state's role.[6] This is a new phase, different from the phase that began with World War I when the state gained almost abolute control over these matters. There are multiple instances that reflect this development. An earlier chapter mentioned that attempts by France and Germany to limit family reunification were blocked by administrative and constitutional courts on the grounds that such restrictions would violate international agreements. The courts have also regularly supported a combination of rights of resident immigrants which have the effect of limiting a government's power over them. Similarly such courts have limited the ability of governments to stop asylum seekers from entering the country. The overall outcome of these diverse processes and of the politicization of immigration and of immigrants has been a gradual convergence in immigration and refugee policy across Western Europe.

The more generalized discussion and understanding that has been produced over the last years is in good part a response to objective

conditions shared by all these countries, from the transnationalization of economic activity to a web of rights of immigrants and refugees upheld in courts and international agreements. This is quite a
marked change compared to only a few years ago. The historical and
cultural heritage of each country is increasingly forced to engage
these contemporary conditions, therewith launching a whole new era
in the role of the state and marking the end of the period that began
with World War I.

CONCLUSION

The facts and arguments presented in this book suggest that migrations do not simply happen. They are produced. And migrations do
not involve just any possible combination of countries. They are patterned. Further, immigrant employment is patterned as well; immigrants rarely have the same occupational and industrial distribution
as nationals in receiving countries. Finally, although it may seem that
migrations are ever present, there are actually distinct phases and
patterns over the last two centuries. In brief, international migrations
are produced, they are patterned, and they are embedded in specific
historical phases.

Acknowledging these traits opens up the immigration policy question beyond the familiar range of border control, family reunion,
naturalization and citizenship law. There are three aspects to this
opening up which are central to the analysis and interpretation in this
book.

One of these is the extent to which labor migrations are embedded
in larger social, economic, and political structures, and the fact that
they are consequently bounded in their geography, duration, and size.
There is a geopolitics of migration and there is the fact that migrations are parts of systems: both set parameters for migrations. Migrations do not assume the form of invasions; they did not in the
nineteenth century when border controls were minimal or nonexist-
ent, and they do not today. Both emigration and immigration always
encompasses only a small fraction of a country's population.

If we can accept that migration is not simply an aggregation of
individual decisions, but a process patterned and shaped by existing
politico- economic systems, then the question of control and regula-

tion becomes more manageable. The systems within which migrations are embedded contain their own regulatory forces. The spill-
over tends to be minor, and clearly when it reaches an excessive point
we see considerable return migration and/or declining levels of immigration; it may take a few years but it happens.

A second condition is the highly differentiated nature of immigration, most particularly the increasingly important distinction between
circular migration and permanent settlement. If we can accept that
immigration is a bounded and differentiated process rather than a
mass invasion from poor countries, then making immigration policy
is more manageable. For instance, policy aimed at ensuring the full
integration of the permanent immigrant population should be less
threatening. Integration along frameworks that recognize cultural
and religious differences is essential and more feasible if we recognize the boundedness of immigration.

A third condition is the de-facto transnationalization of immigration policy making. Both the global linking of economies on the one
hand, and, on the other, the growth of a broad network of rights and
court decisions along with the emergence of immigrants as political
actors, have reduced the autonomy of the state in immigration (and
refugee) policy making. This should not be surprising given the
trends toward transnationalization in economies, in culture, and in
the battle around human rights.

At the end of this journey that has engaged Western European countries with such intensity over the last twenty years, shines a shy
thought: Are the immigrants and refugees who have lived here for so
long the settlers of today? Is postcolonial history, broadly understood,
being enacted partly in these, the former metropolitan nations, and
are our immigrants and refugees part of postcolonial settlement? We
have historically attached positive connotations to the settler for the
hard and dirty work of settling the Western world's frontiers all
around the globe. Are the low-paying, hard and dangerous jobs that
immigrants still disproportionately hold today's frontier in the midst
of our prosperous societies? Have we created a new frontier zone in
the heart of our advanced economies, especially our large cities in the
United States and in Western Europe? And is it because it is in our
midst that this "frontier" cannot become the subject of cleansing

myths? Is unemployment, which hits immigrants and nationals, also a contemporary frontier in our midst that can no longer be displaced to faraway lands through mass emigration?

European nations–from Germany to France in their radically contrasting policies–have been incorporating "foreign" men and women for at least two centuries. It is essential that Europe shed its image and representation as a continent whose migration history is confined to the mass emigrations of the past. This is a partial account to the point of distortion, and it is hampering the achievement of reasonable policy. Immigrations from near and far have been an integral part of Europe's history.

NOTES

1   It should be noted that in its history and certainly today, France has had an ethnocultural line running through the nationality and immigration debates; it emphasized the lack of assimilation potential of many immigrants. Although rather visible at times this line of political thinking rarely succeeded in being dominant. When the government tried to enact a somewhat restrictive reform of citizenship in 1986-87 it wound up giving up in view of public resistance. Yet clearly nationalism and xenophobia can coexist with jus soli, as they have done in various periods and again in the 1980s with the National Front, and to some extent in the public pressure that led to the reform of the Nationality Code in 1993. There is now a new nationalism of the right, more connected to the notion of a community of descent and blood, which is exclusionary rather than assimilationist.

2   In Sweden a 1984 survey found that immigrants married to Swedes expressed a greater willingness to naturalize than other immigrants. Owning property in the country of origin and plans to return reduced the willingness to naturalize. One third did not know whether they wanted to naturalize or not. Hammar (1985) found that Finns in Sweden were willng to naturalize if they could keep their Finnish nationality as well. In Germany a 1984 survey found 13.2 percent of respondents said they were very interested in obtaining German citizenship and 32.1 percent somewhat interested but the rest basically not interested; Greeks and Yugoslavs were the most interested and Turks and Spaniards the least interested. In this survey there was a direct relation between length of residence and interest in citizenship: the longer the residence the higher the interest; for example, among those with fifteen years or more of residence twenty-one percent were very interested. But the share of "not interested" remained the same regardless of length of residence. The shift that results from residence is from those mildly interested to very interested.

3   In its origin the term denizen referred to an alien admitted to citizenship by royal letters patent by the English Crown in the sixteenth century (Cohen 1987). In the contemporary usage, it emphasizes that the traditional sharp distinction between foreigner and citizen has been eroded and that large numbers of foreign citizens have established close, intensive, secure, and long-standing relations with the country of residence. They are members of these countries even if foreign. If it became widely recognized it would provide an alternative to the sharp choice between being a citizen and a noncitizen (Hammar 1990; Layton-Henry 1990). Baubock (1994) has made one of the most detailed analyses of the different forms of citizenship that might be considered.

4 Elsewhere I examine whether there are alternative frameworks to border control for the regulation of immigration, and whether the existence of an increasingly integrated global economy, or free-trade blocks, can provide frameworks through which to regulate such flows. See Sassen (1999), *Immigration Policy in a Global Economy*, prepared for The Century Fund (New York City).

5 The whole idea of a labor market is that workers go where there is a demand, where they are needed. Further, given the concern of the EU to keep its borders closed to new immigrant workers, some have argued that it would make more sense if there were a flexibilization of the immigrant labor force within the EU, such that if one member state has a shortage and needs new supplies of immigrant workers it can resort to the supply in another country which may have high unemployement levels. In my reading of the evidence both for Europe and the United States such rapid adjustments would actually require government action; one could not rely on the market producing the desired outcomes. But this would be a way of adjusting labor supply with labor demand in those occupations/industries where immigrants are prevalent. It would also provide for a geographic decentralization of some immigrant groups and would incorporate immigrant workers in processes of transnational European construction.

6 For example, the International Convention adopted by the General Assembly of the UN on December 18, 1990 on the protection of the rights of all migrant workers and members of their families (Resolution 45/158).

APPENDIX

Tables

The source for all these tables is the same as listed in Table 1.

Table 1
Stocks of foreign population in selected European countries
1986–1996

	Thousands and percentages		
	1986	1990	1996
Austria	314.9	456.1	728.2
% of total population	4.1	5.9	9.0
Belgium	853.2	904.5	911.9
% of total population	8.6	9.1	9.0
Czech Republic	..	..	198.6
% of total population	..	..	1.9
Denmark	128.3	160.6	237.7
% of total population	2.5	3.1	4.7
Finland	17.3	26.3	73.8
% of total population	0.4	0.5	1.4
France	..	3596.6	..
% of total population	..	6.3	..
Germany	4512.7	5342.5	7314.0
% of total population	7.4	8.4	8.9
Hungary	..	..	142.5
% of total population	..	..	1.4
Ireland	77.0	80.0	118.0
% of total population	2.2	2.3	3.2
Italy	450.2	781.1	1095.6
% of total population	0.8	1.4	2.0
Luxembourg	97.3	113.1	142.8
% of total population	26.3	29.4	34.1
Netherlands	568.0	692.4	679.9
% of total population	3.9	4.6	4.4
Norway	109.3	143.3	157.5
% of total population	2.6	3.4	3.6
Portugal	..	107.8	172.9
% of total population	..	1.1	1.7
Spain	293.2	278.7	539.0
% of total population	0.8	0.7	1.3
Sweden	390.8	483.7	526.3
% of total population	4.7	5.6	6.0
Switzerland	956.0	1100.3	1337.6
% of total population	14.7	16.3	19.0
United Kingdom	1820.0	1723.0	1972.0
% of total population	3.2	3.2	3.4

Note: Data are from population registers or from register of foreigners except for France and the United States (Census). Portugal and Spain (residence permits), Ireland and the United Kingdom (Labour Force Survey) and refer to the population on the 31 December of the years indicated unless otherwise stated. Source: These tables are derived from SOPEMI, 1998. *Trends in International Migration. Continuous Reporting System on Migration Annual Report.* Paris: OECD

Table 2

**Inflows of foreign population into selected European countries.
1986–1996**

	Thousands		
	1986	1990	1996
Inflow data based on population registers:			
Belgium	39.3	50.5	51.9
Denmark	17.6	15.1	..
Finland	..	6.5	7.5
Germany	478.3	842.4	708.0
Hungary	..	37.2	9.4
Luxembourg	7.4	9.3	..
Netherlands	52.8	81.3	77.2
Norway	16.8	15.7	17.2
Sweden	34.0	53.2	29.3
Switzerland	66.8	101.4	74.3
Inflow data based on residence and work permits:			
Austria	..	..	224.2
France	38.3	102.4	74.0
United Kingdon	..	..	216.4

Note: Data from population registers are not fully comparable because the criteria governing who gets registered differ from country to country. Counts for the Netherlands, Norway and especially Germany include substantial numbers of asylum seekers.

Table 3
Outflows of foreign population from selected European countries 1986–1996

	Thousands		
	1986	1990	1996
Belgium	31.8	27.0	32.4
Denmark	4.3	4.6	..
Finland	..	0.9	3.0
Germany	347.8	466.0	599.1
Luxembourg	5.5	5.5	..
Netherlands	23.6	20.6	22.4
Norway	8.4	9.8	10.0
Sweden	15.4	16.2	14.5
Switzerland	52.8	59.6	67.7

Note: Data are from population registers.

Table 4
Net migration of foreign population in selected European countries 1986–1996

	Thousands		
	1986	1990	1996
Belgium	7.5	23.4	19.5
Denmark	13.3	10.5	..
Finland	..	5.6	4.5
Germany	130.5	376.4	148.9
Luxembourg	1.9	3.8	..
Netherlands	29.2	60.7	54.8
Norway	8.4	5.9	7.2
Sweden	18.6	37.0	14.9
Switzerland	14.0	41.8	6.5

Note: Data are derived from Tables 2 and 3

Table 5
Inflows of foreign workers into selected European countries 1986–1996

Thousands

	1986	1987	1988	1989	1990	1991	1992	1993	1994	1995	1996
Austria	18.0	15.3	17.4	37.2	103.4	62.6	57.9	37.7	27.1	15.4	16.3
Belgium	2.2	2.4	2.8	3.7	..	5.1	4.4	4.3	4.1	3.0	2.2
Denmark	..	..	3.1	2.7	2.8	2.4	2.4	2.1	2.1	2.2	2.7
France											
Permanents	9.9	10.7	12.7	15.6	22.4	25.6	42.3	24.4	18.3	13.1	11.5
APT[1]	1.4	1.5	1.9	3.1	3.8	4.1	3.9	4.0	4.1	4.5	4.8
Germany	37.2	48.1	60.4	84.8	138.6	241.9	408.9	325.6	221.2	270.8	262.5
Hungary	..	..	..	25.3	51.9	41.7	24.6	19.5	18.6	18.4	14.5
Ireland	..	..	..	1.2	1.4	3.8	3.6	4.3	4.3	4.3	3.8
Italy	..	..	..	..	..	125.5	123.7	85.0	99.8	111.3	129.2
Luxembourg	8.4	10.5	12.6	14.7	16.9	16.9	15.9	15.5	16.2	16.5	18.3
Spain	..	..	..	..	19.8	85.0	52.8	17.4	23.5	36.6	..
Switzerland	29.4	33.6	34.7	37.1	46.7	46.3	39.7	31.5	28.6	27.1	24.5
United Kingdom											
Long term	7.9	8.1	10.4	13.3	16.1	12.9	12.7	12.5	13.4	15.5	16.9
Short term	8.0	9.4	11.8	12.2	13.8	12.6	14.0	13.3	12.9	15.6	16.8
Trainees	2.8	2.9	3.8	4.2	4.8	3.5	3.4	3.5	3.8	4.4	4.0
Total	18.7	20.4	26.0	29.7	34.6	29.0	30.1	29.3	30.1	35.5	37.7

1. Provisional work permits: cannot exceed six months.

Table 6

Inflows of seasonal workers into selected European countries 1986–1996

Thousands

	1986	1987	1988	1989	1990	1991	1992	1993	1994	1995	1996
Austria	..	..	..	24.3	26.3	17.6	20.4	15.8	..	..	..
France	87.7	76.6	70.5	61.9	58.2	54.2	13.6	11.3	10.3	9.4	8.8
Germany	–	–	–	–	–	–	212.4	181.0	155.2	192.8	220.9
Italy	..	..	..	..	..	..	1.7	2.8	5.8	7.6	8.9
Netherlands	..	..	..	..	..	..	1.0	0.9	0.5	–	–
Norway	..	..	..	..	4.3	4.3	4.7	4.6	4.5	5.0	5.4
Switzerland	142.8	150.8	154.0	156.4	153.6	147.5	126.1	93.5	83.9	72.3	62.7
United Kingdom	..	..	..	..	..	..	3.6	4.2	4.4	4.7	5.5

Table 7

Stocks of foreign and foreign-born labour force in selected European countries 1986–1996

Thousands and percentages

	1986	1987	1988	1989	1990	1991	1992	1993	1994	1995	1996
Stocks of foreign labour force											
Austria[1]	155.0	157.7	160.9	178.0	229.5	277.2	295.9	304.6	316.5	325.2	328.0
% of total labour force	5.3	5.4	5.4	5.9	7.4	8.7	9.1	9.3	9.7	9.9	10.0
Belgium	179.2	176.6	179.4	196.4	..	..	..	..	..	..	..
% of total employment	6.2	6.1	6.1	6.5	..	..	..	..	..	..	..
Denmark	60.1	62.7	65.1	66.9	68.8	71.2	74.0	77.7	80.3	83.8	
% of total labour force	2.1	2.1	2.2	2.3	2.4	2.4	2.6	2.7	2.9	3.0	
France	1555.7	1524.9	1557.0	1593.8	1549.5	1506.0	1517.8	1541.5	1593.9	1573.3	1604.7
% of total labour force	6.5	6.3	6.4	6.6	6.2	6.0	6.0	6.1	6.3	6.2	6.3
Germany	1833.7	1865.5	1910.6	1940.6	2025.1	2179.1	2360.1	2575.9	1559.6	2569.2	2559.3
% of total labour force	6.8	6.9	7.0	7.0	7.1	7.5	8.0	8.9	8.9	9.0	9.1
Hungary	..	..	..	..	31.7	33.4	15.7	17.6	20.1	21.0	18.8
% of total labour force	..	..	..	..	..	..	0.4	0.4	0.5	0.5	0.5
Ireland	33.0	33.0	35.0	33.0	34.0	39.3	40.4	37.3	34.5	42.1	52.4
% of total labour force	2.5	2.5	2.7	2.7	2.7	2.9	3.0	2.7	2.5	2.9	3.5
Italy	..	..	..	..	..	285.3	296.8	304.8	307.1	332.2	
% of total employment	..	..	..	..	..	1.3	1.4	1.5	1.5	1.7	
Luxembourg	58.7	63.7	69.4	76.2	84.7	92.6	98.2	101.0	106.3	111.8	117.8
% of total employment	35.6	37.6	39.9	42.4	45.2	47.5	49.2	49.7	51.0	52.4	53.8

Netherlands	169.0	176.0	176.0	192.0	197.0	214.0	229.0	219.0	216.0	221.0	218.0
% of total employment	3.2	3.0	2.9	3.1	3.1	3.2	3.4	3.3	3.2	3.2	3.1
Norway	..	..	49.5	47.7	46.3	46.3	46.6	47.9	50.3	52.6	54.8
% of total employment	..	..	2.3	2.3	2.3	2.3	2.3	2.4	2.5	2.5	2.6
Portugal	..	..	45.5	48.7	51.8	54.9	59.2	63.1	77.6	84.3	86.8
% of total labour force	..	..	1.0	1.0	1.0	1.1	1.3	1.4	1.6	1.8	1.8
Spain	..	..	58.2	69.1	85.4	171.0	139.4	117.4	121.8	139.0	161.9
% of total labour force	..	..	0.4	0.5	0.6	1.1	0.9	0.8	0.8	0.9	1.0
Sweden	215	215	220	237	246	241	233	221	213	220	218
% of total labour force	4.9	4.9	4.9	5.2	5.4	5.3	5.3	5.1	5.0	5.1	5.1
Switzerland	566.9	587.7	607.8	631.8	669.8	702.5	716.7	725.8	740.3	728.7	709.1
% of total labour force	16.4	16.6	16.7	17.0	18.9	17.8	18.3	18.5	18.9	18.6	17.9
United Kingdom	815.0	815.0	871.0	914.0	882.0	828.0	902.0	862.0	847.0	899.0	878.0
% of total employment	3.4	3.3	3.4	3.5	3.3	3.0	3.6	3.4	3.4	3.5	3.4

1. Data for 1990 and 1991 have been adjusted to correct for a temporary over-issue of work permits relative to the number of jobs held by foreigners between August 1990 and June 1991.

Table 8.

Inflows of asylum seekers into selected European countries 1986–1997

Thousands

	1987	1988	1989	1990	1991	1992	1993	1994	1995	1996	1997[1]
Austria	11.4	15.8	21.9	22.8	27.3	16.2	4.7	5.1	5.9	7.0	6.7
Belgium	6.0	4.5	8.2	13.0	15.4	17.6	26.5	14.7	11.7	12.4	11.6
Czech Republic	..	..	..	1.8	2.0	0.9	2.2	1.2	1.4	2.0	2.1
Denmark	2.7	4.7	4.6	5.3	4.6	13.9	14.3	6.7	5.1	5.9	5.1
Finland	–	0.1	0.2	2.7	2.1	3.6	2.0	0.8	0.8	0.7	1.0
France	27.6	34.3	61.4	54.8	47.4	28.9	27.6	26.0	20.4	17.4	21.4
Germany	57.4	103.1	121.3	193.1	256.1	438.2	322.6	127.2	127.9	116.4	104.4
Greece	6.3	9.3	6.5	4.1	2.7	2.0	0.8	1.3	1.4	1.6	4.2
Ireland	..	..	..	0.1	–	–	0.1	0.4	0.4	1.2	3.9
Italy	11.0	1.4	2.3	4.7	31.7	2.6	1.3	1.8	1.7	0.7	1.4
Luxembourg	0.1	0.0	0.1	0.1	0.2	0.1	0.2	0.2	0.2	0.3	0.4
Netherlands	13.5	7.5	13.9	21.2	21.6	20.3	35.4	52.6	29.3	22.9	34.4
Norway	8.6	6.6	4.4	4.0	4.6	5.2	12.9	3.4	1.5	1.8	2.3
Poland	..	..	..	..	..	..	..	0.6	0.8	3.2	2.9
Portugal	0.2	0.3	0.1	0.1	0.2	0.6	2.1	0.8	0.5	0.3	0.4
Spain	3.7	4.5	4.1	8.6	8.1	11.7	12.6	12.0	5.7	4.7	3.7
Sweden	18.1	19.6	30.0	29.4	27.4	84.0	37.6	18.6	9.0	5.8	9.7
Switzerland	10.9	16.7	24.4	35.8	41.6	18.0	24.7	16.1	17.0	18.0	23.9
United Kingdom	5.9	5.7	16.8	38.2	73.4	32.3	28.0	42.2	55.0	37.0	41.5

1. January to September 1997 for Italy, Luxembourg, Poland and Spain.

168

Table 9.

Acquisition of nationality in selected European countries 1986–1996

Thousand and percentages

	1988	1989	1990	1991	1992	1993	1994	1995	1996
Countries where national / foreigner distinction is prevalent									
Austria	8.2	8.5	9.2	11.4	11.9	14.4	16.3	15.3	16.2
% of foreign population	2.5	2.5	2.4	2.5	2.2	2.3	2.4	2.1	2.2
Belgium	..	..	..	8.5	46.4	16.4	25.8	26.1	24.6
% of foreign population	..	..	..	0.9	5.0	1.8	2.8	2.8	2.7
Denmark	3.7	3.3	3.0	5.5	5.1	5.0	5.7	5.3	7.3
% of foreign population	2.7	2.3	2.0	3.4	3.0	2.8	3.0	2.7	3.3
Finland	1.1	1.5	0.9	1.2	0.9	0.8	0.7	0.7	1.0
% of foreign population	6.0	8.1	4.2	4.7	2.3	1.8	1.2	1.1	1.4
France	74.0	82.0	88.5	95.5	95.3	95.5	126.3	92.4	109.8
% of foreign population	..	..	..	2.7	..	..	..	..	
Germany	40.8	68.5	101.4	141.6	179.9	199.4	259.2	313.6	302.8
% of foreign population	1.0	1.5	2.1	2.7	3.1	3.1	3.8	4.5	4.2
Hungary	..	1.1	3.2	5.9	21.9	11.8	9.9	10.0	12.3
% of foreign population	..	..	..	..	..	..	..	7.3	8.7
Italy	..	..	..	4.5	4.4	6.5	6.6	7.4	7.0
% of foreign population	..	..	..	0.6	0.5	0.7	0.7	0.8	0.7
Luxembourg	0.8	0.6	0.7	0.6	0.6	0.7	0.7	0.8	0.8
% of foreign population	0.7	0.6	0.7	0.5	0.5	0.6	0.6	0.6	0.6

Table 9. (*continued*)

Acquisition of nationality in selected European countries 1986–1996

Thousand and percentages

	1988	1989	1990	1991	1992	1993	1994	1995	1996
Countries where national / foreigner distinction is prevalent									
Netherlands	9.1	28.7	12.8	29.1	36.2	43.1	49.5	71.4	82.7
% of foreign population	1.5	4.6	2.0	4.2	4.9	5.7	6.3	9.4	11.4
Norway	3.4	4.6	4.8	5.1	5.1	5.5	8.8	11.8	12.2
% of foreign population	2.7	3.4	3.4	3.5	3.5	3.6	5.4	7.2	7.6
Spain	8.1	5.9	7.0	3.8	5.3	8.4	7.8	6.8	8.4
% if foreign population	2.4	1.6	2.8	1.3	1.5	2.1	1.8	1.5	1.7
Sweden	18.0	17.6	16.8	27.7	29.3	42.7	35.1	32.0	25.6
% of foreign population	4.5	4.2	3.7	5.7	5.9	8.5	6.9	6.0	4.8
Switzerland	11.4	10.3	8.7	8.8	11.2	12.9	13.8	16.8	19.4
% of foreign population	1.2	1.0	0.8	0.8	1.0	1.1	1.1	1.3	1.5
United Kingdom	64.6	117.1	57.3	58.6	42.2	45.8	44.0	40.5	43.1
% of foreign population	3.5	6.4	3.2	3.4	2.4	2.3	2.2	2.1	2.1

Note: Statistics cover all means of acquiring the nationality of a country, except where otherwise indicated. These include standard naturalisation procedures subject to age, residency, etc. criteria, as well as situations where nationality is acquired through a declaration or by option (following marriage, adoption, or other situations related to residency or descent), recovery of former nationality and other special means of acquiring the nationality of a country. The naturalisation rate ("% of foreign population") indicates the number of persons acquiring the nationality of the country as a percentage of the stock of the foreign population at the beginning of the year.

Abadan-Unat, Nermin. "Implications of Migration on Emancipation and Pseudo-Emancipation of Turkish Women," *International Migration Review* 11 (1977) 31-57.

Alter, George. *Family and the Female Life Course: Women of Verviers, Belgium, 1849-1880.* Madison, Wisc.: University of Wisconsin Press, 1988.

Amersfoort, Hans, van. "Ethnic Residential Patterns in a Welfare State: Lessons from Amsterdam, 1970-1990." *New Community* 18 (1992): 439-56

Amman, H. *Die Italiener in der Schweiz: Ein Beitrag zur Fremdenfrage.* Basel, 1917.

Anderson, Michael. *Population Change in North-Western Europe, 1750-1850.* London: Macmillan, 1988.

Arendt, Hannah. *The Origins of Totalitarianism.* New York: Harcourt Brace Jovanovich, 1958.

Aries, P. *Histoire des populations françaises.* Paris: Seuil, 1971.

Bade, K. J. "Massenwanderung und Arbeitsmarkt im deutschen Nordosten von 1880 bis zum Ersten Weltkrig: Uberseeische Auswanderung, interne Abwanderung und kontinentale Zuwanderung," *Archiv fur Sozialgeschichte* 20 (1980): 265-323.

——. "Transnationale Migration und Arbeitsmarkt im Kaiserreich: Vom Agrarstaat mit starker Industrie zum Industriestaat mit starker agrarischer Basis." In *Historische Arbeitsmarktforschung,* edited by T. Pierenkemper and R. H. Tilly. Göttingen: Vandenhoeck and Ruprecht, 1982.

——. "Kulturkampf auf dem Arbeitsmarkt: Bismarcks 'Polenpolitik' 1885–1890." In *Innenpolitische Probleme des Bismarckreichs*, edited by O. Pflanze, 121–42. Munchen: R. Oldenbourg, 1983.

——. *Vom Auswanderungsland zum Einwanderungsland? Deutschland 1880–1980*. Berlin: Colloquium, 1983.

——. "Labor, Migration and the State: Germany from the late 19th Century to the Onset of the Great Depression." In *Population, Labour and Migration in 19th Century and 20th Century Germany*, 59–85 New York: St. Martin's Press, 1987.

Bailyn, Bernard. *Voyages to the West: A Passage in the Peopling of America on the Eve of the Revolution*. New York: Knopf, 1986.

Bairoch, Paul. "International Industrial Levels from 1750–1980." *Journal of European Economic History* 11 (1982):269–333.

Balbo, Laura and Luigi Manconi. *I Razzismi Possibili*. Milano: Feltrinelli, 1990.

Bardet, Ihan and Norman Furniss, eds. *Turkish Workers in Europe: An Interdisciplinary Study*. Bloomington, Ind.: Indiana University Press, 1985.

Baubock, Rainer and Dilek Cinar. "Briefing Paper: Naturalization Policies in Western Europe." *West European Politics* 17(2), 1994.

Benedict, Philip. "Was the Eighteenth Century an Era of Urbanization in France?" *Journal of Interdisciplinary History* 21 (1990): 179–215.

Benveniste, Annie. *Le Bosphore à la Roquette: La communauté judeo-espagnole à Paris, 1914–1940*. Paris: Editions L'Harmattan, 1989.

Berger, John and Jean Mohr. *A Seventh Man: Migrant Workers in Europe*. New York: Vicking Press, 1975.

Berkner, Lutz and Franklin Mendels. "Inheritance Systems, Family Structure and Demographic Patterns in Wertern Europe, 1700–1900." In *Historical Studies of Changing Fertility* edited by C. Tilly, 209–23. Princeton: Princeton University Press, 1978.

Best, Geoffrey. *Humanity in Warfare: The Modern History of the International Law of Armed Conflicts*. New York: Columbia University Press, 1980.

Beteille, Roger. "Les Migrations Saisonnières en France sous le Premier Empire: Essai de synthese," *Revue d'Histoire Moderne et Contemporaine* 17 (1970): 424–41.

Bezza, B. *Gli italiani fuori d'Italia*. Milan: F. Angeli, 1983.

Blanc, M. "Immigrant Housing in France: From Hovel to Hostel to Low-Cost Flats," *New Community*, 11 (1984): 225–33.

Blaschke, J. and A. Germershausen. "Migration und ethnische Beziehungen." *Nord-Sud Aktuell,* 3-4, 1989.

Blaschke, Karlheinz. *Bevolkerungs geschichte von Sachsen bis zur industriellen Revolution.* Weimar: Bohlau 1967.

Blythell, Duncan. *The Handloom Weavers: A Study in the English Cotton Industry during the Industrial Revolution.* Cambridge: Cambridge University Press, 1969.

Body-Gendrot, Sophie. *Ville et Violence: L'irruption de Nouveaux Acteurs.* Paris: Presses Universitaires de France, 1993.

Body-Gendrot, Sophie, Emmanual Ma Mung, Catherine Hodier, eds. "Entrepreneurs Entre Deux Mondes: Les Créations d'Entreprises par les Étrangers: France, Europe, Amérique du Norde." Special issue, *Revue Européenne des Migrations Internationales,* 8, no. 1 (1992): 5-8.

Böhning, W. R. "Integration and Immigration Pressures in Western Europe." *International Labour Review* 130 (1991):4.

——. "Some Thoughts on Emigration from the Mediterranean Basin." *International Labor Review* 3 (March 1975):251-77.

——. and Denis Maillat. *The Effects of the Employment of Foreign Workers.* Paris: Organization of Economic Cooperation and Development, Division of Manpower and Social Affairs, 1974.

——. and M.-L. Schloeter-Paredes (eds). 1994. *Aid in Place of Migration.* Geneva: International Labor Office.

Boissevain, Jeremy. "Les Entreprises Ethniques aux Pays-Bas.". *Revue Européenne des Migrations Internationales* 8, 1 (1992): 97-106.

Boisvert, Colette Callier, 1987. "Working-Class Portuguese Families in a French Provincial Town: Adaptive Strategies." In *Migrants in Europe: The Role of Family, Labor and Politics,* edited by H. Buechler and J. M. Buechler, 61-76. New York: Greenwood Press, 1987.

Bonneff, M. *La vie tragique des travailleurs: enquêtes sur la condition économique et morale des ouvriers et ouvriers d'industrie.* Paris: M. Rivèr and cie., 1914.

Bonnet, Jean-Charles. "Les italiens dans l'agglomeration lyonnaise à l'aube de la 'Belle Epoque,'" *Affari Sociali Internazionali* 3-4 (1977): 87-103.

——. *Les pouvoirs publics français et l'immigration dans l'entre-deux guerres.* Lyon: Centre d'Histoire Économique et Sociale de la Region Lyonnaise, 1976.

Bouvier, Jeanne. *Mes Memoires: Ou 59 années d'activité industrielle, socialle et intellectuelle d'une ouvriere, 1876–1935.* Paris: Maspero, 1983.

Boyer, Armand. Les migrations saisonnieres dans la Cevenne vivaroise." *Revue de géographie alpine* 22(1934):571–609.

Boyer, Robert ed. *La Flexibilité du Travail en Europe.* Paris: La Decouverte, 1986.

Brettell, Caroline. *Men Who Migrate, Women Who Wait: Population and History on a Portuguese Parish.* Princeton, N.J.: Princeton University Press,1986.

Britschgi-Schimmer, I. *Die wirtschaftliche und soziale Lage der italienischen Arbeiter in Deutschland: Ein Beitrag zur ausländischen Arbeitsfrage.* Karlsruhe, 1916.

Brosnan, P. and F. Wilkinson. *Cheap Labour: Britain's False Economy.* London: Low Pay Unit, 1987.

Brown, C. *Black and White Britain.* London: Heinemann, 1984.

Bruan, Rudolf. "Early Industrialization and Demographic Change in the Canton of Zurich." In *Historical Studies of Changing Fertility,* edited by C. Tilly, 289–334. Princeton: Princeton University Press, 1978.

Brubaker, Roger. *Citizenship and Nationhood in France and Germany.* Cambridge: Harvard University Press, 1992.

Brouwer, Lenie and Marijke Priester, 1983. "Living In Between: Turkish Women in Their Homeland and in the Netherlands." In *One Way Ticket: Migration and Female Labour,* edited by A. Phizacklea, ed., London: Routledge and Kegan Paul, 1983.

Brun, F. *Les français d'Algerie dans l'agriculture du Midi mediterranéen.* Gap: Editions Ophrys, 1976.

Bruschi, Christian. "Le droit d'asile: l'Europe à l'heure des choix." In *Migrations Société* 12(1990): 47–72.

Brym, R. "The Emigration Potential of Czechoslovakia, Hungary, Lithuania, Poland and Russia: Recent Survey Results," *International Sociology,* vol. 7 (1992): 387–95.

Buechler, H. and J. M. Buechler eds. *Migrants in Europe: The Role of Family, Labor and Politics.* New York: Greenwood Press, 1987.

Bundesanstalt für Arbeit. Presseinformation 68–91. Nürnberg, Germany, 1991.

Butt Philip, Alan. "European Union Immigration Policy: Phantom,

Fantasy of Fact?" *West European Politics*, edited by Martin A. Schain and Martin Baldwin-Edwards, vol.17 n.2(1994), 168–92.

Cafiero, U. "Inchiesta nei circondari di Sora e di Isernia," *Bollettino dell'Opera di Assistenza,*I 1(1901): 1–17.

Cannistrano, Philip V. and Gianfausto Rosoli. *Emigrazione, Chieza e Fascismo: Lo Scioglimento dell'Opera Bonomelli,* (1922–1928). Rome, 1979.

Canevari, Annapaola. "Immigrati Prima Accoglienza: E Dopo?" *Dis T Rassegna di Studi e Ricerche del Dipartimento di Scienze del Territorio del Politecnico di Milano*, 53–60. 9/Settembre, 1991.

Carlsson, Sten. "Chronology and Composition of Swedish Emigration to America." In *From Sweden to America*, edited by H. Runblom and H. Norman, 114–48.

Castles, Stephen, Heather Booth and Tina Wallace. *Here for Good: Western Europe's New Ethnic Minorities*. London: Pluto Press, 1984.

Castles, Stephen and Godula Kosak. *Immigrant Workers and Class Structure in Western Europe*. London: Oxford University Press, 1973.

Castles, Stephen and Mark Miller. *The Age of Migration*. London: Macmillan, 1993.

CEE. *L'emploi en Europe*. Bruxelles, European Commission, 1990.

CEMAT. *Draft European Regional Planning Strategy, Vol. One and Two*. Luxembourg: CEMAT., 1988.

Central Department of Statistics. *Statistic Yearbook of the GDR*, Berlin, 1990.

Cerase, Francesco. "Expectations and Reality: A Case Study of Return Migration from the United States to Southern Itlay," *International Migration Review* 8(1974):245–62.

Chaliand, Gerard and Yves Ternon. *Le Génocide des Arméniens*. Brussels: Editions Complexe, 1980.

Chatelain, Abel. "Migrations et domesticité feminine urbaine en France, XVIIIe siècle-XXe siecle," *Revue d' histoire économique et sociale* 47(1969):506–28.

——. *Les migrants temporaires en France de 1800 à 1914*, 2 vols. Lille: Publications de l'Université Presses de Lille, 1976.

Cheshire, P. C. and D. G. Hay. *Urban Problems in Western Europe*. London: Unwin Hyman, 1989.

Chesnais, Jean-Claude. *Les migrations d'Europe de l'Est vers l'Europe*

de l'Ouest: de l'histoire (1946–1989) à la prospective (1990–2000).
Rapport au Conseil de l'Europe, 1996.

Chevalier, Louis. *La Formation de la population parisienne au XIXe siècle.* Paris: Presses Universitaires Françaises, 1950.

——. *Classes laborieuses et classes dangereuses à Paris pendant la première moitié du XIXe siècle.* Paris: Plon, 1958. Translated into English as *Labouring Classes and Dangerous Classes in Paris During the First Half of the Nineteenth Century.* London: Routledge and Kegan Paul, 1973.

——. "L'émigration française au XIXe siècle. *Etudes d'Histoire Moderne et Contemporaine* 1(1947): 127–71.

Clark, Peter. "Migration in England During the Late Seventeenth and Early Eighteenth Centuries." *Past and Present* 8(1979): 57–90.

Cohen, R. *The New Helots: Migrants in the International Division of Labour.* London: Avebury, 1976.

Collicelli, Carla. "Il Problema Dei Rientri e la Nuova Immigrazione." Conferenza Internazionale Sulle Migrazioni. Roma: 13–15 Marzo, 1991.

Coquant, Andre. "Du village de Yesilyazi au quartier des Chamarda a Druez (Eure et Loire)." *Hommes et migrations: Documents* 1021(1981):1–23

Corbin, Alain. *Archaisme et modernité en Limosin au XIXe siècle (1845-1880),* 2 vols. Paris: Marcel Riviere, 1975.

Cornelius, Wayne A., Philip L. Martin, and James F. Hollifield (eds). *Controlling Immigration. A Global Perspective.* Stanford: Stanford University Press, 1994.

Costa-Lascoux, J. "Chronique legislative." *Revue Européenne des Migrations Internationales* 2(1984): 179–240.

——. "L'acquisition de la nationalité française, une condition d'installation." In *Question de nationalité: Histoire et enjeux d'un code,* edited by S. Laarcher. Paris: CIEMI, L'Harmatan, 1987.

—— *De l'immigré au citoyen.* Paris: La Documentation Francaise, 1989.

Cressy, David. *Migration and Communication between England and New Negland in the Seventeenth Century.* Cambridge: Cambridge University Press, 1987.

Crew, D. *Town in the Ruhr: A Social History of Bochum, 1860–1914.* New York: Columbia University Press, 1979.

Cross, G. S. *Immigrant Workers in Industrial France: The Making of a*

New Labouring Class. Philadelphia: Temple University Press, 1983.

Curtin, Phillip D. *The Atlantic Slave Trade: A Census.* Madison: University of Wisconsin Press, 1969.

Davis, Natalie Z. *The Return of Martin Guerre.* Cambridge Mass.: Harvard University Press, 1983.

Depauw, Jacques "Amour illegitime et société à Nantes au XVIIIe siècle." *Annales E.S.C.* 27(1972): 1155–81.

de Bryas, Madeleine. *Les Peuples en marche: Les migrations politiques et économiques en Europe depuis la guerre mondiale.* Paris: 1926.

de Michelis, G. *L'emigrazione italiana nella Svizzera.* Roma, 1903.

de Tinguy, A. "Emigration sovietique: quelles perspectives?" In *La Nouvelle Alternative* no. 2, December 1991.

de Vries, Jan. *European Urbanization: 1500–1800.* Cambridge, Mass.: Harvard University Press, 1984.

——. "The Population and the Economy of the Preindustrial Netherlands," *Journal of Interdisciplinary History* 15(1985):661–82.

Deyon, Pierre. *Amiens, capitale provinciale: Étude sur la société urbaine au 17e siècle.* Paris: Mouton, 1967.

Didion, Maurice. *Les Salariés étrangers en France.* Paris: V. Giard and E. Briere, 1911.

Direction de la Documentation Francaise. "Politiques d'Immigration en Europe," *Problèmes Politiques et Sociaux* no. 530, 21 February 1986.

Dollot, Louis. "Les Immigrations humaines" (Paris 1965); *World Migration in Modern Times,* edited by Franklin D. Scott. Englewood Cliffs, N.J.: Prentice Hill, 1968

Drobnic, S. "The Political Participation of Yugoslav Immigrants in Sweden," *European Journal of Political Research* 16(6), 1988.

Dupaqier, James. *Histoire de la population française,* 4 vols. Paris: Presses Universitaires Françaises, 1988.

Dyer, C. *Population and Society in Twentieth Century France.* London: Hodder and Stoughton, 1978.

Eltis, David. "Free and Coerced Transatlantic Migrations: Some Comparisons," *American Historical Review* 88(1983): 253–80.

Fainstein, S., I. Gordon and M. Harloe, 1993. *Divided Cities: Economic Restructuring and Social Change in London and New York.* New York: Blackwell, 1992.

Faist, Thomas. "How to Define a Foreigner? The Symbolic Politics of

Immigration in German Partisan Discourse, 1978–1992." *West European Politics* 17 (2), 1994.

Fassmann, Heinz. "A Survey of Patterns and Structures of Migration in Austria 1850–1900." In *Labor Migration in the Atlantic Economies*, edited by Dirk Hoerder. Westport, Conn.: Greenwood Press, 1985.

Fenske, Hans. "International Migration: Germany in the Eighteenth Century," *Central European History* 13(1980): 332–47.

Fohlen, Claude. *L'industrie textile au temps du Second Empire*. Paris: Plon, 1956.

——. Introduction. In *L'émigration française. Etudes de cas. Algerie, Canada, Etats Unis*. edited by Centre de recherche d'histoire Nord-Américaine. Paris: Publications de la Sorbone, 1985.

Foner, Nancy "Women, Work and Migration: Jamaicans in London," *Urban Anthropology* 4(1975): 229–49.

Fouche, N. Preface, and "Les passeports delivres à Bordeaux pour les Etats-Unis de 1816 a 1889. In *L'émigration française. Etudes de cas. Algerie, Canada, Etats Unis*, edited by Centre de recherche d'histoire Nord-Américaine. Paris: Publications de la Sorbone, 1985.

Fontaine, Laurence. "Solidarités familiales et logiques migratoires en pays de montagne à l'époque moderne," *Annales: E.S.C.* 45(1990): 1433–50

Franzoi, Barbara. *At the Very Least She Pays the Rent: Women and German Industrialization 1871–1914*. Westport, Conn.: Greenwood, 1985.

Frost, Martin and Nigel Spence. "Global City Characteristics and Central London's Employment," *Urban Studies* vol. 30, no. 3 (1992): 547–558.

Fuchs, Rachel G. *Poor and Pregnant in Paris*. New Brunswick, N.J.: Rutgers University Press, 1997.

Furnrohr, W. *Afrika im Geschichtsunterricht europäischer Länder; Von der Kolonialgeschichte zur Geschichte der Dritten Welt*. Munchen. 1982.

Gabaccia, Donna. *From Sicily to Elizabeth Street: Housing and Social Change among Italian Immigrants, 1880–1930*. Albany, N.Y.: SUNY Press, 1984.

Garden, Maurice. *Lyon et les Lyonnais au XVIIIe siècle*. Paris: Belles Lettres, 1970.

——. "Le bilan demographique des villes: Un système complexe." *Annales de demographie historique*, 267–75. 1982.

Gide, C. and M. Lambert "Les troubles d'Aigues Mortes," *Revue d'Économie Politique*, 839-41. Sept.–Oct. 1983.

Gillette, A. and A. Sayad. *L'Immigration Algerienne en France.* Second edition. Paris: Éditions Entente, 1984.

Girard, Alain and Jean Stoetzel. *Français et immigrés: L'attitude française et l'adaptation des Italiens et des Polonais.* INED-Travaux et Documents, Cahiers 19 et 20. Paris: Presses Universitaires de France, 1953.

Goldstein, Sydney. "The Extent of Repeated Migration: An Analysis Based on the Danish Population Register," *Journal of the American Statistical Association.* 59(2064): 1121–32.

Gordon, Ian and Saskia Sassen. "Restructuring the Urban Labor Markets." In *Divided Cities*, edited by S. Fainstein et al., 105-128. Oxford: Blackwell, 1992.

Grafteaux, Serge. *Mme Santerre: A French Woman of the People.* New York: Schoken Books, 1985.

Gravier, J. F. *Paris et le desert français.* Paris: Le Portulan, 1947.

Green, Nancy. "L'Histoire comparative et le champ des études migratoires." *Annales: E.S.C.* 45(1990): 1335–50.

——. "'Filling the Void': Immigration to France Before World War I." In *Labor Migration in the Atlantic Economies*, edited by Dirk Hoerder, Westport, Conn.: Greenwood Press, 1985.

Gridaudi, Maurizio. *Itineraires ouvriers: Espaces et groupes sociaux à Turin au debut du XXe siècle.* Paris: Éditions de l'Ecole des Hautes Études en Sciences Sociales, 1987.

Guey, P. *Peregrination des "barcelonettes" en Mexique.* Grenoble: Presses Universitaires, 1980.

Guillaume, Pierre. *La population de Bordeaux au XIXe siècle: Essai d'histoire sociale.* Paris: A. Colin, 1972.

Guillon, M. "Les étrangers dans les grandes agglomerations françaises, 1962-82," *Espace, Populations, Sociétés* 2(1986): 179-90.

Gullickson, Gay. *Spinners and Weavers of Auffay: Rural Industry and the Sexual Division of Labor in a French Village, 1750–1850.* Cambridge: Cambridge University Press, 1986.

Guttman, Myron. *Toward the Modern Economy: Early Industry in Europe, 1500–1800.* New York: Knopf, 1988.

—— and Etienne van de Walle. "New Sources for Social and Demographic History: The Belgian Population Registers," *Social Science History* 2 (1978): 121–43.

Hagen, William W. *Germans, Poles and Jews: The Nationality Conflict in the Prussian East, 1772–1914.* Chicago, University of Chicago Press, 1980.

Hajnal, John. "Two Kinds of Pre-industrial Household Formation Systems." In *Family Forms in Historic Europe*, edited by R. Wall and P. Laslett, 65–104. Cambridge: Cambridge University Press, 1983.

Hammar, T. *European Immigration Policy: A Comparative Study.* Cambridge: Cambridge University Press, 1985.

Harris, Ruth-Ann. "Seasonal Migration Between Ireland and England Prior to the Famine." In *Canadian Papers in Rural History* vol. 7, edited by D.H. Akenson, 363–86. Gananoque: Langdale Press, 1989.

Hart, Simon. "Gens de mer à Amsterdam au XVIIe siècle." *Annales de demographie historique*, 145–63, 1974.

Harvard Encyclopedia of American Ethnic Groups, edited by S. Thernstrom and A. Orlov, 1036–37. Cambridge, Mass. 1980.

Hausserman, Hartmut and Walter Siebel.*Neue Urbanität.* Frankfurt: Suhrkamp Verlag, 1987.

Head, Anne-Lise. "Quelques remarques sur l'émigration des regions prealpines," *Revue suisse d'histoire*, 29(1979): 181–93.

Heisler, Barbara Schmitter. 1991. "A comparative perspective on the underclass. Questions of urban poverty, race, and citizenship." *Theory and Society*, 20: 455–483.

Heitmann, S. *Soviet Emigration in 1990.* Berichte des Bundesinstituts für Ostwissenschaftliche und Internationale Studien no. 33. Bonn, 1991.

Hily, M. A. "Qu'est-ce que l'assimilation entre les deux guerres? Les enseignements de la lecture de quelques ouvrages consacrés à l'immigration." In *Maghrébins en France: émigrés ou immigrés?*, edited by L. Talha, et al., 71–80. Paris: Editions du CNRS, 1983.

Hitz, H. R. Keil, V. Lehrer, K. Ronneberger, C. Schmid, and R. Wolff. *Financial Metropoles in Restructuring: Zurich and Frankfurt en Route to Postfordism.* Zurich: Rotpunkt Publishers, 1993.

Hobsbawn, Eric. *The Age of Empire, 1875–1914.* New York: Pantheon, 1987.

——. "The Overall Crisis of the European Economy in the Seventeenth Century," *Past and Present* 5(1954): 33–53.

——. "Afterword: Working Classes and Nations." In *Labor Migration in the Atlantic Economies*, edited by Dirk Hoerder. Westport, Conn.: Greenwood Press, 1985.

Hochstadt, Steve. "Stadtische Wanderungsbewegungen in Deutschland 1850–1914." In *von Aretin zum 65 Geburtstag*, 2 vols., edited by R. Melville, C. Scharf., M. Vogt, and U. Wengenroth, 2: 575–98. Stuttgart: Franz Steiner Verlag, 1988.

—— and James Jackson, Jr. "'New' Sources for the Study of Migration in Early Nineteenth Century Germany." *Historical Social Resarch/Historische Sozialforschung* 31(1984): 85–92.

Hoerder, Dirk, ed. *Labor Migration in the Atlantic Economies: The European and North American Working Classes during the Period of Industrialization.* Westport, Conn.: Greenwood Press, 1985.

Hoffmann-Nowotny, Hans-Joachim. 1985. "Switzerland." In *European Immigration Policy*, ed. T. Hammar. Cambridge: Cambridge University Press.

Hogen, Dennis and David Kertzer. "Longitudinal Methods for Historical Migrations Research." *Historical Methods* 18: 20–30.

Hollifield, James F. *Immigrants, Markets and States.* Cambridge: Harvard University Press, 1992.

Husbands, C. "The Dynamics of Racial Exclusion and Expulsion: Racist Politics in Western Europe." *European Journal of Political Research* 16(6), 1988.

International Organization for Migration. *Profiles and Motives of Potential Migrants: An IOM Study Undertaken in Four Countries: Albania, Bulgaria, Russia and Ukraine.* Geneva: IOM, 1993.

Institut national d'études demographiques (INED). *L'argent des immigres. Revue, epargne et transferts de huit nationalites immigres en France.* Cahier de l'INED no. 94. Paris: Presses Universitaires de France, 1981.

Jacini, S. "Die italienische Auswanderung nach Deutschland," *Weltwirtschaftliches Archiv* 5(1915): 121–43.

Jackson, J. A. *The Irish in Britain.* London: Routledge and Kegan Paul, 1963.

Jackson, James, Jr. "Alltagsgeschichte, Social Science History and the

Study of Migration in Nineteenth Century Germany," *Central Europe History* 23(1990): 242–63.

——. "Migration in Duisburg, 1867–1890: Occupational and Familial Contexts," *Journal of Urban History* 8(1982): 235–70.

Jacobson, David. *Rights Across Borders: Immigration and the Decline of Citizenship.* Baltimore: Johns Hopkins Press, 1996.

Jegouzo, Christopher, forthcoming. *The Life and Death of Industrial Languedoc.* Oxford: Oxford University Press.

Joly, Daniele, C. Nettleton and H. Poulton. *Refugees: Asylum in Europe?* London: Minority Rights Group, 1992.

Jones, Garth Stedman. *Outcast London: A Study in the Relationship between Classes in Victorian Society.* Oxford: Oxford University Press, 1970.

Jones, K and A. Smith. *The Economic Impact of Commonwealth Immigration.* London: Cambridge University Press and National Institute of Economic and Social Research, 1970.

Journal fur Entwicklungspolitik. Special Issue: *Migration.* Vol. XI, nr. 3, 1995. (Frankfurt: Brandes & Apsel Verlag).

Kaelble, Hartmut. "Historical Research on Social Mobilty. Western Europe and USA in the Nineteenth and Twentieth Centuries" New York: Columbia University Press, 1981.

——. "Social Mobility in America and Europe: A Comparison of 19th Century Cities." Urban History Yearbook. Leicester: Leicester University Press 1981, 24–38.

Kalvemark, Ann-Sofie. "The Country that Keeps Track of Its Population: Methodological Aspects of Swedish Population Records." In *Time, Space and Man: Essays on Microdemography,* edited by J. Sundin and E. Söderlund, 221–43. Atlantic Highlands, N.J.: Humanities Press, 1979.

Kamphoefner, Walter. *The Westfalians: From Germany to Missouri.* Princeton: Princeton University Press, 1987.

Katan, Y. "Le voyage 'organisé' d'émigrants: parisiens vers l'Algérie, 1848–49." In *L'émigration française. Etudes de cas: Algérie, Canada, États-Unis,* edited by Centre de Recherches d'Histoire Nord-Américaine, 17-47. Paris: Publications de la Sorbonne, 1985.

Kaufman, Franz-Xaver. *Bevölkerungsbewegung zwischen Quantitat und Qualitat: Beitrage zum Problem einer Bevölkerungspolitik in industriellen Gesellschaften* Stuttgart: Ferdinand Enke Verlag, 1975.

Kero, Reino. "Emigration of Finns from North America to Soviet Kare-lia in the Early 1930s." In *The Finnish Experience in the Western Great Lakes Region: New Perspectives,* edited by Michael G. Karni, 212–21. Vammala, 1975.

Kertzer, David and Dennis Hogan. "On the Move: Migration in an Italian Community, 1865–1921," *Social Science History* 9 (1985): 1–23.

Khader, Bichara "Le Méditerranée entre les tentations solitaires et les projets solidaires." In *Développement du Maghreb dans la per-spective du Marche Unique,* 1991.

——. "Immigration maghrebine face à l'Europe, 1992." In *Migrations Société CIEMI, Immigration maghrebine et Europe* 92, vol. 3, no. 15(1991): 17.

Kindleberger, C.P. *Europe's Postwar Growth: The Role of Labor-Supply.* Cambridge: Harvard University Press, 1967.

Kintz, Jean-Pierre "La mobilité humaine en Alsace: Essai de présen-tation statistique, XIVe-XVIIIe Siècles," *Annals de demographie historique* (1970), 157–83.

Kish, Herbert. "The Textile Industries in Silesia and the Rhineland: A Comparative Study in Industrialization." In *Industrialization Be-fore Industrialization: Rural Industry in the Genesis of Capital-ism.* edited by P. Kriedte, H. Medick, J. Schlumbohm. Cambridge: Cambridge University Press, 1981.

Klee, Ernst, ed. *Gastarbeiter Analysen und Berichte.* Frankfurt: Suhr-kamp Verlag, 1975.

Knoke, A. *Ausländische Wanderarbeiter in Deutschland.* Leipzig. 1977.

Koch, Fred C. *The Volga Germans in Russia and the Americas from 1763 to the Present.* University Park: Pennsylvania State Univer-sity Press, 1977.

Kollmann, W. *Bevölkerung in der industriellen Revolution: Studien zur Bevölkerungsgeschichte Deutschlands.* Gottingen: Vandenhoeck und Reprecht, 1974.

Kulischer, Eugene M. *Europe on the Move: War and Population Changes, 1917–47.* New York: Columbia University Press, 1948.

Kunzmann, K. R. and M. Wegener. *The Pattern of Urbanisation in Western Europe 1960–1990.* Report for the Directorate General XVI of the Commission of the European Communities as part of the study "Urbanisation and the Function of Cities in the European Community." Dortmund, Germany: Institut fur Raumplanung, 15 March, 1991.

Kurlic, Joseph. "L'immigration et l'identité de la France: mythe et réalité." *Pouvoirs*, no. 47 (1988).

Kussmaul, Ann. *Servants in Husbandry in Early Modern England.* Cambridge: Cambridge University Press, 1981.

Langewiesche, D. "Wanderungsbewegungen in der Hochindustrialisierungsperiode: Regionale, interstädtische und innerstädtische Mobilität in Deutschland 1880–1914." *Vierteljahrschrift fur Sozial und Wirtschaftsgeschichte*, 64(1977): 1–40.

Larrabee, F. St. "Down and Out in Warsaw and Budapest: Eastern Europe and East-West Migration," *International Security* vol. 16, no. 4 (spring, 1992).

Layton-Henry, Zig ed. *The Political Rights of Migrant Workers in Western Europe.* Newbury Park: Sage Publications, 1990.

Lebon, A. and G. Falchi. "New Developments in Intra-European Migration since 1974," *International Migration Review* 14(1980): 539–79.

Lequin, Yves. *Les Ouvriers de la region lyonnaise (1848–1914).* Lyon: Presses Universitaires de Lyon, 1977.

LeRoyLadurie, Emmanuel. *Histoire de la France rurale, L'âge classique des paysans, 1340–1789*, vol. 2. Paris: Seuil, 1975.

——. *Histoire de la France urbaine, La ville classique*, vol. 3. Paris: Seuil, 1981.

Levine, David. *Family Formation in an Age of Nascent Capitalism.* New York: Academic Press, 1977.

——. *Reproducing Families: The Political Economy of English Population History.* Cambridge: Cambridge University Press, 1987.

Lis, Catharine and Hugh Soly. *Poverty and Capitalism in Pre-Industrial Europe.* Atlantic Highlands, NJ: Humanities Press, 1979.

Livian, Marcel. *Le Parti Socialiste et l'immigration.* Paris: Anthropos, 1982.

Lottin, Alain. "Naissance illégitimes et filles-mères à Lille au XVIIIe siècle." *Revue d'Histoire Moderne et Contemporaine* 17(1970): 278–322.

Lowe, William J. *The Irish in Mid-Victorian Lancashire: The Shaping of a Working-Class Community.* New York: Peter Lang, 1989.

Lucassen, Jan. *Migrant Labor in Europe 1600–1900: The Drift to the North Sea.* Wolfeboro, N.H.: Croom Helm, 1987.

——. "Dutch Migration, 1600–1900." Paper presented at the 17e Congrès International des Sciences Historiques, Madrid. July, 1990.

Macartney, C. A. *National States and National Minorities.* London: Oxford University Press, 1934.

MacDonagh, Oliver. *A Pattern of Government Growth, 1800–1869: The Passenger Acts and Their Enforcement.* London: McGibbon and Kee, 1961.

Marchalck, P. *Deutsche Uberseeauswanderung im 19. Jahrhundert.* Stuttgart, 1973.

Marie, C. "L'immigration clandestine en France." *Hommes et Migrations* 1059(1983): 4–21.

Marrus, Michael R. *The Unwanted: European Refugees in the Twentieth Century.* New York: Oxford University Press, 1985.

Mauco, Georges. *Les Etrangers en France: Leur rôle dans l'activité économique.* Paris, 1932.

Mayer, Margit. "Shifts in the Local Political System in European Cities since the 80s." In *Competition, Regulation and the New Europe,* edited by Mick Dunford/Grigoris Kafkalas. London: Belhaven, 1993.

Meijide, Pardo. *La emigración Gallega intrapeninsular en el siglo XVIII.* Madrid: Instituto Balmes de Sociología, 1960.

Mendels, Franklin. "Protoindustrialization: The First Phase of the Industrialization Process," *Journal of Economic History* 32(1972): 241–61.

Messance. *Recherches sur la population des généralités d'Auvergne, de Lyon, de Rouen.* Paris: Durand, 1766. Reprint, Paris: Éditions d'Histoire Sociale, 1973.

Miles, Robert and Annie Phizacklea. *White Man's Country: Racism in British Politics.* London: Pluto Press, 1984.

Milza, P. "L'integration des italiens dans le mouvement ouvrier français à la fin du XIXe siècle et au debut duXXe siècle: le cas de la région marseillaise," *Affari Sociali Internazionali* 3–4(1973): 171–207.

Mingione, E. and E. Pugliese. "La questione urbana e rurale: tra superamento teorico e problemi di confini incerti," *La Critica Sociologica* 85(1988): 17–50.

Mitter, S., ed. *Information Technology and Women's Employment: The*

Case of the European Clothing Industry. Berlin and New York: Springer Verlag, 1989.

Moch, Leslie Page. "Government Policy and Women's Experience: The Case of Teachers in France." *Feminist Studies* 14(1988): 301–24.

——. "Infirmities of the Body and Vices of the Soul: Migrants, Family and Urban Life in Turn-of-the-Century France." In *Essays on the Family and Historical Change*, edited by L. P. Moch and G. Stark, 35–64. College Station, Tex.: Texas A&M University Press, 1983.

Moch, Leslie Page, et al. "Family Strategies: A Dialogue." *Historical Methods* 20(1987): 113–25.

Moch, Leslie Page and Louise Tilly. "Joining the Urban World: Occupation, Family, and Migration in Three French Cities." *Comparative Studies in Society and History* 27(1984): 33–56.

Mockmeier, W. *Die deutsche überseeische Auswanderung.* Jena, 1912.

Molle, Willem. *The Economics of European Integration: Theory, Practice, Policy.* Aldershot: Dartmouth Publishing Company, 1990.

Moltmann, Günther. "American-German Return Migration in the Nineteenth and Early Twentieth Centuries," *Central European History,* 13(1980): 378–92.

Morawska, Eva. "Labor Migration of Poles in the Atlantic Economy, 1880–1914," *Comparative Studies in Society and History* 31(1989): 237–72.

Morgan, David. *Harvesters and Harvesting, 1840–1900.* London: Croom Helm, 1982.

Morokvasic, Mirjana. "Une migration pendulaire: les Polonais en Allemagne." *Hommes et Migrations* vol. 1155 (June 1992): 31–37.

——, ed. *Women in Migration: International Migration Review,* Special Issue, 18(4) winter 1984.

—— and Anne de Tinguy. "Between East and West: A New Migratory Space." In *Bridging States and Markets: International Migration in the Early 1990s,* edited by Hedwig Rudolf and Mirjana Morokvasic. 1993. Berlin: Die Deutsche Bibliothek, 1993.

Mouillon, Marthe-Juliette. "Un exemple de migration rurale: De la Somme dans la capitale. Domestique de la Belle Époque à Paris." *Études de la region parisienne* 44(1970): 1–9.

Munoz-Perez, F. and M. Tribalat. "Mariages d'étrangers et mariages mixtes en France: évolution depuis la première guerre," *Population* 39(1984): 427–62.

Nansen, Fridtjof. *Russia and Peace.* New York: Macmillan, 1924.

Neubach, Helmut. *Die Ausweisungen von Polen und Juden aus Preussen 1885/86.* Wiesbaden: Otto Harrassowitz, 1967.

Nichtweiss, J. *Die Ausländischen Saisonarbeiter in der Landwirtschaft der ostlichen und mittleren Gebiete des Deutschen Reiches.* Berlin, 1959.

Noiriel, Gerard. *Longwy: Immigres et proletaires, 1880–1980.* Paris: Presses Universitaires de France, 1984.

——. "L'immigration en France: une histoire en friche," *Annales: Économies, Societes, Civilisations* 41(1986): 751–69.

——. *Le creuset français: Histoire de l'immigration, XIXe–XXe siècles.* Paris: Seuil, 1988.

Nugent, Walter. "Frontiers and Empires in the Late Nineteenth Century," *The Western Historical Society* 20(1989): 393–406.

Oberndörfer, Dicker. *Die Offene Republik. Zur Zukunft Deutschlands und Europas.* Feiburg: Herder, 1989.

OECD. *Economic Survey: Germany 1989/1990.* Paris: OECD Publications, 1990.

Office International de Migrations (OIM). *Mouvements migratoires des pays d'Europe centrale et orientale vers l'Europe occidentale.* Rapport au Conseil de l'Europe, 1990.

Ogden, P. E. *Foreigners in Paris: Residential Segregation in the Nineteenth and Twentieth Centuries.* Occasional Paper 11, Department of Geography, Queen Mary College, University of London, 1977.

——. "Immigration, Cities and the Geography of the National Front in France." In *Foreign Minorities in Continental European Cities,* edited by G. Glebe and J. O'Loughlin, 163–83. Wiesbaden: Steiner Verlag, 1987.

—— and Paul E. White. "Migration in Later Nineteenth and Twentieth Century France: Social and Economic Context." In *Migrants in Modern France: Population Mobility in the Later Nineteenth and Twentieth Centuries,* edited by P. E. Odgen and Paul White. London: Unwin Hyman, 1989.

Okólski, M. "Poland" In *The Politics of East-West Migrations,* edited by S. Ardittis, 1992.

——. *Mouvements migratoires en provenance des pays d'Europe centrale et orientale.* Rapport au Conseil de l'Europe, 1989.

Paine, Suzanne. *Exporting Workers: The Turkish Case.* Cambridge University Press. 1974.

Parnreiter, Christof. *Migration und Arbeitsteilung. Auslander Innen-beschaftigung in der Weltwirtschaftskrise.* Wien: Promedia, 1994.

Penninx, Rinus. "Immigrant Populations and Demographic Develop-ment in the Member States of the Council of Europe," *Population Studies* no. 13 (1984) Strasburg.

Perkins, J. A. "The Agricultural Revolution in Germany, 1850–1914," *Journal of European Economic History* 10 (1981):71–118

Perrot, Michelle. *Les ouvriers en grève, France, 1870–1890* 2 vols. Paris: Mouton, 1974.

Petras, Elizabeth McLean. "The Role of National Boundaries in a Cross-National Labor Market," *The International Journal of Ur-ban and Regional Research* 4, 2(1980): 157–195.

Phizacklea, Annie, ed. *One Way Ticket: Migration and Female Labour.* London: Routledge and Kegan Paul, 1983.

Pinchemel, Philippe. *Structures sociales et depopulation rurale dans les campagnes picardes de 1836 à 1936.* Paris: Colin, 1957.

Plender, Richard. *International Migration Law.* Leyden: A. W. Sythoff, 1972.

Pluyette, Jean. *La Selection de l'immigration en France et la doctrine des races.* Paris, 1930.

Poinard, Michel and Michel Roux. "L'émigration contre le dévelop-ment: Les cas Portugais et Yougoslave." *Revue Tiers-Monde* 18 (Janvier-Mars 1977): 21–53.

Poitrineau, Abel. "Aspects de l'émigration temporaire et saisonnière en Auvergne à la fin du XVIIIe siècle et au debut du XIXe siècle." *Revue d'histoire moderne et contemporaine* 9(1962): 5–50.

——. *Remues d'hommes: Essai sur les migrations montagnardes en France, aux 17e-18e siècles.* Paris: Aubier Montaign, 1983.

——. *La vie rurale en Basse Auvergne au XVIIIe siècle.* Paris: Presses Universitaires Françaises, 1966.

——. *Les espagnols de l'Auvergne et du Limousin du XVIIe au XIXe siècle.* Aurillac: Malvoux-Mazel, 1985.

Portes, Jacques. "Les voyageurs français et l'émigration française aux États-Unis (1870–1914)." In *L'émigration française. Études de cas. Algerie, Canada, États-Unis,* Centre de Recherches d'Histoire Nord-Américaine, 259–69. Paris: Publications de la Sorbonne, 1985.

Poussou, Jean-Pierre. *Bordeaux et le sud-ouest au XVIIIe siècle.* Paris: Éditions de l'École des Hautes Études en Sciences Sociales, 1988.

Prost, A. "L'immigration en France depuis cent ans." *Esprit*, special edition,(1966), 532–45.

Pugliese, E. "Aspetti dell' Economia Informale a Napoli," *Inchiesta* 13, 59–60 (January–June 1983): 89–97.

Quante, P. *Die Flucht aus der Landwirtschaft*. Berlin, 1933.

Rabb, Theodore. "The Effects of the Thirty Years' War on the German Economy," *The Journal of Modern History* 34(1962): 40–51.

Rabut, O. "Les étrangers en France," *Population* 28(1974): 147–160.

Raman, Michael. "Mesure de la croissance d'un centre textile: Roubaix de 1789 à 1913." *Revue d'histoire économique et sociale* 51(1973): 470–501.

Rath, Jan. "Voting Rights." In *The Political Rights of Migrant Workers in Western Europe*, edited by Zig Layton-Henry. London: Sage, 1990.

Ravenstein, Ernest. *The Laws of Migration*. Reprint. New York: Arno Press, 1976.

Redford, Arthur. *Labour Migration in England, 1800–1850*. Manchester: Manchester University Press, 1976.

Renooy, P. H. *Twilight Economy: A Survey of the Informal Economy in the Netherlands*. Research Report, Faculty of Economic Sciences, University of Amsterdam, 1984.

Rogers, Rosemarie, ed. *Guests Come to Stay: The Effects of European Labor Migration on Sending and Receiving Countries*. Boulder, Colo.: Westview Press, 1985.

Roncayolo, M. *L'Imaginaire de Marseille*. Marseille: Chambre de Commerce et d'Industrie de Marseille, 1990.

Rosoli, G., ed. *Un secolo d'emigrazione italiana: 1876–1976*. Rome: Centro studi emigrazione, 1978.

Roudie, P. "Long Distance Emigration from the Port of Bordeaux, 1865–1920," *Journal of Historical Geography* 11(1985): 268–79.

——. "Italian Migration to European Countries from Political Unification to World War I." In *Labor Migration in the Atlantic Economies*, edited by Dirk Hoerder. Westport, Conn.: Greenwood Press, 1985.

Roy, Olivier. "Ethnicité, Bandes et Communautarisme," *Esprit*, Fevrier 1966, 37–47.

Rudolph, Hedwig and Mirjana Morokvasic.*Bridging States and Markets: International Migration in the Early 1900s*. Berlin: Die Deutsche Bibliothek, 1993.

Sabean, David. "Household Formation and Geographic Mobility: A Family Register Study for a Wurttemberg Village, 1760–1900," *Annales de demographie historique* (1970) 275–94

Sandicchi, P. "I fornaciai italiani in Baviera," *Bollettino dell'Emigrazione* 12(1912): 3–34.

Sarna, Jonathan. "The Myth of No Return: Jewish Return Migration to Eastern Europe, 1800–1914." In *Labor Migration in the Atlantic Economies*, edited by D. Hoerder, 423–34. Westport, Conn.: Greenwood, 1981.

Sartorius von Waltershausen, A. *Die italienischen Wanderarbeiter.* Leipzig, 1903.

Sassen, Saskia. 1998. *Globalization and Its Discontents*. New York: New Press.

——. 1996. *Losing Control? Sovereignty in an Age of Globalization.* The 1995 Columbia University Leonard Hastings Schoff Memorial Lectures. New York: Columbia University Press.

——. *The Global City: New York, London, Tokyo.* Princeton: Princeton University Press, 1991.

——. *The Mobility of Labor and Capital: A Study in International Investment and Labor Flow.* New York: Cambridge University Press, 1988.

Schain, Martin A. "Immigrants and Politics in France." in *The French Socialist Experiment*, edited by John S. Ambler. Philadelphia: ISHI, 1985.

Schechtman, Joseph. *European Population Transfers, 1939–1945.* New York: Oxford University Press, 1946.

Schiaparelli, E. "Il traffico dei minorenni italiani per le vetrerie francese." *Bollettino dell'Opera di Assistenza, I*, 3–4. 1901.

Schiller, Günther. "Auswirkungen der Arbeitskraftwanderungen in den Herkunftslandern." In *Ausländerbeschäftigung und Internationale Politik; Zur Analyse Transnationaler Sozial Prozesse*, edited by Lohrmann and Manfrass. München: Oldenburg, 1974.

Schnapper, Dominique. "Centralisme et federalisme culturels: les émigrés italiens en France et aux États-Unis," *Annales E.S.C.* (October 1974): 1141–59.

——. *La France de l'integration: Sociologie de la nation en 1990.* Paris: Gallimard, 1991.

Schofield, Roger. "Age-Specific Mobility in an Eighteenth Century Rural English Parish." *Annales de demographie historique* (1970) 261-74.

Schor, R. *L'opinion française et les étrangers en France, 1919-1939.* Paris: Publications de la Sorbonne, 1985.

Sennett, Richard. *Flesh and Stone: The Body and the City in Western Civilization.* New York: Norton, 1994.

——. *The Uses of Disorder: Personal Identity and City Life.* New York: Norton, 1970.

Senior, Carl. "German Immigration in Jamaica, 1834-38." *Journal of Caribbean History* 10-11(1978): 25-53.

Sewell, W. H. *Structure and Mobility: The Men and Women of Marseille 1820-1870.* Cambridge: Cambridge University Press, 1985.

Sik, E. "Policy Networks to Cope with Crisis: The Case of Transylvanian Refugees in Contemporary Hungary," *Innovation* vol. 3, no. 4 (1990): 729-748.

Snell, Keith D.M. *Annals of the Labouring Poor: Social Change and Agrarian England 1660-1900.* Cambridge: Cambridge University Press, 1985.

Soboul, Albert. *La Civilisation et la Révolution Française.* Paris: Arthaud, 1970.

SOPEMI (Système d'observation permanente pour les migrations). *Annual Report.* Paris: OECD, Directorate for Social Affairs, Manpower and Education, 1977.

——. *Annual Report* Paris: OECD Directorate for Social Affairs, Manpower and Education, 1992.

——. *Annual Report* Paris: OECD Directorate for Social Affairs, Manpower and Education, 1998.

Sori, E. *L'emigrazione italiana dall'Unita alla seconda guerra mondiale.* Bologna: Il Mulino, 1979.

Souden, David. "Movers and Stayers in Family Reconstitution Population, 1660-1780." *Local Population Studies* 33(1984): 11-28.

Soysal, Yasmin. *Limits of Citizenship.* Chicago: University of Chicago Press, 1994.

Spencer, Michael. *1992 and All That: Civil Liberties in the Balance.* London: Civil Liberties Trust, 1990.

Statistical Office of the European Community. Demographic and Labour Force Analysis Based on Eurostat Data Banks. Luxembourg, 1987.

Statistisches Bundesamt. *Statistisches Jahrbuch 1991 fur das vereinte Deutschland.* Wiesbaden: Metler-Poeschl, 1992.

Tapinos, G. *L'immigration étrangère en France, 1946–1973.* Cahier de l'INED no. 71. Paris: Presses Universitaires de France, 1975.

——. "Pour une introduction au debat contemporain." Extrait de "La Mosaique en France, Histoire des etrangers et de l'immigration en France" sous la direction de Yves Lequin. Paris: Larousse, 1988.

Tartakower, Arieh and Kurt R. Grossmann. *The Jewish Refugee.* New York: Institute of Jewish Affairs of the American Jewish Congress and World Jewish Congress, 1944.

Thernstrom, Stephan and Ann Orlov, eds. *Harvard Encyclopedia of Ethnic Groups.* Cambridge, Mass.: Harvard University, 1980.

Tedebrand, Lars-Goran, "Remigration from America to Sweden." In *Labor Migration in the Atlantic Economies,* edited by D. Hoerder, 357-80. Westport, Conn.: Greenwood Press, 1985.

Thomas, Brinley. *Migration and Economic Growth: A Study of Great Britain and the Atlantic Economy,* second edition. Cambridge: Cambridge University Press, 1973.

Thomas, Dorothy Swaine. *Social and Economic Aspects of Swedish Population Movements, 1750–1933.* New York: Macmillan, 1941.

Thranhardt, Dietrich (ed.) *Europe: A New Immigration Continent.* Hamburg: Lit Verlag, 1992.

Tilly, Charles. *Coercion, Capital, and European States, AD 990–1990.* Cambridge, Mass.: Basil Blackwell, 1990.

——. "Flows of Capital ad Forms of Industry in Europe, 1500–1900," *Theory and Society* 12(1983): 123–42.

——. "Did the cake of custon break?" In *Consciousness and class experience in nineteenth century Europe,* edited by J. M. Merriman, 17–44. New York: Homes & Meier, 1979.

Tilly, Louise. "Occupational Structure, Women's Work and Demographic Change in Two French Industrial Cities, Anzin and Roubaix, 1872–1906." In *Time Space and Man: Essays in Microdemography,* edited by J. Sundin and E. Söderlund, 107–32. Atlantic Highlands, N.J.: Humanities Press, 1979.

Tilly, Louise and Joan Scott. *Women, Work and Family.* New York: Holt, Rinehart and Winston, 1978.

Tilly, Louise, Joan Scott, and Miriam Cohen. "Women's Work and

European Fertility Patterns," *Journal of Interdisciplinary History* 6(1976): 447–76.

Todd, Emmanuel. "Mobilité geographique et cycle de vie en Artois et en Tascae au XVIIIe siècle," *Annales E.S.C.* 30(1975): 726–44.

Tribalat, M. "Chronique de l'immigration," *Population* 38(1983): 137–59.

——. "Chronique de l'immigration," *Population* 40(1985): 131–54.

——, J.-P. Garson, Y. Moulier-Boutang, and R. Silberman. *Cents Ans D'Immigration, Étrangers D'Hier Français D'Aujourd'Hui.* Paris: Presses Universitaires de France, Institut National d'Études Demographiques, 1991.

Turpin, Dominique. "Les solutions françaises: rapport général," In *Immigrés et réfugiés dans les democraties occidentales,* 38–30. Paris: Economica, 1981.

United Nations, Department of International Economic and Social Affairs: Centre for Social Development and Humanitarian Affairs. "Migrant Workers, No., 2: The Social Situation of Migrant Workers and Their Families." New York, 1986.

Universita Bocconi. "L'immigrazione Straniera in Italia: Esame, Interpretazione e Valutazione Comparate di significative Esperienze Europee." Conferenza Nazionale Della'Immigrazione, 1990.

U.S. Committee for Refugees. *World Refugee Sumary.* Washington, D.C. 1993.

van de Walle, E. *The Female Population of France in the Nineteenth Century.* Princeton: Princeton University Press, 1974.

Vandervelde, Emile. *L'exode rural et le retour aux champs.* Paris: Alcan, 1903.

Verbunt, G. "France." In *European Immigration Policy: A Comparative Prespective,* edited by T. Hammar, 127–64. Cambridge: Cambridge University Press, 1985.

Vertone, T. "Antecedents et causes des evenements d'Aigues Mortes." *Affari Sociali Internazionali* 3–4(1977): 107–38.

Veuglers, John W. P. "Recent Immigration Politics in Italy: A Short Story." In Martin Baldwin-Edwards and Martin A. Schain, eds. *West European Politics* vol. 17 no. 2(1994): 33-50.

Vieillard-Baron, Herve. "Le Risque du Ghetto," *Esprit,* Fevrier 1991, 14–22.

Voisard, Jacques and Christiane Ducastelle. *La question immigrée dans la France d'aujourd'hui.* Paris: Calmann-Levy, 1988.

Wareing, John. "Migration to London and Transatlantic Emigration of Indentured Servants, 1683–1775," *Journal Of Historical Geography* 7(1981): 356–78.

Watkins, Susan Cotts. *From Provinces into Nations: Demographic Integration in Western Europe, 1870–1960.* Princeton: Princeton University Press, 1991.

Weil, Patrick. *La France et ses étrangers.* Paris: Calman- Levy, 1991.

Wentz, Martin, ed. *Stadtplanung in Frankfurt: Wohnen, Arbeiten, Verkehr.* Frankfurt, New York: Campus, 1991.

Werner, Heinz. "Migration and Free Movement of Workers in Western Europe." In *Les travailleurs étrangers en Éurope occidentale,* edited by Philippe Bernard, 65–85. Paris: Mouton, 1976.

Werth, Manfred and Heiko Korner eds. *Social Europe: Immigration of Citizens from Third Countries into the Southern Member States of the European Community.* Luxembourg: Office for Official Publications of the European Communities, 1991.

Wihtol de Wenden, Catherine. *Les immigrés et la politique.* Paris: Presse de la FNSP, 1988.

——. "The Absence of Right: the Position of Illegal Immigrants." In *The political Rights of Migrant workers in Western Europe,* edited by Zig Layton-Henry. London: Sage, 1990.

——. "Les migrations Est-Ouest," *Migrations Societe.* CIEMI, 92, vol. 3, no. 15(1991): 9.

——. "Immigrants as political actors in France." In Martin Baldwin-Edwards and Martin A. Schain eds. *West European Politics* vol. 17 no. 2(1994): 91–110.

Willcox, F. W. and I. Ferenczi eds. *International Migrations,* 2 vols. New York, National Bureau of Economic Research 1929, 1931.

Wilson, W. J. *The Truly Disadvantaged: The Inner City, the Underclass and Public Policy.* Chicago: University of Chicago Press, 1987.

Wischenbart, Rudiger. "National Identity and Immigration in Austria-Historical Framework and Political Dispute." In Martin Baldwin-Edwards and Martin A. Schain eds. *West European Politics* vol .17 no.2(1994): 72–90

Wlocevski, S. *L'installation des italiens en France.* Paris, 1934.

Wrigley, E. Anthony. "The Growth of Population in 18th. century England: A Conumdrum Resolved." *Past and Present* 98(1983): 121–50

Zeroulou, Z. "Mobilisation familiale et réussite scolaire." *Revue Européenne des Migrations Internationales* 1(1981): 107–17.

Zolberg, Aristride R. "International Migration Policies in a Changing World System." In W. J. McNeill and R. S. Adams, 241–81. *Human Migration: Patterns and Policies.* Bloomington: Indiana University Press, 1978.

——. "Contemporary Transnational Migrations in Historical Perspective: Patterns and Dilemmas." In *U.S. Immigration and Refugee Policy: Global and Domestic Issues,* edited by Mary M. Kritz, 18–19. Lexington, Ky.: Lexington Books, 1983.

INDEX

Printed in the USA
CPSIA information can be obtained
at www.ICGtesting.com
LVHW091514080824
787695LV00001B/99